National

BY JOHN WALKER DIRECTOR EMERITUS

FOREWORD BY J. CARTER BROWN, DIRECTOR

Gallery of Art

WASHINGTON

HARRY N. ABRAMS, INC. PUBLISHERS NEW YORK

TO PAUL MELLON   A PERFECT TRUSTEE

Library of Congress Cataloging in Publication Data

Walker, John, Dec. 24, 1906–
  National Gallery of Art, Washington, D. C.

1. United States. National Gallery of Art.
2. Paintings—Washington, D. C.   I. Title.
N856.W33 1975   708'.153   74-10716
ISBN 0-8109-0336-9

Library of Congress Catalogue Card Number: 74-10716.
All rights reserved. No part of the contents of this book may be reproduced without the written permission of the publishers, Harry N. Abrams, Incorporated, New York. Printed and bound in Japan. Designed by Howard Morris

Note: Parts of this book have been previously published in *Art in America, Ladies' Home Journal, National Geographic Magazine, Twin Editions, Great Paintings of the World, Connoisseur, Atlantic Monthly,* and certain National Gallery of Art publications and catalogues. I am very grateful for permission to reprint this material.   J.W.

Acknowledgments

The present volume began as an amplification of my much smaller book, published in 1963, about the National Gallery of Art. Although some of the text is repeated, this is now a totally new book, including sections on sculpture and drawings and illustrating all the major works of art in the Gallery's collections.

Without the assistance of Carolyn H. Wells I would not have undertaken this work. She has done much of the research and aided me in every way in preparing the text. But the book was made possible only by the full cooperation which I received from the staff of the National Gallery of Art.

My successor as Director of the Gallery, J. Carter Brown, has written the foreword and some passages of the introductory text. His unfailing interest and encouragement, despite the pressure of his multitudinous duties, has been invaluable. I am most grateful also to Charles P. Parkhurst, Assistant Director, who brought together the resources of the various curatorial departments to assist me, and to Elizabeth Foy, Administrative Assistant to the Director. I greatly appreciate the specialized advice, in their respective fields, of David A. Brown, Curator of Early Italian Painting; William P. Campbell, Curator of American Painting; E. A. Carmean, Jr., Curator of Twentieth-Century Art; Sheldon Grossman, Curator of Northern and Later Italian Painting; John O. Hand, Curator of Northern European Painting; Parker Lesley, Curator of Decorative Arts; David E. Rust, Curator of French Painting; Anna Voris, Museum Curator; Ross Watson, Curator of British Painting; and Arthur K. Wheelock, Jr., Curator of Flemish and Dutch Painting. Miss Voris was also of the greatest assistance in reading proof.

Douglas Lewis, Curator of Sculpture, and Andrew Robison, Curator of Graphic Arts, advised me in the selection of works of art in their departments and contributed introductory essays which add greatly to the reader's understanding of the Gallery's collections in fields other than painting.

Kathleen Ewing, Coordinator of Photography, and her staff accomplished in record time the tremendous task of furnishing color transparencies for the more than one thousand color plates which illustrate my text. Henry B. Beville, retired Chief Photographer, returned to work long hours to complete the necessary photography.

I am also indebted to J. M. Edelstein, Chief Librarian; David Scott, Planning Consultant; Richard Bales, Assistant to the Director for Music; and Margaret Bouton, Curator in Charge of Education, for information on those functions of the Gallery under their supervision.

The chapter on scientific work at the Gallery is based on a report prepared for me by Dr. Robert Feller, Senior Fellow, National Gallery of Art Research Project. His investigations, together with those of his colleague Dr. Bernard Keisch, in a program begun in 1950 at the Mellon Institute, Carnegie-Mellon University, Pittsburgh, have led to the discovery of many vital tools for the preservation and authentication of works of art.

I am particularly grateful to the two eminent scholars cataloguing the Samuel H. Kress Collection of paintings, Dr. Fern Rusk Shapley and Dr. Colin Eisler, who made their notes available to me in advance of publication. Professor John Rewald was good enough to allow me to use his notes on the *Portrait of the Artist's Father* by Cézanne. I would also like to thank Miss Mary Davis, Vice-President of the Samuel H. Kress Foundation, for her constant helpfulness.

Finally, to Harry N. Abrams, my thanks for his exciting concept for this book, and for the professionalism of his staff, in particular Darlene Geis, Margaret Kaplan, Patricia Gilchrest and Howard Morris, who brought that concept into being.

John Walker

Contents

were made, Mr. Mellon became Ambassador to the Court of St. James's, where he remained from 1932 to 1933. It was a happy year in his life. From the time of his earliest trips to Europe he had gone repeatedly to look at the pictures in the British National Gallery. It had become his favorite collection. The size, the installation, the high level of quality, all appealed to him. He determined that it should be the model for the Washington National Gallery of Art. One might have seen this delicate, patrician, impeccably dressed figure with his high cheekbones, his carefully trimmed gray moustache, his silver-white hair, sometimes alone, sometimes accompanied by David Finley, intensely scrutinizing paintings, teaching himself to discriminate, trying always to learn what made certain works of art greater than others.

This world of aesthetic contemplation, however, did not last. The Depression arrived and Herbert Hoover went down in defeat. On the election of Franklin D. Roosevelt, lawyers from the Department of Justice and the Treasury descended on Mr. Mellon. President Roosevelt and his followers, who had victoriously overthrown twelve years of Republican supremacy, looked upon Andrew Mellon as a symbol of all they opposed. They were determined to discredit him. They asserted that he had committed fraud on his federal income-tax return. On these grounds they attempted to procure a criminal indictment, but the grand jury flatly refused to indict. A civil trial to collect penalties dragged on, overshadowing the last years of his life. When the court finally handed down the verdict, it was a complete vindication of any wrongdoing, but Mr. Mellon was no longer alive.

Yet, during a trial of extraordinary bitterness, he never lost his stoical detachment, never permitted the cruelty of the attack to cause him to deviate from his purpose of building a great national gallery in Washington. In December 1936 he wrote to Mr. Roosevelt, "My dear Mr. President: Over a period of many years I have been acquiring important and rare paintings and sculpture with the idea that ultimately they would become the property of the people of the United States and be made available to them in a national art gallery to be maintained in the city of Washington for the purpose of encouraging and developing a study of the fine arts." And on

December 26, Mr. Roosevelt replied, "My dear Mr. Mellon: When my uncle handed me your letter of December 22 I was not only completely taken by surprise but was delighted by your very wonderful offer. . . . This was especially so because for many years I have felt the need for a national gallery of art in the Capital. . . . Furthermore, your offer of an adequate building and an endowment fund means permanence in this changing world."

All during the tax trial Mr. Mellon continued to collect, spending vast sums to assemble the works of art he felt would provide the nucleus for the Gallery. In the last twelve months of his life he acquired twenty-six paintings, ranging from works by Cimabue and Masaccio to Gainsborough's *Landscape with a Bridge*. Only a few weeks before his death he acquired Duccio's *Nativity*, once part of the *Maestà* of the Cathedral of Siena. This marvelous panel had been exchanged by the Kaiser Friedrich Museum in Berlin for a German painting to satisfy the wishes of Hitler for more Teutonic art.

Andrew Mellon wanted his collection to provide a framework on which the collection of the National Gallery of Art might grow. Therefore he intended his pictures to recapitulate the development of Western painting. His gift begins with a Byzantine Madonna of the thirteenth century and ends with a Turner landscape of the nineteenth century. Between these terminal paintings there is an example by almost every artist who strongly influenced the development of style. Though his collection contains only 115 pictures, exclusive of American portraits, these were chosen with such discrimination that they provide a nearly complete outline of seven centuries of European painting.

He did not collect paintings of the second half of the nineteenth century. He rightly considered American collections to be very rich in the work of the French Impressionists and Post-Impressionists, the most significant schools of the last hundred years, and he believed that the Gallery through gifts would ultimately receive an ample representation of these movements—a judgment which has been proved correct.

But American painting he did wish to provide and to that end he bought *en bloc* the most important private collection of American portraits ever assembled, the Thomas B. Clarke Collection. He knew that the quality of these portraits, ranging from our pioneer painters to Frank Duveneck, was uneven; but he wished the National Gallery of Art and a future National Portrait Gallery, which he hoped would be established, to be enriched by a judicious selection from among them.

Originally it was Andrew Mellon's intention to restrict his gift to painting, but he came to the conclusion that to understand the development of Italian art it is also necessary to know the works of the great sculptors of the Renaissance. With this in mind, especially during the last months of his life, he began to acquire magnificent statues of the fifteenth and sixteenth centuries, when Florentine sculpture reached the peak of its development.

Like the collection of paintings, the number of pieces of sculpture he bought is small, just over a score, principally from the famous Dreyfus Collection. But in both painting and sculpture the quality of the works of art shows an exacting connoisseurship. Mr. Mellon wished his collection to establish a measuring rod which would guide future Trustees in their acceptance of gifts for the Gallery. Thus he set himself the difficult task of acquiring nothing but masterpieces, an undertaking which can fail with even the greatest financial resources. Andrew Mellon, however, was astoundingly successful.

Unfortunately he did not live to see his collection installed in the National Gallery. Thus he did not witness and enjoy that moment which would have meant so much to him, when, with all his paintings and sculptures in place, he might have said to himself in Louis MacNiece's words, "Hundreds of windows are open . . . on a vital but changeless world, a daydream freed from doubt."

P. A. B. and Joseph E. Widener

Of the principal donations to the National Gallery of Art, the Widener Collection is the only one assembled for the most part before 1920. It was brought together when two factors were uniquely in balance: opportunities of purchase and sophistication of judgment.

Peter A. B. Widener and his son, Joseph, were introduced into the world of art by a poker-playing friend, John G. Johnson. Mr. Johnson was among the few dedicated American collectors of his generation. Compared to the Wideners, he was merely well-to-do, but he loved his collection of paintings, a very mixed bag with a few works of outstanding importance, yet for the most part consisting of minor examples that appealed to him. He was, however, a true dilettante in the eighteenth-century sense, and unlike most of the American millionaires of the time, he collected with no ulterior social motive.

P.A.B. Widener was a very different type. According to his grandson the motivation for his collecting was directly related to Philadelphia society. He wished to rise above their snobbery on the wings of his art collection, and he triumphantly succeeded, though his son, Joseph, seems to have remained permanently embittered. P.A.B. Widener in his portrait by Sargent looks as though he might have been a recently enriched alderman; Joseph Widener, in his portrait by Augustus John, looks more like a neurotic peer. The evolution of American families is rapid.

When P.A.B. Widener died in 1915 he left his son the disposition but not the ownership of the collection. Under his will the Widener works of art could be given to a museum in Philadelphia, New York, or Washington, or they could be sold for the benefit of the Widener family. Meanwhile they were displayed at Lynnewood Hall, where the Wideners lived, a house which over the years became a pilgrimage site to all who were interested in art.

In the 1930s Andrew Mellon and Joseph Widener discussed the proposed National Gallery and the future of the Widener Collection without a definite decision being reached. After Mr. Mellon's death, and when the construction of the Gallery was under way, David Finley went to Lynnewood Hall and urged Mr. Widener to give his collection to the National Gallery in Washington. Mr. Widener seemed inclined to do so. David Finley, with his wonderful intuition of how to persuade donors to give collections, asked Otto Eggers, the successor to John Russell Pope as architect of the Gallery, to make renderings of the rooms where the Widener Collection might be placed, showing each work of art installed. Joseph Widener was entranced, but still reluctant to decide. After an agonizing period of uncertainty, he finally offered to designate the National Gallery of Art the fortunate museum provided three conditions could be met: a) that the collection should be shown as a unit; b) that the entire collection including Chinese porcelain, Renaissance furniture, tapestries, ceramics, jewelry, and rock crystals, and French eighteenth-century decorative arts, books, and engravings be accepted; c) that the gift be without taxes of any kind to the Widener estate.

The Widener Collection was a museum in itself and its acquisition of greatest importance to the new National Gallery. The first condition, that the collection be shown as a unit, would, however, have nullified Mr. Mellon's desire for a strictly chronological installation. This principle of an arrangement showing the historical development of painting and sculpture has remained a basic Gallery policy; but it is one that has cost the National Gallery of Art two collections only a little less important than the Widener Collection. The first demand, therefore, the Trustees refused, and Joseph Widener finally accepted a compromise which has been satisfactorily employed with other collectors. He agreed that the Widener Collection should not be shown in contiguous rooms; but in return the Trustees also agreed that when there were enough paintings by one artist or a single school of artists, these would be kept together. The location of the room in which they would be shown, however, would conform with the pattern of the Gallery's chronological arrangement. Thus all the Widener van Dycks are placed in one room, but this room is adjacent to another gallery containing further works by van Dyck from various collections. In a similar way the Widener English paintings are installed in two rooms, at the opposite end of the building, where there are other galleries devoted to this school.

The second condition, that all the important Widener works of art, including decorative arts, be accepted, was easier to satisfy. The original edifice of the National Gallery is built on two floors. The main floor has a skylight with natural illumination in the daytime and artificial illumination at night. It provides ample space for a collection somewhat larger than the collection on exhibition in the Na-

tional Gallery in London. The ground floor, beside areas for temporary exhibitions, a print cabinet, and storage rooms, offered an ideal location for the Widener decorative arts. Though such works of art fall outside the scope of the collection as planned by Andrew Mellon, they represent some of the greatest masterpieces in the Gallery, objects of inestimable value—for instance, the Suger Chalice, one of the most renowned examples in the world of the minor arts of the Middle Ages; the Mazarin Tapestry, the outstanding illustration in the United States of the achievement of Flemish weaving about 1500; and a superbly chosen collection of Renaissance jewels, rock crystals, and Chinese porcelains.

The third condition, that the gift should be tax free, was the most difficult to fulfill. Pennsylvania was one of the states in the Union which assessed a tax on bequests made to charitable institutions located outside the state. Ironically, under the Pennsylvania law, if Joseph Widener had decided to sell the Widener Collection for the benefit of his father's heirs, there would have been no state tax; but if these works of art were to be given to the federal government, then a 5 percent tax would have to be paid to Pennsylvania. Efforts were made by the Gallery to have this law altered, but to no avail. The Pennsylvania legislators proved obdurate and difficult. They refused to estimate the value of the collection until the Gallery agreed to pay the tax, but to accede to this meant accepting an unlimited commitment. The problem therefore seemed insoluble.

President Roosevelt took a personal interest and sent a message to Congress asking that the tax to Pennsylvania be paid regardless of the amount. The bill was passed and may well represent the only blank check ever written by Congress. It was this blank check which finally made possible one of the greatest donations in the history of museums.

There remained only the question of a valuation. The State of Pennsylvania appointed an appraiser, as did the Treasury and the National Gallery of Art. The results were significant. The date of the appraisal was 1940, when the gift was made. The three appraisals in the order mentioned were: $7,141,060; $3,877,010; and $4,953,060.

From documents in our files it is evident that

P.A.B. and Joseph Widener paid between $20 and $25 million for their collections during the first two decades of the twentieth century, when the purchasing power of the dollar was very high. Yet by 1940 the value of the collection had declined 72 percent in terms of more inflated dollars. It is often assumed that the monetary value of works of art steadily increases. This is not true. The fluctuations are staggering. Today with $200 million I could not begin to assemble another Widener Collection. Yet thirty years ago its value for tax purposes was just over $7 million.

There is about the Widener Collection a certain unity of selection difficult to describe. Both father and son showed a concentration of rare intensity in their collecting. They were the type of devoted amateur that has become scarce in the world today. Although they sought advice from scholars and experts, the ultimate decision was always theirs, and for this reason, perhaps, they soon freed themselves from those fads and fashions that have characterized modern taste. Barbizon canvases, which once hid the walls of American houses under drifts of gray-green foliage, they avoided or disposed of, being satisfied with a few magnificent Corots. The present ubiquitous vogue of the Impressionists they anticipated by half a century. Manet's *The Dead Toreador* entered the collection in 1894, to be followed by important works by Degas and Renoir, at a time when these artists were still not fully appreciated even in their own country.

Yet the instinctive taste of the Wideners was for an earlier age and an earlier style. Their real feeling was for the grand manner: for the High Renaissance in Italy, for the seventeenth century in the Netherlands, and the eighteenth century in England. Their aesthetic sense was close to that of the English milords, those landed amateurs portrayed by Reynolds and Gainsborough, whose galleries showed their love of Raphael, Titian, van Dyck, and Rembrandt. For it is the work of these masters of the grand style which both Wideners tirelessly sought throughout Europe and which today makes up the great treasures of their collection.

Like eighteenth-century connoisseurs, Mr. Widener and his son felt no interest in the styles of the thirteenth and fourteenth centuries, so highly esteemed in our time. Castagno, Neroccio de' Landi, Lorenzo di Credi, Mantegna, along with a few other fifteenth-century artists, seemed sufficiently archaic to indicate the origins of the Italian school. One painting by each of these masters was acquired, but what paintings they are! The unparalleled shield by Castagno; the rare example of Sienese portraiture of the fifteenth century by Neroccio; the only existing self-portrait by Lorenzo di Credi; as well as one of the most marmoreal and exquisitely preserved of Mantegna's panels—these and a few superb paintings by less well-known artists represent the Quattrocento.

Similar panels one might occasionally have found hanging on the walls of great eighteenth-century houses; but wonderful as such paintings now seem, they would once have been considered, and perhaps should still be considered, secondary to other pictures in the Widener Collection, such as *The Small Cowper Madonna* by Raphael, which Lord Cowper bought in Italy nearly two centuries ago; *The Feast of the Gods*, that most harmonious but enigmatic work of collaboration between Giovanni Bellini and Titian, which was formerly the greatest treasure in the collection of the Duke of Northumberland; and the *Venus and Adonis* by Titian, which so impressed John Evelyn, the seventeenth-century

Decorative Arts from the Widener Collection

Upper left: Necklace with pendant representing a sphinx. Italian, Florence, c. 1580. Enameled gold, rubies, emeralds, and pearls; pendant: 14⅜ x 2 x ⅝"

Upper right: Pyx in the form of a dove. French, Limoges, XIII century. Copper gilt with champlevé enamel, 7⅛ x 8⅞ x 7½"

Lower left: Reliquary. French, Limoges, c. 1180. Vermiculated copper gilt with champlevé enamels mounted on a wooden support, 7⅜ x 10½ x 4⅞"

Lower right: The Chalice of Abbot Suger. French, Saint Denis, c. 1140. Sardonyx cup with silver-gilt mounting, encrusted with filigree, jewels, pearls and glass; 7¼ x top diam. 4⅞"; base diam. 4⅝"

small salary had accumulated enough capital to buy a stationery and novelty store in northern Pennsylvania. His enterprise succeeded, and he expanded, selecting the South and West for the chain of stores he later established. These proved to be immensely profitable; and partly for business reasons, partly for pleasure, he began to make annual trips to Europe.

He began collecting quite by chance. He was not a man who could ever be idle; and that European ennui, which affects so many American businessmen vacationing abroad, impelled him to seek an outlet for his indefatigable energy. A friend introduced him to a dealer, Count Contini-Bonacossi, in the hope that this recently ennobled Florentine might interest him in art and thus render his European vacations less boring. The cure for boredom worked beyond all expectations and cost in the end between $50 million and $100 million. Through his contact with the Count, as Mr. Kress affectionately called him, he was soon infected with the collector's virus, succumbing almost immediately to that passion from which he never recovered, much to the benefit of cities in various parts of the United States and particularly of the National Gallery in Washington.

But Mr. Kress's collecting was, at the beginning, of a special kind. Perhaps because of his life as a storekeeper, he often referred to his works of art in a naive but charming way as "items." These "items" were to provide the most complete and systematic collection of Italian art ever brought together. Count Contini persuaded him to assemble works not only by the principal geniuses of the Italian schools but also by their entourage, those lesser-known painters and sculptors whose work, he said, explains and gives scale to the greater artists.

Such an emphasis on the form and structure of art represents a shift in the focus of appreciation from that shared by Mr. Mellon and Mr. Widener. The Kress Collection, in its first phase, reflected a point of view which Contini encouraged and which has grown out of the characteristic twentieth-century interest in art history. It showed the full effect of the scientific approach introduced into connoisseurship, especially of Italian art, by Morelli. This system of attributing paintings was perfected by Berenson, whose remarkable, intuitive scholarship made a deep impression on Samuel Kress. In the dossier of nearly every object which he gave the Gallery were written opinions not only by Berenson, but also by Fiocco, Longhi, Van Marle, Perkins, Suida, and Adolfo Venturi.

Samuel Kress's first purchases of Italian art were made in the most logical place, in Italy, and principally from his mentor, Count Contini. But he discovered that the Italian private collections had long before yielded their greatest treasures either to the museums of their own country or to the collections of England, France, and Germany. He realized that if he were to bring together distinguished works not only by minor artists but also by the great masters, he would have to search beyond the wares being offered by a single Italian dealer. This realization, however, presented Mr. Kress with a dilemma. When he began collecting, he once told me, Andrew Mellon dominated the international art market, and everything was offered to him first. Samuel Kress was reluctant to buy what had already been, he suspected, turned down. He therefore refused for many years to trade with the principal dealers. With the death of Andrew Mellon in 1937 the situation changed, and Samuel Kress became the most important private collector in the world. But in 1938 the Kress Collection still consisted chiefly of what Mr. Kress had bought from Count Contini.

Although Samuel Kress admired Andrew Mellon as a collector, he had no idea of giving his own collection to the museum Mr. Mellon had established. The fact that in the end the Kress Collection came to Washington was almost a matter of chance. In the winter of 1938 while the Gallery was being erected, two friends, Herbert Friedmann, the Curator of Birds at the Smithsonian Institution, and Jeremiah O'Connor, the Curator of Painting at the Corcoran Gallery, made a trip to New York, intent on their favorite pastime, to see as many private collections as possible. On this expedition they arranged to visit the Kress Collection, at that time scarcely known. Although neither was an expert in Italian art, both were astute enough to realize what Samuel Kress had already collected. On their return they described to David Finley the extraordinary paintings and sculpture they had seen. They went further and wrote Mr.

Kress, urging him to give his collection to Washington. They knew he was contemplating a private museum like the Frick Collection, and they argued eloquently against such an arrangement and in favor of a donation to a museum supported by the federal government where, they pointed out, the Kress Collection would be seen by more persons and have a more secure future. The result of the correspondence was an invitation from Mr. Kress to Mr. Finley, asking him to come to New York to discuss the new museum in Washington.

Mr. Kress and Mr. Finley had met once on shipboard, though with characteristic modesty Samuel Kress had scarcely mentioned his collection. When the new Director of the National Gallery of Art saw what his steamship companion had brought together, he realized the collection must be procured for Washington. He had arrived at three in the afternoon; he left at ten in the evening. During those seven hours, with his inimitable powers of persuasion, he induced Samuel Kress to give up his plan for a private museum, for which property was already under option and architectural drawings prepared, and to send his works of art instead to the National Gallery. Had David Finley not arrived when he did, the Kress Collection would have remained on Fifth Avenue in its own building.

But even after Samuel Kress had decided that the National Gallery of Art would be the recipient of his collection, there was a strong possibility that the Trustees of the Gallery would be unwilling to receive it. The problem was that Andrew Mellon had insisted that a clause be inserted in the Act of Congress establishing the Gallery stating that "no work of art shall be included in the Permanent Collection of the National Gallery of Art unless it be of similar high standard of quality to those in the Collection acquired from the donor." Mr. Kress insisted that we take a minimum of 375 paintings and 18 sculptures, and a majority of these did not meet Mr. Mellon's qualifications. David Finley was able to negotiate an arrangement whereby a segment of the gift was constituted a Study Collection. But there remained 281 paintings and 18 pieces of sculpture which Samuel Kress insisted should be shown as part of the Permanent Collection. The Trustees of the Gallery were dubious, and they asked me whether these paintings

and sculptures met Andrew Mellon's stipulations. If I believed they did, would I attest to this in writing?

I faced a dilemma. On the one hand, if the Gallery opened with only the 125 paintings and the 23 sculptures provided by Andrew Mellon, the vast building with 3¼ acres of exhibition space would be so empty that visitors might have to ask the guards to direct them to the next work of art. I foresaw budgetary problems with Congress, and knowing that politicians, like nature, abhor a vacuum, I was apprehensive about what we might be forced to exhibit. Moreover, I was convinced that Samuel Kress intended to improve his collection. He had the wealth, and I could see that the virus of collecting had entered his veins.

On the other hand, the standards of the Mellon Collection were as high as those of the Frick and the Widener collections, to name the two greatest in America. What Contini had sold Mr. Kress was different in character. All the lesser Italian masters were well represented, but apart from the Allendale *Nativity* by Giorgione, which Mr. Kress had bought from Duveen, there were relatively few paintings of world renown. The sculpture was no more impressive.

I was deeply perplexed. Samuel Kress was reluctantly enthusiastic about the new Gallery, and he had no intention of modifying his terms. We accepted what he offered, he stated, or he built his own museum. In the end I felt I had no choice. I signed an affidavit that the Kress Collection met Andrew Mellon's stipulations. Luckily events proved it was the right thing to do. Of the 393 paintings and sculptures in this first gift from Samuel Kress, only 131 remain on exhibition. Those that have been removed have been replaced by the greatest masterpieces available for purchase during the 1940s and 1950s, the last two decades when acquisitions on a large scale were possible.

It must have been very hard for Samuel Kress to face parting with all these works of art, for in many ways his paintings and sculpture were a substitute for the children he never had. After the final selection for Washington had been made, David Finley said to me, as we were leaving the Kress apartment, that our new friend seemed to look upon us with the questioning and dubious reflection of a father estimating the character of his future sons-in-law. It was an astute observation, and this somewhat delicate relationship continued for several years. About once a month we would go to New York, and Mr. Kress would walk with us on the terrace of his penthouse or sit with us in his living room, where the blank walls seemed to accuse us of the treasures which had been removed. We would discuss the collection: how it looked, how it could be improved. Even in the last tragic years, when he was almost completely paralyzed, any mention of the National Gallery of Art would stimulate him to the effort of a reply. In the end we knew to our great joy that he was satisfied with the disposition of his collection, which he had originally looked on with considerable doubt.

After Samuel Kress was stricken, his much younger brother, Rush Kress took over the direction of the Samuel H. Kress Foundation and devoted much of its resources to collecting for the National Gallery of Art.

The two brothers somewhat resembled one another, except that in place of Samuel Kress's shrewd, appraising glance, Rush Kress's look was open, even ingenuous. He was certainly the handsomer of the two, and his appearance was less that of a shopkeeper than of a president of an inherited firm. He did, in fact, become president of the company and of the Foundation when his brother fell ill. It was he who was responsible for the really great Kress Collection purchases. Perhaps because Samuel Kress had made the money, he was a little parsimonious in parting with it. Rush Kress, on the other hand, felt that his brother's collection, as he always called it, should contain the noblest masterpieces which could be acquired. Although he constantly repeated that he had no real interest in collecting, but was simply completing a plan begun by his brother, urged on by the director of the Foundation's artistic program, Guy Emerson, and by Mario Modestini, the curator of the Kress Collection, he grew fascinated by the quest for masterpieces. Between 1945 and 1956 the Kress Foundation spent more than $25 million on works of art. As the Gallery had the first choice of nearly all acquisitions, and considerable influence on their selection, this vast sum of money was in many ways a purchase fund, undoubtedly the largest capital expenditure disbursed in so short a time in the history of museums.

It was an extraordinary investment, as art prices subsequently have soared, and the value of what was purchased has tripled or quadrupled in the last fifteen years. Moreover, Rush Kress allowed me to distill the collection as I wished to do from the beginning, and he broadened the Kress acquisitions from an overwhelming concentration on Italian painting and sculpture to include Flemish, Spanish, French, Dutch, and German art.

Each rise of the tide of economic prosperity in the various countries has left behind incrustations of beauty; and very little of the residuum of this treasure can be removed. In recent years, through increased export restrictions, these possessions have become still more firmly embedded. It is remarkable that the Kresses, forming their collection so late in history, could have found so many masterpieces still susceptible to the ebb and flow of wealth. But private collections in England yielded the noble Allendale Giorgione and the uncompromising *Portrait of a Condottiere* by Giovanni Bellini; in France, a number of eighteenth-century paintings, including the rare Boucher portrait of Madame Bergeret; and in Germany, in this case from museums, the Filippo Lippi *Madonna and Child* and the Raphael *Portrait of Bindo Altoviti*.

In Europe it is customary to think that works of art cross the Atlantic in only one direction. During the Depression, however, a number of the greatest artistic possessions of the United States returned to Europe. For economic laws, which govern the movement of works of art, have not always been in our favor. In the thirties when our gold reserves were being drawn to Europe, their magnetic force pulled from us, among other masterpieces, the Mackay Sassettas (now in the National Gallery, London), the Kahn Carpaccio and Frans Hals, and the Morgan Ghirlandaio (now in the Thyssen Collection, Lugano), all supreme achievements by these artists.

Only the purchases made by a few American private collectors, among whom Andrew Mellon and Samuel and Rush Kress were outstanding, checked this outflow of works of art from the United States. Samuel Kress stopped further exportation of the Mackay and Kahn pictures and bought most of the

Goldman Collection as well as many fine paintings from the collections of Robert Lehman and Dan Fellows Platt. Thus the original Kress Collection contained large parts of five of the most important private collections formed in this country.

During the war a number of paintings were sent to the United States for safekeeping, and from among these Rush Kress was able to make exceptional purchases. From the Cook Collection he acquired seventeen pictures, including the famous *Adoration of the Magi* by Fra Angelico and Fra Filippo Lippi; from the Thyssen Collection the wonderfully preserved *St. Veronica* by Memling, and other paintings; and from the collection of Count Cini, the *Giuliano de' Medici* by Botticelli and the *Dance of Salome* by Gozzoli.

After the war, at Rush Kress's instigation, dealers went to Europe in a continuing search for paintings and sculpture. This resulted above all in magnificent acquisitions from the greatest of Viennese collections, those of Count Czernin and of Prince Liechtenstein. Moreover, whatever of outstanding importance came on the New York, London, or Paris markets was likely to be offered first to the Kress Foundation. The purchases in these years altered the character of the Kress Collection. More masterpieces were acquired and less attention paid to the minor Italian artists. The schools north of the Alps received new emphasis. A room devoted to German masters was assembled; two rooms of early Flemish and Hispano-Flemish paintings were added. Two galleries of seventeenth- and eighteenth-century French paintings supplemented those Samuel Kress had given; and Spanish, Dutch, and later Flemish pictures were bought.

Some idea of the magnitude of the purchases made between 1945 and 1956 by the Kress Foundation under Rush Kress's leadership may be gained from the Kress exhibitions held in 1951 and 1956 to celebrate the tenth and fifteenth anniversaries of the opening of the National Gallery of Art. In the two exhibitions there were 208 paintings and 46 pieces of sculpture. From these shows the Kress Foundation offered the National Gallery of Art the choice of as many works of art as would strengthen and enrich the collection in Washington. The Gallery finally decided to retain 167 paintings and all the sculptures.

The rapid expansion of the Kress Collection presented the Gallery with an unusual problem. There was a danger that the collection in Washington might grow too rapidly, with undue duplication, with too many minor masters, and with unwarranted emphasis on the Italian schools. Rush Kress was well aware of the law of diminishing returns, which plagues museums with collections insufficiently distilled. He decided that his brother's conception of a study collection and a permanent collection, both located in Washington, was not the most efficient way to utilize the vast number of paintings and sculpture the Kress Foundation had acquired. He concluded that works of art in storage are of little use; whereas the same paintings and sculpture shown in a community deficient in art might have a profound effect. He therefore determined to make important donations to eighteen museums in cities stretching from Miami in the East to Honolulu in the West. He bought a number of important works for these galleries, and asked that the National Gallery of Art return to the Foundation in exchange for new gifts whatever it could spare from the Kress Foundation's previous donations.

The staff of the National Gallery of Art was thus presented with one of the most fascinating series of decisions in museum history. To discuss only paintings, the Kress Foundation owned over 1,300 canvases and panels, of which there were at least 600 up to the standard of the National Gallery of Art. The space decided upon for the Kress Collection in Washington, more than a third of the main floor of the Gallery, would hold without crowding between 350 and 400 pictures. To reduce the Kress Collection to the present 377 paintings required eliminations which were often heartbreaking. But these were made less distressing by the realization that the 250 or more pictures surrendered by the Gallery would be enjoyed elsewhere in the United States.

Although the Kress Collection has been dispersed in this way, it is recorded in a nine-volume catalogue. These books reunite and present to the world one of the greatest collections formed in this century. That the most significant part of this collection should have ended in Washington has helped to give the National Gallery of Art its high rank among museums.

Chester Dale

The sources of the principal collections given to the National Gallery of Art are interestingly varied. Andrew Mellon bought from only two firms, M. Knoedler and Company and Duveen Brothers. The Wideners and the Kresses were patrons of all the important art dealers in Europe and America. But Chester Dale alone was shrewd enough to become a partner of a dealer—the Galerie Georges Petit, one of the best-known companies dealing in Impressionist and Post-Impressionist canvases. This allowed him to scrutinize what was going on behind the scenes. His knowledge of the world centers of the art trade—Fifty-seventh Street in New York, Bond Street in London, and the rue de la Boëtie in Paris—was unique among American collectors. It enabled him to enter the art market with complete assurance and to carry off from dealers, private collectors, and, above all, the great auctions of Europe and America, unsurpassed treasures of French painting of the last one hundred and fifty years.

That Chester Dale would one day become a great collector must have seemed unlikely to his parents. A dropout from school, he started life as a runner on the New York Stock Exchange. His first collection had nothing to do with art; it was devoted to inactive and unlisted railway bonds. His connoisseurship in these recondite securities enabled him eventually to become a partner in Langley and Company. Gifted with an amazing memory and a quick intuitive judgment, he pioneered successfully in buying public-utility holding companies, a field of investing then relatively unfamiliar even to the investment bankers of his generation. A redhead, wiry, and quick on his feet as a welterweight boxer (which he had once been), Chester Dale with his determination and inexhaustible vitality proved himself a formidable opponent among the financiers of his time. Wall Street was a challenge to him, a place to play a game with skill and daring. He played well, and ultimately retired to devote his intensely competitive nature to a different game, the acquisition of works of art.

Here he was fortunate enough to receive indispensable assistance. Maud Dale, his first wife, was a painter and art critic who would have had a successful career in either field, had her days not been fully occupied arranging art exhibitions and finding paintings for her husband to buy. In the early years of their collecting it was she who would point to the quarry; Chester Dale would track it down and secure it. Masterpieces have their own protective coloration and are not always easy to discern. But Mr. Dale's perceptive instinct soon developed, and with its development came a passion for works of art equaled by few collectors. His paintings, and the National Gallery of Art, became the major interests of his life. He gave unstinted devotion to both. For it was the essence of his character to commit himself entirely.

When Maud Dale died in 1953 one might have supposed that he would stop collecting. They had worked so closely together that the collection was in a way a joint enterprise. But such a supposition would have been wrong, He continued buying. In spite of the growing scarcity of masterpieces, some of his greatest acquisitions were made after her death.

The great period of purchase by the Dales, however, was during the 1920s. This was a time when the values of stocks and bonds were increasing daily until they were inflated beyond all reason, whereas the prices being paid for the work of the Impressionist and Post-Impressionist painters whom the Dales especially collected were, though costly, excellent investments in relation to the market today. When the crash came, securities fell to a fraction of their former prices; but the value of French painting held up remarkably well, supported largely by Chester Dale's continuing purchases. Since 1929 stocks have risen to an average somewhat less than twice their previous high, whereas French paintings now bring many times the highest prices ever paid in the twenties. Of all the collections in the Gallery, judged in purely monetary terms, the Chester Dale Collection has had far and away the greatest increase in value.

I had known Chester Dale in the late twenties, when two friends and I, while undergraduates, were running a gallery we had established in Harvard Square. We had temporary shows of what was then considered avant-garde art, and we borrowed extensively from the Dales, who were generous lenders. In the autumn of 1940, with David Finley, I renewed my acquaintance with Chester and Maud Dale. After a long and earnest conversation during which we stressed our need for American and French painting, we felt we had infected them with our enthusiasm for the new Gallery, but it was too close to the time of the opening, in 1941, to install a number of rooms devoted to their collection. Nevertheless, they sent seven American pictures on indefinite loan to bolster our American section. A few months later twenty-five French nineteenth-century paintings arrived to give the Gallery its first representation of Impressionism and Post-Impressionism. In 1942 more paintings of the same period were added, and in 1951 and 1952 the School of Paris canvases previously on loan to Chicago and Philadelphia were concentrated in Washington. All these paintings were only on loan, though we tried to give the impression that they had been donated.

Meanwhile the Samuel H. Kress Foundation was acquiring and sending to Washington incredible masterpieces of earlier painting and sculpture, but Rush Kress decided that as long as Chester Dale would not make a gift, the new Kress acquisitions would maintain the same status. These concealed loans were a source of constant anxiety. At one time in the late 1950s almost half of the works of art on display at the National Gallery seemed likely to be whisked away by these two potential but rival donors, whose good manners concealed a fervent dislike. This was a critical time. It ended when in 1961 the last of the Kress loans were finally converted into gifts, and when at Chester Dale's death in 1962 his loans also became the property of the Gallery.

The National Gallery of Art has acquired its collection by taking chances. Coming so late on the museum scene, the Director and Trustees had to have faith in a few collectors. To show the brilliance of French painting during the last century and a half they had to rely on Chester Dale. For a long time there were no Dale gifts, and while this was admittedly disconcerting, they refused to let it be disheartening. They knew the magnitude of the Dale Collection and they gambled that Chester Dale's fluctuating satisfaction with the Gallery would end happily. It did; the result was a bequest of 252 paint-

ings and sculptures, a sizable purchase fund, and money for fellowships for students in art history.

Lessing J. Rosenwald

Another of the Founding Benefactors, Lessing J. Rosenwald, has given the National Gallery of Art his collection of prints and drawings, as well as some paintings.

A retired businessman who looks more like a medieval monk, Lessing Rosenwald was at one time chairman of Sears, Roebuck and Company. In his retirement the collecting of prints, drawings, and illustrated books, once his avocation, became an all-absorbing vocation. From the beginning he has sought excellence rather than volume. Nevertheless, he has brought together over twenty-five thousand drawings, woodcuts, engravings, etchings, mezzotints, lithographs, and prints in other media. This is not an enormous collection, but considering that it was assembled by one collector and that the impressions are extremely fine, it is an amazing achievement. In thirty years a single individual has formed a collection rivaling in quality, if not in quantity, the most important private collections of graphic art ever formed.

In the past, print collectors like the Abbé de Marolles wanted every print ever executed. In the seventeenth century, when the abbé lived, one hundred thousand impressions would have represented print-making completely. Today millions of examples would be required and such comprehensive collecting would be folly. Selectivity has become essential. Rosenwald has discriminated carefully, basing his judgment on four criteria: beauty, content, rarity, and, above all, quality. As he has said himself, "Quality is infinitely more difficult to attain than quantity. It is dependent on at least two variables, the ability to recognize the excellence of an impression from experience and knowledge and the availability of fine prints."

Print collecting requires a special erudition. A discriminating eye, though basic, is in itself insufficient.

There are matters of rarity, brilliance of impression, paper, margins, states, innumerable facts which the collector must know. In all these matters Rosenwald's knowledge is exceptional.

In recent years the availability of outstanding prints and drawings has been on the whole greater than that of paintings or sculpture. There have been wonderful opportunities for acquisition from European collections like that of Count Harrach of Vienna, and from many of the European print cabinets which, since the war, have been increasingly inclined to dispose of their duplicates. Moreover, as prints and drawings are easy to transport, refugees from Nazi and Communist persecution have brought these precious leaves of paper to the auction rooms of Europe and America. Consequently, in some areas of print collecting Lessing Rosenwald has assembled examples unmatched elsewhere. His collection of fifteenth-century wood- and metal-cuts, for example, is one of the finest of its kind in the world. An entire year's collecting is rewarded if a few excellent impressions of these rare prints can be found. Yet, because of several extraordinary opportunities, he has assembled close to four hundred examples, many of which are unique. There are other areas of print collecting in which the Rosenwald Collection is outstanding: engravings by Northern Gothic masters and by Dürer, Lucas van Leyden, Rembrandt, and Nanteuil, to select a few artists.

Lessing Rosenwald has built a small museum near Philadelphia where the collection is housed during his lifetime. From there selected prints and drawings are brought to the main Print Room at the National Gallery in Washington as they are needed for study or exhibition. Traveling exhibitions and loans also show many choice items from the Rosenwald Collection throughout the United States.

The Rosenwald Collection has been constantly augmented, and, since it was presented to the National Gallery of Art in 1943, it has more than doubled in size. This great donation deserves a more detailed treatment, and some beginnings toward that may be found in the section on drawings at the end of this volume, as well as in the series of scholarly exhibition catalogues published by the National Gallery on the miniatures and the Old Master prints in its collection.

Paul Mellon

The Founding Benefactors represent three generations of collecting: the first, Andrew Mellon (1855–1937), P.A.B. Widener (1834–1915), and Samuel Kress (1863–1955); the second, Joseph Widener (1871–1943), Rush Kress (1877–1963), Chester Dale (1883–1962), and Lessing Rosenwald (b. 1891); and the third, the son and daughter of Andrew Mellon, Paul Mellon (b. 1907) and Ailsa Mellon Bruce (1901–1969). Paul Mellon, though serving on the boards of the Mellon Bank and T. Mellon and Company, which handles the Mellon financial affairs, has spent his life not making money but giving it away. The Andrew W. Mellon Foundation, the result of gifts from him and his sister, is one of the largest in the United States. Philanthropy, collecting, and sport have been his major interests. A graduate of Yale and of Clare College, Cambridge, he is a self-admitted Anglophile. For a few precious weeks each year he races and hunts in England.

While I was Chief Curator, from 1939 to 1956, I had no idea that someone I had known from a mutual Pittsburgh childhood would become one of the great collectors of recent years. But lurking in his unconscious, perhaps planted there by heredity and nurtured by environment, was a love of art; and there was an instinct for collecting evident already in his library. He once tried to explain the impulse to collect, which has played such an important part in the lives of his wife and himself: "There seems to be a built-in or inherited desire to own, enjoy, to savor, and to conserve rare and beautiful things, a desire which must infuse all collectors. It begins in childhood, or is perhaps there even at birth. It is the childish pleasure of searching for odd or rare or beautiful shells on a beach, the immediate and delighted relationship between the shell lying in the afternoon sun in the wet sand and the clear, unclouded vision of the child."

When fairly late in life he turned to collecting paintings, his first important purchases were canvases of the French Impressionists and Post-Impressionists. Here his second wife, a remarkably creative woman in gardening, architecture, and decorating, was certainly influential. There was also the influence of Chester Dale. But as Paul Mellon has said, "We almost never buy a painting or a drawing we would not want to live with or see constantly," and the wall space in his houses soon vanished. The collection continued to grow; as had been the case with Chester Dale, the National Gallery has benefited by loans from this overflow of masterpieces.

Although Paul Mellon has always felt himself only a temporary custodian of the treasures he has gathered, the ephemeral nature of possession has not affected the character of his collecting. As he has written, "Although obviously some day many of our works of art will be in a public museum or museums, we have only in rare instances bought with this in mind. . . . We do not believe in giving a work of art to a museum or other institution, even anonymously, if we do not personally feel affection toward it."

Such sensibilities have given the French pictures lent from the collection of the Paul Mellons to the National Gallery of Art a particularly personal quality. French paintings, however, represent numerically the smaller part of the collection. Paul Mellon's holdings of British art are far more extensive. Here his interest was somewhat fortuitous. He had for many years collected in a desultory way English pictures and books, but it was not until after 1959 that his collection took on something of its present magnitude. In that year the Virginia Museum of Fine Arts, of which he has been a Trustee for many years, asked him to help organize an exhibition entitled *Sport and the Horse*. Basil Taylor, then an official of the Royal College of Art in London, was employed as adviser. A remarkable show was assembled, and in the process of borrowing from British museums and private collectors Paul Mellon became engrossed in English art, not the full-length official or society portraits his father had bought, but scenes of sport, conversation pieces, topographical paintings, and genre and story-telling pictures, whatever offered an insight into English life between 1650 and 1850. He was enchanted by the poetry of nature in the landscapes of Wilson, Constable, and Turner; the social insight of the canvases of Hogarth and the watercolors of Rowlandson; the technical virtuosity underlying the chiaroscuro of Joseph Wright of Der-

by, and equally reflected in the vitreous surfaces of Stubbs; the depiction of every aspect of that delectable existence, which was the good fortune of the English upper classes in the eighteenth century, glimpsed in scenes delineated with captivating charm by scores of artists like Johann Zoffany, Arthur Devis, George Morland, and others. Some of these paintings may one day be given to the National Gallery, but the greater part will form the collection of the Yale Center for British Art and British Studies.

Apart from important gifts of paintings, including Cézanne's monumental portrait of his father, his magnificent portrait of his friend Antony Valabrègue, and Manet's *The Plum*, as well as over 350 oils by Catlin and canvases by Canaletto and Devis, Paul Mellon's most significant donations have been financial. His support made possible the A. W. Mellon Lectures in the Fine Arts and their publication. These have constituted since 1952 the most distinguished lectureship on the general subject of art and aesthetics in the United States and recently have been paralleled by the Wrightsman Lectures at the Metropolitan Museum.

Paul Mellon has been deeply interested in scholarship. His Center for British Art and British Studies has infused new vitality into art history. He also supported the Gallery's request to the foundations established by him and his sister for graduate fellowships for students intending to become curators, a project so successful that the Samuel H. Kress Foundation gave still larger grants for the same purpose and added an annual stipend for a Samuel H. Kress Professor in Residence at the National Gallery. On Chester Dale's death further funds became available for similar fellowships. Consequently the Gallery now annually finances the postgraduate studies of nine or ten young men and women.

Ailsa Mellon Bruce

The two recently merged Mellon foundations had always worked in close conjunction, and the National Gallery has benefited by many mutual donations. But the greatest gifts of money received by the Gallery from one person have come from Ailsa Mellon Bruce herself. Her untimely death was the most disastrous blow the Gallery has sustained. She gave more than money. She had a deep love of the institution her father established. She was determined that it should become the greatest of its kind. Whenever difficulties seemed insurmountable, her support and enthusiasm always enheartened us.

Like her brother she became a collector fairly late in life. Her first important acquisition was the purchase of the entire Molyneux Collection—roughly ninety French Impressionist and Post-Impressionist pictures, all intimate in scale but of the highest quality. To this nucleus she added such masterpieces as Goya's *Condesa de Chinchón*, Monet's *The Artist's Garden at Vétheuil*, Renoir's *Pont Neuf, Paris*, Cézanne's *Riverbank*, and many more French paintings. At her death her whole collection of paintings was left to the National Gallery of Art.

I always discussed with Ailsa Mellon Bruce the pictures we intended to buy with the immense resources she provided, and almost all the greatest works of art the Gallery acquired with its own funds are the result of her generosity. To some she responded with excitement, to others with a personal indifference which, she assured me, was not to matter so long as I felt they would enrich the Gallery. When we bought Leonardo da Vinci's *Ginevra de' Benci*, it took me over a year to persuade her to allow her name to be connected with the purchase. Because of speculation as to the picture's value she thought it would be ostentatious to be mentioned as having made its acquisition possible. Such modesty is not found often among collectors and donors.

I talked to her frequently about the goal I had long dreamed of for the National Gallery of Art, a goal suggested to me over thirty years ago by Bernard Berenson. It was to create in Washington a modern equivalent of the ancient library at Alexandria, which had burned in A.D. 391. This was the center of Hellenistic scholarship. It seemed to me the National Gallery could provide the same environment—a superb collection, a magnificent library adjacent, and a group of scholars to work in both. She immediately understood and enthusiastically backed the project.

Paul Mellon also saw that this was an opportunity for the National Gallery to assist scholarship in a way never attempted by any other museum since the destruction of the Alexandrine Library. He and his sister agreed to provide the enormous resources necessary to erect an additional building at the entrance to the Mall, a building which has been described in an earlier chapter.

Other Individual Donations

Opposite the panel at the entrance to the National Gallery of Art listing the Founding Benefactors there is a second panel recording additional donors who have been exceptionally generous. This second roll of honor, which is steadily lengthening, pays tribute to gifts which have varied in number from the unique collection of 215 American Primitives given by Colonel and Mrs. Edgar W. Garbisch to a single great canvas by Manet, *Gare St.-Lazare*, bequeathed by Horace Havemeyer, a great Mondrian given by Herbert and Nannette Rothschild, and the supremely beautiful Vermeer, *A Lady Writing*, given by Horace Havemeyer's sons in his memory.

There have been many distinguished gifts of Old Masters such as the Bellini, Boltraffio, Tintoretto, Cranachs, and Strigels donated by Mr. and Mrs. Ralph Harmon Booth of Detroit; the superb portraits by Goya and other paintings given by Mr. and Mrs. Peter Frelinghuysen, who are the son-in-law and daughter of one of the greatest American collectors, Mrs. Henry O. Havemeyer; and the magnificent English paintings donated by the family of Gov. Alvan T. Fuller of Massachusetts, to mention only a few.

Just as the National Gallery belongs to the whole country, not to a single part, these gifts have come from all over the United States. But there have also been five remarkably generous Washingtonians. One was Duncan Phillips, who not only gave several important paintings but as a Trustee contributed for many years his wisdom and counsel, always valuable but especially so when the Gallery was in its formative stage and badly in need of experience. A second was Mrs. Eugene Meyer, a remarkable connoisseur in Western and Oriental art, who gave her magnificent Cézannes, her Manet *Still Life*, her

Renoir, Despiau, Rodin, and Brancusi, all acquired in the beginning of this century when such acquisitions represented an adventurous appreciation. A third was Averell Harriman, who with his first wife assembled one of the most distinguished collections of Impressionist and Post-Impressionist paintings brought together in this country. Governor Harriman has given indications that his generosity will continue. The fourth was Oscar L. Milmore, a foreign service officer who made his permanent home in Washington. Following his wife's death, he established a trust fund in her memory, which has grown to substantial size. The income from this fund is to be used in perpetuity for the purchase of works of art. The donation of a fifth Washingtonian, an economist and former member of the Federal Reserve Board, Adolph Caspar Miller, was motivated in an unexpected way. He used to come to the Gallery regularly to sit on a sofa facing the self-portrait of Rembrandt. A few weeks before Mr. Miller died, I saw him in his usual place. He said he wanted to speak to me, then told me of his decision to leave his collection and a large donation to the National Gallery of Art. He explained that he had only one motive in making the bequest, namely to repay what he had learned from years of scrutiny of a single portrait. It was a bequest really to Rembrandt, and Mr. Miller could think of no better way of expressing his gratitude.

Some other bequests to the Gallery have been unusual. Mrs. Lillian S. Timken of New York, for example, left her large collection to both the National Gallery and the Metropolitan Museum in New York, without indicating which works of art should go to which institution. The directors tried to divide the collection into equal groups, but in the end the presidents of the two Boards of Trustees had to toss a coin for works by such artists as Moroni, Titian, Rembrandt, van Dyck, Rubens, Boucher, Fragonard, Turner, and others.

There have also been friends who have come to the financial assistance of the Gallery when a particularly desirable painting or piece of sculpture has appeared on the market. Through her very generous donations, Miss Syma Busiel of Chicago has made it possible to acquire outstanding works of art for the Gallery. The W. L. and May T. Mellon Foundation and Mrs. Maude Monell Vetlesen of New York have bought important American paintings.

Many donors continue to show interest in the future of the Gallery. Robert and Clarice Smith have given fellowships as well as important Dutch paintings and Old Master drawings; Burton and Emily Tremaine have made over a large collection of modern paintings and graphics with indications that their entire collection will eventually be coming. David K. E. Bruce has established a vital purchase fund for the newly expanded library's acquisitions. In addition, a nationwide Collectors' Committee has been established to underwrite the commissioning of major works of art for the East Building.

The Gallery continues to depend exclusively on the generosity of private citizens for the growth of the collections and can only rejoice in the fact that over its brief history it has so often been able to compete for whatever painting or sculpture of exceptional merit has been offered for sale.

Policies

When the Gallery was established by Andrew Mellon, he had in mind, as I have said, modeling it on the example of the British National Gallery. His original concept was modified during his lifetime by the inclusion of sculpture, and after his death by the acceptance of the Widener decorative arts. But works by living artists continued to be excluded from exhibition as they are in London.

For many years I strongly advocated this restriction. During the Joseph McCarthy period, and when Representative George A. Dondero was an influential member of Congress, modern art was anathema on the Hill. Our support in the Senate and the House might have been jeopardized had we shown avant-garde work. It was essential to establish the image of the Gallery as a great repository of traditional painting and sculpture before entering the controversial field of contemporary art.

When the Kennedy administration, however, was inaugurated, there was a cultural change in the country. Washington became much more sophisticated. Congressman Dondero was defeated and the atmosphere on the Hill was transformed. Modern art was no longer considered a manifestation of communism, as it had been, even though everybody was aware that only the most reactionary examples were permitted to be shown in Russia. The Kennedys knew and spoke to many painters and sculptors. They represented a new attitude in the White House, one of sympathy and understanding for the arts. During the Kennedy administration Washington became as stimulating as it had been in the days of Franklin Roosevelt.

Chester Dale in 1951 placed his modern French paintings on loan, and there were no protests over Picasso hanging on the same floor with Perugino. Nevertheless, the Trustees' policy of discouraging the acquisition of works by painters who had not died at least twenty years earlier continued. But there was no restriction on loans, and we held a series of shows of contemporary art. When Chester Dale died in December 1962, however, the Trustees were confronted with a problem. The penalty for refusing to show the work of living painters would have been the loss of an invaluable collection. For, according to Chester Dale's will, his gift to the National Gallery of Art was subject to the condition that "said Trustees of the National Gallery of Art shall agree to accept *all* [my italics] of the property bequeathed to it." And his collection contained superb paintings by Derain, Picasso, Matisse, and Braque, all of whom were still living or had not been dead twenty years.

It did not take the Trustees long to revise their thinking. They recognized that pragmatism is of necessity the philosophy of museums. By their acceptance of the Chester Dale Collection, in January 1963, they automatically had an obligation to exhibit the work of living painters.

They went further. They began a search for important collections of contemporary artists. This quest has continued, and the Gallery has now in its possession, or has been promised, a superb nucleus of work of the most significant painters and sculptors of our time.

In this book I have not, however, included works by living artists. My reason is that the number of such works in the Gallery's collection, still small, is growing at such a rapid rate that the choice I might make at this time could not be a representative one.

Activities

Education

The visual arts are playing an increasingly important role in American education. Primary schools, secondary schools, colleges, and graduate schools all over the country are teaching painting and sculpture, and to a lesser extent the history of art.

This has created responsibilities and opportunities for museums. As Carter Brown has said, in no area is creativity more easily shared than in art. A work of art exists for us today as a self-contained entity whose original purpose was communication, communication not invalidated by the obsolescence of theory, as in science; or by the barrier of language, as in literature; or, even, by the mediation of a performer, as in the sister art of music. At the National Gallery of Art one looks at an image put on canvas by Rembrandt's own hand, and one contemplates greatness directly.

It is the purpose of the Gallery's Education Department to make people aware of the vast reservoir of pleasure and enlightenment the collections represent. We have established in the Education Department two divisions, one to look after visitors to the Gallery, the other for extension activities. The total staff devoted to educational work numbers more than twenty. Each day there are three types of

tours: general tours of the whole collection, tours dealing with a special field or a single school, and a lecture (of which mimeographed summaries are available) on a particular painting or sculpture. These are free and are attended annually by nearly eighty thousand people. Tours and lectures for groups of fifteen or more people are frequently arranged by appointment.

The Extension Service of the National Gallery is the nation's largest museum producer and distributor of educational lending programs. All programs are lent free of charge and are circulated annually to over four thousand communities in all fifty states.

A new and far-reaching educational project, developed by the Gallery in cooperation with Scholastic Magazines, Inc., is *Art & Man*, designed to provide eight monthly multi-media packages during the school year, relating the visual arts to classroom subjects such as English, history, social sciences, and modern languages.

At the Mall entrance to the Gallery an Orientation Center has been established to serve visitors more efficiently. It is staffed by five desk-docents. The Education Department also trains volunteer docents from the Junior League and the American Association of University Women. These in turn work closely with the schools near Washington and take about 60,000 schoolchildren a year through the Gallery.

Many persons, however, prefer to wander through

Schoolchildren enrich their knowledge of art through group visits and lectures

Richard Bales conducts the National Gallery Orchestra

The Gallery offers artists opportunities to study major works

Rubens' Daniel in the Lions' Den *enthralls three young visitors*

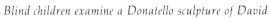

Blind children examine a Donatello sculpture of David

the collections by themselves. To allow them to listen to talks about the works of art at their own pace, electronic guides are available. They are extremely popular, and they enable the visitor to look and listen at the same time.

For those who would rather read than listen, in each of the sixty-six rooms there are leaflets describing the works of art in that particular gallery. The leaflets are free and can be taken home. Our visitors seem to realize that, when the leaflets are assembled from all the galleries, they form a free handbook of the collections and are therefore worth preserving.

On Sunday afternoons there are free lectures in the auditorium given by authorities on different aspects of art. A series of six lectures, known as the A. W. Mellon Lectures in the Fine Arts, is delivered annually. These lectures are published by the Princeton University Press as part of the Bollingen Series.

An interesting educational instrument located at the Gallery is the Index of American Design. During the Depression in the mid-1930s the government, wishing to help artists, organized over 660 painters throughout the United States and gave them the task of recording the decorative arts and crafts of this country from the seventeenth century to the end of the nineteenth century. A remarkably exacting technique of watercolor rendering was taught to these artists, and the resulting facsimiles of many varied craft products form a vivid and permanent record of the development of American folk and decorative arts. Exhibitions from this vast corpus of more than 17,000 illustrations are constantly circulated by the Gallery; publishers and industrial designers, too, frequently draw upon this source of Americana.

Music

The National Gallery of Art, so far as is known, is unique among museums in having its own orchestra, with a conductor-composer working on its staff full time. Each Sunday evening, except during the summer months, the Gallery presents a free concert in its East Garden Court. These concerts are regularly broadcast and have resulted in a number of recordings which have sold widely. The orchestra has also appeared in a telecast series of pretaped concerts, during which paintings appropriate to the musical selections are shown.

The concerts were begun during World War II, owing to the generosity of Chester Dale, and were continued with funds provided by the A. W. Mellon Educational and Charitable Trust. Recently they have received generous support from the Calouste Gulbenkian Foundation of Lisbon, and the J. I. Foundation, Inc., and from funds bequeathed by William Nelson Cromwell and F. Lammot Belin. It is a moving experience to see the crowds, seated and standing, who attend these Sunday evening performances, which have become an important part of the cultural life of Washington.

Each spring the Gallery presents a festival of American music, often giving a first hearing to contemporary compositions. A modest beginning has been made toward commissioning works composed especially for the Gallery. Another recent development is the formation of the National Gallery Strings, a group of first-chair players from the National Gallery Symphony, which frequently plays at the openings of special exhibitions.

In the informality of the setting, in the type of small orchestra with its conductor-composer, and in its emphasis on new native compositions, the National Gallery of Art is continuing the eighteenth-century tradition of musical performances under a *Kapellmeister*, which distinguished so many German and Austrian courts.

Science

The last century and a half has seen an advance in applied science unparalleled in history. We make better steel, build longer bridges, travel in faster vehicles than ever before and live a life completely changed by technological discoveries. Yet there are exceptions to this technical progress. While the tools used to fabricate nearly every commodity have changed, those used to produce art have remained much the same. We paint with pigments not very different and often less lasting than those of the Renaissance, and we apply them in ways generally less durable than the methods of the Old Masters.

Various reasons can be found for this technical backwardness in the fine arts, but the major explanation remains a lack of interest in the kind of full-time research which has made other scientific advances possible. Until recently there has been very little support for serious scientific investigation of artists' materials. In the late 1920s Harvard established at the Fogg Art Museum the first significant laboratory experiments in the United States related to the preservation of art objects. Funds for this program, however, were never abundant and scientific investigation had to be combined with restoration and teaching. Nevertheless, during the last war, when Harvard found it necessary to curtail work in the Fogg laboratory, American museums suffered a severe loss.

In 1950 the National Gallery of Art began a program of research in artists' materials. Funds for this project were provided by the Old Dominion and Avalon foundations, and support for the continuation of this important research has been provided by the Andrew W. Mellon Foundation, with contributions from the National Science Foundation, the Atomic Energy Commission, the National Endowment for the Arts, and the Ciba-Geigy and David L. Kreeger foundations. These funds have made possible a continuation of the work begun at the Fogg Museum. The Gallery's program, however, differs in a significant way from the Harvard program. The scientists have no teaching or restoration responsibilities, and consequently their investigations can proceed without interruptions of this nature. The project is located at the Carnegie-Mellon Institute of Research at Carnegie-Mellon University in Pittsburgh. This immense center for scientific investigation, one of the best-equipped laboratories in the world, offers important advantages. Not only are the most modern tools available, equipment often rare and costly, but scientists working on artists' materials have an opportunity for discussing their research with scores of other scientists doing related work.

It was decided when the National Gallery program began that it would be more practicable to take a chemist and make him aware of the problems of restoration rather than to take a restorer and teach him chemistry. The National Gallery of Art representative at the Carnegie-Mellon Institute, a distinguished chemist, has become familiar with the difficulties confronting museums in preserving paintings. He in turn has trained his assistants. He has worked closely not only with restorers at the National Gallery of Art but also with those in other museums in the United States and abroad.

All museums today are desperately in need of scientific advice. They are faced with many problems of a practical nature related to the conservation of their collections which the scientist alone can solve. To give only three examples: (1) the fading of pigments due to museum illumination; (2) the control of excessive heat from spotlights; (3) the discoloration of areas of repaint.

It is luck, to some extent, that the Old Masters are still as brilliant in color as they are. Most paintings in the past were intended for dimly lit churches and dark palaces. In the nineteenth century, for the first time, these panels and canvases were placed in galleries with skylights, where the natural illumination reaching the walls was often a hundred times as great as the light in the buildings where the paintings originally hung. Until recently the damage which might have been caused by this vast increase in brightness of illumination had been kept to a minimum by varnishes which had in due course turned yellow. In the past, moreover, whenever pictures seemed dull and lusterless, instead of cleaning, as we would do today, the usual procedure was to revarnish. This series of yellow coatings, like layers of yellow glass, provided an effective filter, removing to a great extent the ultra-violet rays, and reducing, with the help of a good deal of dirt, the total amount of light from the rest of the spectrum reaching the pigments themselves. Then came the modern taste for pictures cleaned of their old varnish. The protective coat of yellow dammar or mastic was thus removed along with the dirt; and the pigments, covered with only a colorless, transparent varnish, usually a synthetic resin, were exposed under gallery skylights to illumination as high as 100 foot-candles, as against five or six in the average day-lit interior of a palace or church.

The National Gallery of Art's research program is

investigating the many types of damage that light can cause. It was demonstrated that the effect of light on fugitive pigments is additive, that the light waves of the whole spectrum are deleterious, though ultraviolet rays are generally the most destructive, and that more pigments than we had realized are fugitive. Experimentation is being pushed to improve ultraviolet filters, which can be used over the skylights of galleries and, possibly, infused into the varnish of the pictures themselves; and other methods of reducing the destructive effect of the invisible radiation in the light are being sought. If this search fails to find satisfactory ways of lessening the damaging power of natural light, museums may be compelled to abandon daylight altogether and resort to artificial illumination. The damaging factor in such illumination can be precisely controlled, but there is frequently a loss of aesthetic pleasure. It is to be hoped that science can offer a suitable solution to the use of natural light.

Natural illumination creates heat, but this can be controlled by air conditioning. Much more serious is the heat derived from the spotlights increasingly in use not only for photography but for exhibition purposes. The problem became critical at the National Gallery of Art when plans were made to exhibit the original waxes modeled by Degas and from which his bronzes were later cast. It became obvious, as one of these ballet dancers leaned over in a posture never sanctioned by the School of Ballet, that she was sagging under the heat of the display and threatening to melt. The first problem was to determine how hot she was. A piece of equipment was used to measure the temperature of the wax figures by determining the infrared radiation they emitted. Known as a "heat-detecting gun," this device registers the surface temperature of any work of art at which it is pointed. Once the temperature could be measured, refrigeration was introduced into the case and the ballerinas now promise to hold their poses permanently. This heat-detecting gun has since proved invaluable to the Gallery staff when it becomes necessary to measure the amount of heat to which paintings are exposed during photography, especially filming for movies and television. One stands "offstage," simply pointing the gun at a painting while it is being photographed, and without

touching, the temperature is continually monitored.

Light not only fades paintings and may overheat them, but it also causes a variety of photochemical reactions. In recent years an epidemic of whitening of repaint appeared to have broken out in many galleries in Europe and the United States. Bluish white areas suddenly began to appear on paintings, like a rash. These always occurred in repainted places which were, on the whole, light in tone. Such areas, of course, had previously matched the surrounding color. In the course of a thorough investigation of the problem it has been discovered that certain restorers use mixtures of zinc white, colored pigment, and dammar varnish when they retouch lost or damaged areas. Occasionally, a form of photochemically active titanium white was also detected. The effect of light on this mixture of white pigment and varnish caused the repaint to deteriorate and take on a whitish appearance. The discovery has been widely publicized among restorers, and it is to be hoped that in the future they will avoid the combination of these particular materials.

Similar studies of pigments, supports, varnishes, solvents, adhesives, light, and other problems related to the preservation of works of art are being undertaken by an increasing number of major laboratories, particularly in European countries, and the most heartening aspect of this scientific research into the nature of artists' materials is the amount of international cooperation taking place. We are rapidly catching up with technical advances in other fields. In the next ten years it seems likely that restorers will be given new materials as revolutionary and as useful as antibiotics in medicine. For this reason it is the policy of the National Gallery of Art to restrict restoration to work necessary for preservation, and to clean paintings as little as possible consistent with their conservation.

One of the problems confronting every restorer is the introduction of new synthetic materials in place of the traditional ones. How can he be sure that these will last equally well? There are on the market today a number of synthetic resins which exhibit little tendency to discolor, but is it possible that the use of these materials will have distressing side effects? For example, research showed that it is possible for certain synthetic varnishes to become so tough over a

Proper illumination is a major concern of the Gallery staff

period of time that it will be almost impossible to remove them without damaging the paint underneath. The laboratory initiated an elaborate program of "accelerated aging tests" to provide evidence for and against the use of new materials. The findings were reported in a handbook, *On Picture Varnishes and Their Solvents*, first published in 1959. It proved to be so valuable to conservators that it was revised and enlarged in 1971.

But the scientist's usefulness is not limited to the restorer's studio. He can also assist a curator in determining authenticity. One of the most helpful tools developed through the National Gallery of Art's sponsorship of this research program has been the ability to determine the age of white lead pigments. In the past white lead was used by artists in virtually every picture painted. The scientists at the Carnegie-Mellon Institute of Research knew that lead-bearing minerals exhibit a low degree of radioactivity owing to the presence of uranium as an impurity which produces a radioactive variety of lead, known as lead-210. They speculated that when the ore was refined and the·uranium removed, the decomposing lead-210 would soon decay, losing half of its radioactivity every twenty years. Thus paint in which lead-210 had vanished almost entirely would be roughly a century old, whereas paint with a measurable amount of lead-210 could be judged to be of more recent manufacture.

Many tests were made to prove the validity of this assumption. A worldwide search for samples of lead of known date and origin was instituted. Among others the radioactivity of the white lead in the forgeries of Vermeer done by van Meegeren was measured. In every case the results proved the

hypothesis to be correct.

The newest twist in this search for greater skills in identifying the white lead used by an artist is the use of a mass-spectrometer that is able to count the kind of lead atoms in the pigment. By this means scientists at Carnegie-Mellon University now can tell us the country and sometimes even the mine itself that the lead came from.

The Atomic Energy Commission became interested in the National Gallery of Art's project and as a joint venture a program was undertaken to determine radioactive contamination of artists' materials by the atmosphere. Because of the explosion and testing of atom and hydrogen bombs there has been a great increase in the amount of radioactive carbon in the air. Linseed oil and paper made from growing plants that have existed in the atomic era contain a significantly high proportion of carbon-14, which has been released by such explosions. The possibility of detecting this by advanced scientific methods of analysis now makes it impossible for a forger to use modern linseed oil and paper to fabricate works of art that are supposedly more than a decade or two old.

From these advances in the scientific study of works of art it might seem as though connoisseurship would someday come out of a test tube. It never will. The scientists' contributions increase the range of capabilities that aid the curator and the conservator to do their work, but no laboratory or computer center can measure "quality." And quality is that indescribable property of the greatest masterpieces which Andrew Mellon insisted should be evident in every painting and piece of sculpture in the National Gallery.

Conclusion

Visitors to the Gallery often express surprise when they learn that it opened as recently as 1941. Since then, the National Gallery of Art has had a growth which might never have occurred if it had been established a few years later. Coming when it did, it has proved to be a magnet for those last great American collections not already given or promised elsewhere. Thus, in the Gallery's few decades of life, treasures have flowed to Washington at an unprecedented rate. It is difficult to believe that there will ever again be a similar influx of masterpieces to any museum.

The National Gallery of Art holds a unique position in America. Over its short history, the Gallery has been called upon to undertake many of the functions performed elsewhere by Ministries of Fine Arts. These responsibilities have varied from assisting in the designs of stamps and inaugural medals to organizing exhibitions offered by foreign governments. The Gallery's creation thus helped to fill a void in the governmental structure.

Its establishment presented the President and the Congress with the challenge of maintaining a federal art museum for which there was no real precedent. Until then the government's support of museums was directed mainly to the outstanding departments of science and history at the Smithsonian Institution. But with the acceptance of Andrew Mellon's gift the experiment of creating a distinguished National Gallery was undertaken. This book is in some ways a balance sheet of accomplishment.

Italian Schools

XIII THROUGH EARLY XVI

CENTURY

21

22

23

17   Attributed to Cimabue (Florentine, mentioned 1272–1302): *Christ between St. Peter and St. James Major.* Soon after 1270. Wood, center panel, 31 x 21¾" (79 x 55 cm.). Andrew W. Mellon Collection

18   Bernardo Daddi (Florentine, active 1312–c. 1348): *St. Paul.* Dated 1333. Wood, 92 x 35⅛" (234 x 89 cm.). Andrew W. Mellon Collection

19   Agnolo Gaddi (Florentine, active 1369–1396): *The Coronation of the Virgin.* Probably c. 1370. Wood, 64 x 31¼" (162.6 x 79.4 cm.). Samuel H. Kress Collection

20   Attributed to Cimabue: *Madonna and Child with the Baptist and Saint Peter.* Probably c. 1290. Wood, 13½ x 9¼" (34.3 x 24.8 cm.). Samuel H. Kress Collection

21   Bernardo Daddi: *Madonna and Child with Saints and Angels.* 1330s. Wood, 19¾ x 9½" (50.2 x 24.2 cm.). Samuel H. Kress Collection

22   Agnolo Gaddi: *Madonna Enthroned with Saints and Angels.* c. 1380/90. Wood, 80⅝ x 96⅝" (205 x 245 cm.). Andrew W. Mellon Collection

23   Master of the Fabriano Altarpiece and Allegretto Nuzi (Florentine, active probably c. 1335–c. 1365; Umbrian, active 1345–1373): *Madonna Enthroned with Saints.* Dated 1354. Wood, center panel 42¾ x 23⅜" (108.6 x 59.4 cm.). Andrew W. Mellon Collection

Masaccio

(FLORENTINE, 1401–1428)

24   PROFILE PORTRAIT OF A YOUNG MAN

Giotto's attainment of the suggestion of sculptural form died with him. His followers lost sight of his objective. They were seduced by a love of accessories, by a desire to represent rich stuffs for their own richness, by graceful gestures for their own grace. Thus these artists sacrificed form for pattern and modeling for calligraphy. This attractive heresy culminated in the so-called International Style, which at the end of the fourteenth century flourished throughout Europe.

At the beginning of the fifteenth century, however, Florentine artists were recalled to the true faith, so to speak, by a fanatic for form, Tommaso di Ser Giovanni Guidi, called Masaccio. His panel paintings are extremely rare. Bernard Berenson, the great critic of Italian art, lists only fourteen. Though it is difficult to attribute with complete conviction profile portraits of the fifteenth century, the qualities of sculptural form which distinguish this painting tend to support Berenson's ascription of the panel to Masaccio. Note its subtle qualities of relief achieved by delicate transitions of value from light to shade, which model the lid of the eye, the concavity under the jaw, and the plastic convolutions of the ear.

Rendering three-dimensional form with a new flexibility, Masaccio adapted it to new purposes. The discovery in the fifteenth century of classical coins and busts stimulated a desire for portraiture and the perpetuation of personality which it can give. Masaccio endowed his sitters with this immortality. Like Shakespeare, he could assert:

> So long as men can breathe, or eyes can see
> So long lives this, and this gives life to thee.

Collections: Artaud de Montor, Paris. *Andrew W. Mellon Collection*, 1937. Painted c. 1425. Wood, 16⅝ x 12¾" (42 x 32 cm.).

75

25

25 Lorenzo Monaco (Florentine, c. 1370–1422/24): *Madonna and Child.* Dated 1413. Wood, 46 x 21¾" (117 x 55 cm.). Samuel H. Kress Collection

26, 27 Masolino da Panicale (Florentine, 1383/84– active to 1432): *The Archangel Gabriel, The Virgin Annunciate.* Probably c. 1420/30. Wood, each panel 30 x 22⅝" (76 x 57 cm.). Samuel H. Kress Collection

28 Gentile da Fabriano (Umbrian, c. 1360/70–1427): *A Miracle of St. Nicholas.* 1425. Wood, 14¼ x 14" (36 x 35 cm.). Samuel H. Kress Collection

29 Gentile da Fabriano: *Madonna and Child.* c. 1422. Wood, 37¾ x 22¼" (96 x 57 cm.). Samuel H. Kress Collection

30 Andrea del Castagno (Florentine, c. 1417/19– 1457): *Portrait of a Man.* c. 1450. Wood, 21¼ x 15⅞" (54 x 40.5 cm.). Andrew W. Mellon Collection

31 Masolino da Panicale (Florentine, 1383/84–active to 1432): *The Annunciation.* Probably c. 1425/30. Wood, 58¼ x 45¼" (148 x 115 cm.). Andrew W. Mellon Collection

The grace and charm of the International Style referred to in the note to *Profile Portrait of a Young Man* (plate 24) are brilliantly illustrated in the Annunciation by Masolino da Panicale (plates 26, 27) and the *Madonna and Child* by Lorenzo Monaco (plate 25), Masolino's somewhat older contemporary. The dissemination of this International Style is to be seen in Germany, France, and Spain. It is evident all over Italy, most es-

26

27

28

29

pecially in the work of the first great Umbrian Master, Gentile da Fabriano. The discursive naturalism and linear beauty of late Gothic painting did not last, however, and one of the finest portraits in Florentine art, Castagno's *Portrait of a Man* (plate 30), introduces the severe, uncompromising realism which was a reaction against a sweetness that had begun to cloy.

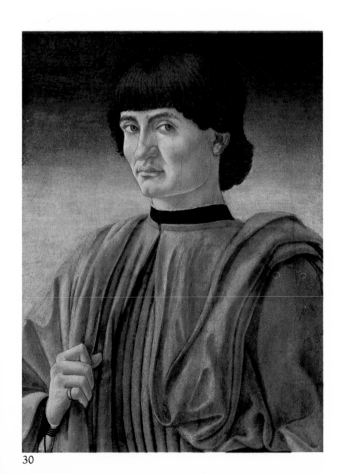

30

31

Sassetta and Assistant

(SIENESE, ACTIVE 1423–1450)

32   THE MEETING OF ST. ANTHONY AND ST. PAUL

In the early decades of the fifteenth century the late Gothic style flowered in such enchanting paintings as this. In spite of medieval characteristics such as the high horizon line and the method of continuous narration whereby three scenes from the life of St. Anthony are shown at once, Sassetta reveals a sensitive observation of nature as advanced as any painter of his age. The landscape with its arid hills, its groves of dark, dense foliage, is the distilled essence of the *Senese*, of that beautiful region of Tuscany near Siena where Sassetta lived and worked.

Sassetta was one of the most gifted of narrative painters. In a series of predella panels, four of which are in the National Gallery of Art (plates 32, 33, 34, 35), he has told, more poetically than any other artist, the legend of St. Anthony Abbot. The panel reproduced here, the seventh of the series, tells of his journey to meet St. Paul. The tradition is that St. Anthony, after having a vision of a fellow hermit, St. Paul, who had attained greater sanctity, decided to pay him a visit. In the upper left-hand corner, staff in hand, St. Anthony sets out on his travels. On his way he meets a centaur, a symbol of the gods of paganism, fast vanishing from the Christian world. The centaur, holding a palm branch, beats on his breast as a sign of his penitence, and receives a blessing—an indication of the conversion to Christianity of the ancient divinities of the woods.

At the bottom of the picture the two old men at last find each other. Their deep emotion is beautifully suggested by their tender embrace. As they incline their bodies one toward the other, their halos overlap, and the two figures form a pyramid whose shape is echoed in the opening of the cave and in the barren hill beyond. The intensity of feeling Sassetta conveys gives this small panel an impressive grandeur, making it one of the noblest creations of Sienese painting.

Collections: G. E. H. Vernon, Nottinghamshire; Wentworth Blackett Beaumont, First Lord Allendale; Viscount Allendale, London. *Samuel H. Kress Collection*, 1939. Painted c. 1440. Wood, 18¾ x 13⅝" (47.5 x 34.5 cm.).

33

34

33 Sassetta (Sienese, active 1423–1450) **and Assistant**: *St. Anthony Distributing His Wealth to the Poor.* c. 1440. Wood, 18⅝ x 13⅝" (47.5 x 34.5 cm.). Samuel H. Kress Collection

34 Sassetta and Assistant: *St. Anthony Leaving His Monastery.* c. 1440. Wood, 18½ x 13¾" (47 x 35 cm.). Samuel H. Kress Collection

35 Sassetta and Assistant: *The Death of St. Anthony.* c. 1440. Wood, 14⅜ x 15⅛" (36.5 x 38.3 cm.). Samuel H. Kress Collection

36 Francesco di Giorgio (Sienese, 1439–1501/2): *God the Father Surrounded by Angels and Cherubim.* c. 1470. Wood, 14⅜ x 20⅜" (36.5 x 51.8 cm.). Samuel H. Kress Collection

37 Giovanni di Paolo (Sienese, active 1420–1482): *The Annunciation.* c. 1445. Wood, 15¾ x 18¼" (40 x 46 cm.). Samuel H. Kress Collection

38 Neroccio de' Landi (Sienese, 1447–1500): *Madonna and Child with St. Anthony Abbot and St. Sigismund.* c. 1495. Wood, 62⅜ x 55⅞" (158.5 x 142 cm.). Samuel H. Kress Collection

39 Giovanni di Paolo: *The Adoration of the Magi.* c. 1450. Wood, 10¼ x 17¾" (26 x 45 cm.). Andrew W. Mellon Collection

38

35

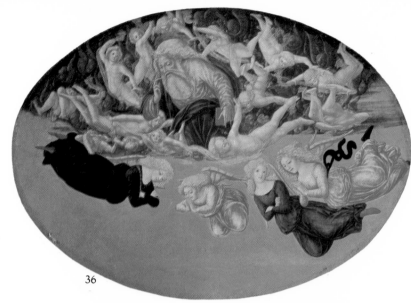

36

37

With *The Meeting of St. Anthony and St. Paul* (plate 32) we return to the International Style. Three more panels by Sassetta and his Assistant from the same altarpiece are reproduced in plates 33, 34, and 35. Paintings by Sienese contemporaries and followers of Sassetta are shown in the other reproductions. All these paintings have in common the characteristics of late Gothic art: linear beauty and languid grace. Siena was a center of stylistic conservatism. Forty miles away Florentines were experimenting with anatomy and perspective. Portraiture also flourished in Florence, whereas Sienese painters ignored these new trends. The portrait by Neroccio (plate 41) is virtually unique in Sienese art. Why, one wonders? The Sienese were known to be amazingly superstitious; perhaps having one's portrait painted was considered unlucky. There seems to be no other rational explanation.

39

40

40 **Master of the Griselda Legend** (Umbrian-Sienese active late XV century): *Eunostos of Tanagra*. c. 1495/1500. Wood, 34⅞ x 20⅝″ (88.5 x 52.5 cm.). Samuel H. Kress Collection

41 **Neroccio de' Landi** (Sienese, 1447–1500): *Portrait of a Lady*. c. 1490. Wood, 18⅜ x 12″ (46.5 x 30.5 cm.). Widener Collection

42 **Benvenuto di Giovanni** (Sienese, 1436–c. 1518): *The Adoration of the Magi*. c. 1470. Wood, 71¾ x 54⅛″ (182 x 137 cm.). Andrew W. Mellon Collection

43 **Andrea di Bartolo:** (Sienese, first mentioned 1389–1428): *Joachim and the Beggars*. c. 1400. Wood, 17⅜ x 12¾″ (44.2 x 32.4 cm.). Samuel H. Kress Collection

44 **Andrea di Bartolo**: *The Nativity of the Virgin*. c. 1400. Wood, 17⅜ x 12¾″ (44.2 x 32.4 cm.). Samuel H. Kress Collection

45 **Andrea di Bartolo**: *The Presentation of the Virgin*. c. 1400. Wood, 17⅝ x 12¾″ (44.2 x 32.4 cm.). Samuel H. Kress Collection

43

41

42

44

45

93

Botticelli

(FLORENTINE, 1444/45–1510)

61   THE ADORATION OF THE MAGI

With this *Adoration of the Magi* we reach the last quarter of the fifteenth century and the reign of Lorenzo de' Medici. Florence had become a center of Greek studies, Neoplatonism almost a religion. Refinement, a fastidious sensibility, a mood of poetic reverie had come into fashion. It was a time when pageants and ceremonials were popular and families took pride in having themselves portrayed as the principal actors in the dramas of Christianity. In the present painting, which Botticelli probably executed during his sojourn in Rome while he was working in the Sistine Chapel, the portraits have never been identified in spite of their incisive characterizations.

But the wonder of this *Adoration* does not consist so much in these portrait studies as in the subtle disposition of the figures, their vibrant movement, and their poetic setting. Amid the ruins of the classical world, symbolized by fragments of ancient architecture, the new order of Christianity is born. From the calmness of the central group, from the mystical yet human serenity of the Madonna and Child, movement radiates in waves of increasing activity through the gestures of awe and of prayer of the onlookers, and reaches a climax in the youthful grooms on the far right.

Beyond this human activity stretches a landscape suggestive of the serene spaces of the Campagna. It is impossible to let the eye travel into the tranquil beauty of this countryside without some relief of the spirit, some sense of refreshment and calm. The breadth, serenity, and restraint which are so conspicuous in this *Adoration* disappeared shortly thereafter from Botticelli's work. With the exile of the Medici he came under the spell of Savonarola, and his last years were overclouded by the feverish visions of the Dominican reformer.

Collections: Purchased in Rome by the engraver Peralli, it was acquired in 1808 for the Hermitage Gallery, Leningrad, by Czar Alexander I. *Andrew W. Mellon Collection*, 1937. Painted early 1480s. Wood, 27⅝ x 41" (71 x 103.5 cm.).

62

63

The paintings reproduced here are by two of the greatest Florentine masters working at the turn of the fifteenth century: Botticelli and Filippino Lippi. Their styles are so similar that it is hard to distinguish one from the other. For example, both *Portrait of a Youth* (plate 64) and the *Coronation of the Virgin* (plate 62), now generally considered to be by Filippino, were once ascribed to Botticelli. This confusion is evidence of the difficulties of attributing unsigned pictures. But the portrait of Giuliano de' Medici, aesthetically and historically one of the most important of Florentine paintings, shows the handwriting of Botticelli so clearly that no other authorship has ever been suggested.

64

62 Filippino Lippi (Florentine, probably 1457–1504): *The Coronation of the Virgin.* c. 1480. Wood, 35½ x 87½″ (90 x 222 cm.). Samuel H. Kress Collection

63 Filippino Lippi: *Tobias and the Angel.* Probably c. 1480. Wood, 12⅞ x 9¼″ (32.5 x 23.5 cm.). Samuel H. Kress Collection

64 Filippino Lippi: *Portrait of a Youth.* c. 1485. Wood, 20 x 13⅞″ (51 x 35.5 cm.). Andrew W. Mellon Collection

65 Botticelli (Florentine, 1444/45–1510): *Giuliano de' Medici.* c. 1478. Wood, 29¾ x 20⅝″ (75.6 x 52.6 cm.). Samuel H. Kress Collection

66 Botticelli: *The Virgin Adoring the Child.* c. 1480–90. Wood, diameter 23⅜″ (59.6 cm.). Samuel H. Kress Collection

67 Botticelli: *Portrait of a Youth.* Early 1480s. Wood, 16¼ x 12½″ (41.2 x 31.8 cm.). Andrew W. Mellon Collection

65

66   67

97

Leonardo da Vinci

(FLORENTINE, 1452–1519)

69   GINEVRA DE' BENCI

68   Leonardo da Vinci (Florentine, 1452–1519): Reverse of *Ginevra de' Benci*

On the reverse of the portrait of Ginevra de' Benci is the only painted still life by Leonardo da Vinci, if so heraldic a design can be thus designated.

The cost per square inch of paint of the portrait of Ginevra de' Benci is the greatest in the history of collecting. Why is the likeness of a young, seemingly disgruntled Florentine heiress so precious? Paintings by Leonardo da Vinci are indeed rare, but rarity in itself is only a cipher, dependent on the numbers that precede it. Furthermore, how can one be sure the picture is by that most extraordinary genius? True, all recent critics have agreed to this attribution, but on what is their judgment based? First, there is external evidence. We know from contemporary sources that Leonardo painted someone called Ginevra de' Benci. The juniper bush, so prominent in the portrait and repeated symbolically on the back, is considered to identify the sitter as that lady, the name *Ginevra* being a dialect form, in the feminine, of the Italian word for juniper (*ginepro*). A pun of this kind would certainly have appealed to Leonardo. Second, and much more important, is the internal evidence. The portrait reveals Leonardo's incomparable technical skill. There are passages, such as the modeling of the lips, which Leonardo never surpassed in delicacy. Such value transitions are miracles of technique, and Leonardo was the first painter to have the perfect control of his medium necessary to make light and shade merge imperceptibly.

In his notebooks, Leonardo compares curls of hair to swirling water. The ringlets which frame Ginevra's face resemble cascading whirlpools. These curls are so like Leonardo's rendering both of hair in his other paintings and of water in his drawings as to be a virtual signature. Lastly, there are Leonardo's colored reflections, discussed at length in his *Treatise on Painting*. In Ginevra's portrait such reflected colors reverberate through the painting and cause the flesh to glow as if, like the moon, it reflected some hidden radiance.

But we still have not answered the question of why the portrait is of such significance. The answer is that this is the first psychological portrait ever painted. Leonardo's tremendous innovation was developed in his three portraits of women. Each expresses a different mood: the earliest, *Ginevra*, withdrawn sadness; the next, *Cecilia Gallerani*, now in Krakow, appealing wistfulness; and the last, the *Mona Lisa*, mirthless amusement. Of these, the most original is the enigmatic melancholy of Ginevra de' Benci. Sadness has rarely been represented in portraiture. I know of no other instance in painting before the seventeenth century, and even then the tragic view of life was usually conveyed by portraits of men, not of women.   *(continued)*

91

92

91   Ambrogio de' Predis (Milanese, c. 1455–c. 1508): *Bianca Maria Sforza*. Probably 1493. Wood, 20 x 12¾" (51 x 32.5 cm.). Widener Collection

92   Giovanni Bellini (Venetian, c. 1430–1516): *Portrait of a Young Man in Red*. c. 1480. Wood, 12½ x 10⅜" (32 x 26.5 cm.). Andrew W. Mellon Collection

93   Giovanni Bellini: *St. Jerome Reading*. c. 1480/90. Wood, 19¼ x 15½" (49 x 39 cm.). Samuel H. Kress Collection

94   Ercole Roberti (Ferrarese, active 1479–1496): *Giovanni II Bentivoglio*. c. 1480. Wood 21⅛ x 15" (54 x 38 cm.). Samuel H. Kress Collection

95   Ercole Roberti: *Ginevra Bentivoglio*. c. 1480. Wood, 21⅛ x 15¼" (54 x 39 cm.). Samuel H. Kress Collection

96   Venetian School (c. 1505): *Portrait of a Young Man*. Wood, 11 x 9" (28 x 23 cm.). Widener Collection

93

94

95

96

Portrait painters at the turn of the fifteenth century placed their sitters either in the old-fashioned profile pose or in the newer three-quarter view. The more primitive method was derived from classical coins and medals, which were passionately collected during the Renaissance; the more innovative style, with the sitter's head turned three-quarters, usually to the right, illustrated by *Portrait of a Condottiere* (plate 90) and by plates 92 and 96, seems to have been first developed in the North. With the model in silhouette there is very little opportunity for psychological characterization, but by delineating the two eyes and two cheeks, the painter has a much greater opportunity to convey his sitter's personality.

Andrea Mantegna

(PADUAN, 1431–1506)

97   JUDITH AND HOLOFERNES

The search for actuality and the discovery of archaeology molded fifteenth-century Italian painting. Padua, where Mantegna was born, was a center of antiquarianism. Even in a scene from the Old Testament, Judith decapitating Holofernes, we find the Jewish drama transformed into a Greek tragedy. Thus the actors, in spite of the gruesomeness of the event, are as impersonal as the sculptured figures of the Parthenon. Judith turns away from her bloody prize with a look of calm detachment; she accepts impassively her predestined triumph. The stone-colored panel seems chiseled rather than painted, like an enlarged cameo which has survived from the ancient world.

Such Classicism appealed strongly to seventeenth-century taste, especially in England. The first recorded owner of this panel was Charles I, who believed it to be by Raphael. Later he exchanged it with the Earl of Pembroke for paintings by Bellini and Parmigianino. Thus it escaped one of the tragic consequences of Cromwell's Revolution, the dispersal of the Royal Collection. It remained in England instead, a part of the famous Pembroke Collection at Wilton House, until brought to America by P. A. B. Widener. The subject of Judith and Holofernes was treated several times by Mantegna and his school. Among the drawings of this scene are one in the Uffizi, Florence (dated 1491), and one in the Samuel H. Kress Collection, National Gallery of Art. A grisaille of almost identical dimensions, showing the same subject, with the composition in reverse, is in the National Gallery, Dublin. Judith, the unscrupulous murderer of tyrants, was the most popular heroine of the Renaissance.

Collections: King Charles I of England; Pembroke Collection, Wilton House. *Widener Collection*, 1942. Painted c. 1495. Wood, 11⅞ x 7⅛" (30 x 18 cm.).

98

99

100

98 **Andrea Mantegna** (Paduan, 1431–1506): *Portrait of a Man*. Probably c. 1460. Transferred from canvas to Masonite, 9½ x 7½" (24.3 x 19.1 cm.). Samuel H. Kress Collection

99 **North Italian School** (c. 1460): *Portrait of a Man*. Wood, 22¼ x 15¾" (56.5 x 40 cm.). Samuel H. Kress Collection

100 **Andrea Mantegna**: *The Christ Child Blessing*. Probably c. 1480/90. Canvas, 27⅝ x 13¾" (70.3 x 35 cm.). Samuel H. Kress Collection

101 **Andrea Mantegna**: *St. Jerome in the Wilderness*. c. third quarter of XV century. Wood, 31¾ x 21⅝" (80.5 x 55 cm.). Andrew W. Mellon Collection

102 **Carlo Crivelli** (Venetian, active 1457–1493): *Madonna and Child Enthroned with Donor*. c. 1470. Wood, 51 x 21⅜" (129.5 x 54.5 cm.). Samuel H. Kress Collection

103 **Cosimo Tura** (Ferrarese, c. 1430–1495): *Madonna and Child in a Garden*. c. 1455. Wood, 20¾ x 14⅝" (53 x 37 cm.). Samuel H. Kress Collection

104 **Francesco del Cossa** (Ferrarese, c. 1435–c. 1477): *The Crucifixion*. Soon after 1470. Wood, diameter 25⅛" (64 cm.). Samuel H. Kress Collection

105 **Francesco del Cossa**: *St. Florian*. Soon after 1470. Wood, 31¼ x 21⅝" (79 x 55 cm.). Samuel H. Kress Collection.

101

102

104

103

105

The National Gallery's collection is especially rich in the work of Mantegna and of the numerous artists who came under his influence in Lombardy, Venice, Ferrara, and even as far south as Sicily, the home of Antonello da Messina. Mantegna's imprint on his followers was extremely strong; thus it is quite possible that the panel representing St. Jerome (plate 101), which is usually attributed to him, was painted by some contemporary Paduan. This picture, of jewel-like beauty, shows the saint kneeling in his flinty desert and beating his breast with a stone. The *Portrait of a Man* (plate 98) and *The Christ Child Blessing* (plate 100), ascribed with more certainty to the master, also show his sculptural style.

Crivelli, active in Venice, also models his elegantly mannered figures as though they were made of some tangible precious stone. Ercole Roberti,

(continued)

106

107

108

106 Francesco del Cossa (Ferrarese, c. 1435–1477): *St. Lucy*. Soon after 1470. Wood, 31¼ x 22" (79 x 56 cm.). Samuel H. Kress Collection

107 Antonello da Messina (Sicilian, active 1456–1479): *Madonna and Child*. c. 1475. Wood, 23¼ x 17¼" (59 x 44 cm.). Andrew W. Mellon Collection

108 Antonello da Messina: *Portrait of a Young Man*. Probably 1475. Wood, 13 x 9¾" (33 x 25 cm.). Andrew W. Mellon Collection

109 Ercole Roberti (Ferrarese, active 1479–1496): *The Wife of Hasdrubal and Her Children*. c. 1480/90. Wood, 18½ x 12" (47.1 x 30.6 cm.). Ailsa Mellon Bruce Fund

(continued)

Cosimo Tura, and Francesco del Cossa, the greatest Ferrarese artists, also looked to Padua and to Mantegna for their sharply delineated contours and infrangible surfaces. This austere, Mantegnesque style, with its hard, monumental forms, was softened and humanized by Antonello da Messina. He was one of the painters who introduced into Italy the use of oil as a medium, a procedure he must have learned through some contact with Northern artists. This new method of painting, which gradually replaced *tempera*, gives his figures a glow of light which seems to come from some interior illumination. It represents a technical innovation which was destined to have a profound effect all over Italy, but especially in Venice, Antonello's adopted city.

109

Northern Schools

XV AND XVI CENTURY

Jan van Eyck

(FLEMISH, 1380/1400–1441)

110   THE ANNUNCIATION

In many ways the founder of all Northern painting was Jan van Eyck, who died in Bruges in 1441. He is traditionally considered the discoverer of oil painting, a technique in which linseed oil serves as the solvent for pigment, rather than egg, which was used in the Italian technique of tempera. This made possible a new flexibility and delicacy of handling.

Whether or not van Eyck actually did discover oil painting may be debated, but certainly he was the first to achieve a naturalistic rendering of interior space, or in less technical terms, the effect of looking through an open window or door into a room. It is this new power of representation which is van Eyck's most salient characteristic. Note his masterful suggestion of atmosphere through subtle gradations of light, and his supreme skill in the definition of detail. Contrast the barely visible frescoes at the top of the dimly lit walls of the church, painted with an impalpable delicacy, and the hard microscopic clarity of the jewels on the angel's robes. No artist has ever had a greater range of visual effects. *The Annunciation*, however, is more than a record of new technical attainment; it is a masterpiece of Christian symbolism. It expounds the significance of the Annunciation, the momentous event in history which divides the Era of Law from the Era of Grace, the Dispensation of the Old Testament from the New. The dark upper part of the church with its single window on which is depicted Jehovah, the Lord of the Old Testament, is contrasted with the lower half illumined by three windows, symbolic of the Trinity, through which shines the Light of the World. The angel addresses Our Lady with the words *Ave Gratia Plena*, to which She answers *Ecce Ancilla Domini*, the words reversed and inverted so they can be read by the Holy Ghost, descending in rays of light.

The building cannot be identified with an existing church, but it suggests the late Romanesque style of Maastricht and Tournai. It would seem as though van Eyck designed this building in an architectural style which had not been practiced for several centuries, perhaps the first example of "revivalism" in architecture.

Collections: Thought to have been ordered by Philip the Good, Duke of Burgundy, for a church in Dijon; William II, King of the Netherlands; Hermitage Gallery, Leningrad. *Andrew W. Mellon Collection*, 1937. Painted c. 1425/30. Transferred from wood to canvas, 36½ x 14⅜" (93 x 36.5 cm.).

Petrus Christus

(FLEMISH, c. 1410–1472/73)

113   THE NATIVITY

111, 112 Petrus Christus (Flemish, c. 1410–1472/73): *A Donor and His Wife.* c. 1455. Wood, two panels, each 16½ x 8½" (42 x 21.6 cm.). Samuel H. Kress Collection

Glimpses of landscape in Flemish painting are always rewarding. The background of the Petrus Christus *Nativity* shows how pleasant the countryside must have been in the fifteenth century. The town walls kept building within bounds. There were no suburbs. One stepped from the gate of the city directly into meadowland. Nothing could seem closer to an earthly paradise than the world the Flemish artists portrayed. Fortunately, the smells, the dirt, the lack of sanitation of urban life in the Middle Ages had no place in the visual arts.

Painters were not paid to represent the facts of life. Theirs was a different task—to portray the facts of religion. In the foreground of his painting Petrus Christus tells us the story of Man's Fall and Redemption; Adam and Eve stand on columns supported on the backs of stooped figures, symbolizing mankind burdened with Original Sin. Above on the arch are scenes showing the Expulsion from Eden, Cain slaying Abel, and other episodes from the Old Testament. In the spandrels are two battling figures, mankind in hopeless conflict and enmity as a consequence of sin.

These simulated sculpture groups provide the historical antecedents for the action in the center, where Mary and Joseph, accompanied by angels, worship the Redeemer. This moment of dramatic stillness, so portentous for mankind, must often have been acted out in a similar way in mystery plays, even to the wooden shoes of Joseph, which lend a sense of actuality to the scene. In the middle distance are four spectators, symbols of humanity, for whose Redemption the Incarnation has taken place. Confronted by a vision of compelling eloquence their indifference, so characteristic of mankind, remains tragically unchanged.

Collections: Prince Manuel Yturbe, Madrid; Duchess of Parcent, Madrid. *Andrew W. Mellon Collection*, 1937. Painted c. 1445. Wood, 51¼ x 38¼" (130 x 97 cm.).

114

115

Petrus Christus was a superb portrait painter as well as a painter of altarpieces. His double portrait *A Donor and His Wife* (plates 111, 112) once formed the wings of a triptych, the center panel of which has been lost. Another Flemish portraitist of exceptional skill was Dirk Bouts, who like Petrus Christus was strongly influenced by Jan van Eyck. The newly perfected technique of painting in oils made possible the minute realism of these likenesses. From Flanders, realism spread to France; its influence is evident in the somewhat unusual representation of Our Lady pregnant with the Saviour.

116

117

118

119

120

114 School of Amiens (French, c. 1437): *The Expectant Madonna with Saint Joseph*. Wood, 27⅝ x13⅝" (70.2 x 34 cm.). Samuel H. Kress Collection

115 Hispano-Dutch School (probably last quarter XV century): *The Adoration of the Magi*. Wood, 73 x 65⅜" (185.4 x 166.1 cm.). Samuel H. Kress Collection

116 Dirk Bouts (Dutch-Flemish, c. 1420–1475): *Portrait of a Donor*. c. 1455. Wood, 10⅛ x 8" (25.6 x 20.4 cm.). Samuel H. Kress Collection

117 Franco-Flemish School (early XV century): *Profile Portrait of a Lady*. c. 1415. Wood, 20⅜" x 14⅜" (52 x 36.5 cm.). Andrew W. Mellon Collection

118 Miguel Sithium (Flemish, c. 1469–1525): *A Knight of the Order of Calatrava*. c. 1515. Wood, 13⅛ x 9¼" (33.5 x 23.5 cm.). Andrew W. Mellon Collection

119 Master of Flémalle and Assistants (Flemish, first half XV century): *Madonna and Child with Saints in the Enclosed Garden*. Wood, 47⅛ x 58½" (119.9 x 148.8 cm.). Samuel H. Kress Collection

120 Circle of Rogier van der Weyden (c. 1460): *Christ Appearing to the Virgin*. Wood, 64 x 36⅝" (163 x 93 cm.). Andrew W. Mellon Collection

121 Rogier van der Weyden (Flemish, 1399/1400–1464): *St. George and the Dragon*. c. 1432. Wood, 5⅝ x 4⅛" (14.3 x 10.5 cm.). Ailsa Mellon Bruce Fund

Rogier van der Weyden's *St. George and the Dragon* (plate 121), reproduced here actual size, is the smallest painting in the National Gallery. It is also among the most valuable. It was bought at auction, and the final bid represented a price of $26,552 per square inch. Among the other reproductions shown here, the Franco-Flemish *Portrait of a Lady* (plate 117) is particularly interesting. Formerly ascribed to Pisanello, it was long considered a masterpiece of Italian art. The costume, however, is Burgundian, and the picture is now correctly placed on the other side of the Alps. This example demonstrates the international character of late Gothic portraiture.

121

140 **Miguel Sithium** (Flemish, c. 1469–1525): *The Assumption of the Virgin.* c. 1500. Wood, 8⅜ x 6½" (21.2 x 16.4 cm.). Ailsa Mellon Bruce Fund

141 **Juan de Flandes** (Hispano-Flemish, active 1496– c. 1519): *The Annunciation.* Probably c. 1510. Wood, 43¼ x 31¼" (109.9 x 79.4 cm.). Samuel H. Kress Collection

142 **Juan de Flandes**: *The Nativity.* Probably c. 1510. Wood, 43½ x 31" (110.5 x 83.2 cm.). Samuel H. Kress Collection

143 **Juan de Flandes**: *The Baptism of Christ.* Probably c. 1510. Wood, 49½ x 32" (125.7 x 81.1 cm.). Samuel H. Kress Collection

144 **Juan de Flandes**: *The Adoration of the Magi.* Probably c. 1510. Wood, 49⅛ x 31¼" (124.8 x 79.4 cm.). Samuel H. Kress Collection

145 **Juan de Flandes**: *The Temptation of Christ.* c. 1500. Wood, 8¼ x 6¼" (21 x 15.8 cm.). Ailsa Mellon Bruce Fund

140

141

142

During the latter part of the fifteenth century, several provinces of the Netherlands became linked to Burgundy and Spain as a result of political alliances. A consequence of this union was that a number of artists trained in the Low Countries and eastern France traveled south. Many of them settled in Spain, where a fusion of Northern and Hispanic artistic traditions took place. Two of these itinerant artists collaborated on an altar for Queen Isabella, Sithium painting two scenes and Juan de Flandes, the court painter, forty-five. A panel by each artist is shown (plates 140, 145). Albrecht Dürer wrote of the altarpiece, which he saw in the Netherlands, "I saw about 40 little panels in oil color, such as I have never seen for precision and excellence."

The other pictures reproduced here show further work by Juan de Flandes, the finest of these Hispano-Flemish artists: four panels painted for the High Altar of the Cathedral of Palencia.

143

144

145

Master of St.Gilles

(FRANCO-FLEMISH, ACTIVE c. 1500)

146   THE BAPTISM OF CLOVIS

The Flemish technique of painting spread over northern Europe and Spain. The panel reproduced is by an artist strongly influenced by Hugo van der Goes. His birthplace is unknown, but his Parisian residence is certain. The baptism is shown as occurring in Sainte-Chapelle on the Île de la Cité in Paris. The upper church is suggested by the statue on the central pier and the door on the right, but otherwise the scene seems to take place on the ground level. Through the door of the chapel can be seen the former royal palace and its courtyard, Place du Parvis, as they appeared about 1500. The gabled edifice and the corner tower were built about 1323 and are thought to have housed the king's chaplains. Just beyond, one has a glimpse of the royal apartments. This picture and a companion piece (plate 148), also in the National Gallery of Art, are, except for manuscript illumination, the earliest accurate views of the city of Paris. Thus, apart from the beauty of the paintings, they are archaeological documents of outstanding significance.

Clovis was baptized at Rheims, not Paris, and William M. Hinkle has suggested that the scene represents instead the baptism of Lisbius by St. Denis. Lisbius was the first Christian martyr of Paris. His martyrdom was brought about by the denunciation of his wife, Larcia, who is identified as the grim lady standing behind the baptismal font. Colin Eisler, however, has found an illustration of 1488, approximately the date of the panel reproduced, which shows the scene in much the same fashion. He believes the forbidding expression of the lady in the background was due less to hostility toward her husband than to repainting by an inept restorer. Thus she and her two companions are more likely to have been donors. That the figure being baptized wears a crown indicates that he could be Clovis, who was king of the Franks. Assuming that the naked man with the far-away look is the king, the description of his baptism, one of Gibbon's most delightful passages, is worth quoting: "The important ceremony was performed in the cathedral of Rheims, with every circumstance of magnificence and solemnity that could impress an awful sense of religion on the minds of its rude proselytes. The new Constantine was immediately baptized, with three thousand of his warlike subjects; and their example was imitated by the remainder of the *gentle Barbarians*, who, in obedience to the victorious prelate, adored the cross which they had burnt, and burnt the idols which they had formerly adored."

Collections: Probably commissioned for the church of St.-Leu–St.-Gilles, Paris; Chevalier Lestang-Parade; Comte Melchior de Lestang-Parade, Aix-en-Provence; Baron E. de Beurnonville; M. Watil, Paris. *Samuel H. Kress Collection*, 1952. Painted c. 1500. Wood, 24¼ x 18⅜" (61.6 x 46.7 cm.)

141

153

168

170

169

171

154

168 **Bernhard Strigel** (German, 1460/61–1528): *Margaret Vöhlin, Wife of Hans Rott*. Dated 1527. Wood, 17¼ x 12¼" (43.8 x 31.1 cm.). Ralph and Mary Booth Collection

169 **Bernhard Strigel**: Reverse of *Margaret Vöhlin, Wife of Hans Rott*

170 **Bernhard Strigel**: *Hans Rott, Patrician of Memmingen*. Dated 1527. Wood, 17¼ x 12¼" (43.8 x 31.1 cm.). Ralph and Mary Booth Collection

171 **Bernhard Strigel**: Reverse of *Hans Rott, Patrician of Memmingen*

172 **Nicolaus Kremer** (German, c. 1500–1553): *Portrait of a Nobleman*. Signed with initials, and dated 1529. Wood, 23½ x 17⅜" (59.9 x 44.5 cm.). Ralph and Mary Booth Collection

173 **Hans Schäufelein** (German, c. 1470/85–1538/40): *Portrait of a Man*. Dated 1507. Wood, 15⅝ x 12⅝" (40 x 32 cm.). Andrew W. Mellon Collection

173

German painters were often superb portraitists, although few reached the level of Dürer. The painting attributed to Schäufelein bears the false initials "A.D." (Albrecht Dürer), a favorite device to give a picture greater importance. This brilliant characterization, however, needs no misrepresentation to be considered a masterpiece. The sitter's ruthless and determined face reveals the fanaticism that made possible the cruelty and intolerance of the Reformation. The portraits by Strigel of Hans Rott and his wife, two patricians from Memmingen, seem by comparison far too mild and inexpressive. Their coats of arms on the reverse are more interesting than their likenesses. This often happens with German painters who delighted in decorative calligraphy for its own sake.

172

Hans Holbein the Younger

(GERMAN, 1497-1543)

174   SIR BRIAN TUKE

As Hazlitt said, Holbein's portraits are like state documents. In them we find recorded objectively, but with impressive dignity, the great figures who surrounded Henry VIII. Sir Brian Tuke was Governor of the King's Post "in England and in other parts of the King's domain beyond the sea." He was also secretary and treasurer of the royal household, and he has been credited with the responsibility of bringing Holbein to England, possibly to paint this portrait, which is the finest of a number of versions.

Droit et avant (upright and forward) was the sitter's personal motto, one that seems to have been justified by his life. On the folded paper near his hand can be discerned with difficulty the Latin words from Job 10:20, "Are not my days few? cease then, and let me alone, that I may take comfort a little." Sir Brian was fifty-seven when he was painted, an old man by the standards of his time. He accepted that he had but a short while to live, for in the Renaissance death was always imminent. The plague still ravaged Europe, and an outbreak of the pestilence in London some years later carried off Holbein himself when only forty-six and at the peak of his career. If a courtier escaped death by disease there was still the enmity of his monarch to be feared, and this could be mortal, too, as it was in the case of St. Thomas More, the friend of both Tuke and Holbein, who died with many others for refusing to say "yes" to the King. Sir Brian never lost his sovereign's favor, but in his twisted smile, full of pain, and in the wistful plea on the folded paper, we sense the desperate insecurity of life in the England of Henry VIII.

Collections: Philip Sidney, Third Earl of Leicester; Sir Paul Methuen and descendants, among whom the last owner was Paul, First Lord Methuen, Corsham Court, Chippenham, Wiltshire; Richard Sanderson, Edinburgh; Richard, Second Marquess of Westminster; Lady Theodora Guest, Inwood, Templecombe, England; Watson B. Dickerman, New York. *Andrew W. Mellon Collection*, 1937. Painted c. 1527. Wood, 19⅜ x 15¼" (49 x 39 cm.).

175

175 Jan Gossaert (Mabuse) (Flemish, c. 1478–1532): *Portrait of a Banker.* c. 1530. Wood, 25 x 18¾″ (63.6 x 47.5 cm.). Ailsa Mellon Bruce Fund

176 Hans Holbein the Younger (German, 1497–1543): *Portrait of a Young Man.* c. 1520. Wood, 8⅝ x 6¾″ (21.9 x 17 cm.). Samuel H. Kress Collection

177 Ambrosius Benson: *Niclaes de Hondecoeter.* Dated on reverse 1543. Wood, 10 x 7⅞″ (25.5 x 19.9 cm.). Gift of Adolph Caspar Miller

178 Ambrosius Benson (Flemish, active c. 1519-1550): *Wife of Niclaes de Hondecoeter.* 1543. Wood, 10⅛ x 7⅞″ (25.9 x 19.9 cm.). Gift of Adolph Caspar Miller

179 Peter Gertner (German, active 1530–1540): *Portrait of a Man.* Dated 1539. Paper, 17½ x 12¾″ (44.4 x 32.3 cm.). Gift of Adolph Caspar Miller

180 Peter Gertner: *Portrait of a Lady.* Dated 1539. Paper, 17½ x 12¾″ (44.4 x 32.3 cm.). Gift of Adolph Caspar Miller

181 British School (c. 1597): *The Earl of Essex.* Wood, 45⅛ x 34½″ (114.7 x 87.7 cm.). Gift of Mrs. Henry R. Rea

176

177

178

179

180

181

The fascination of portraits comes partly from the way they entrap the past. They catch in the mirror of art the reflections of a vanished life. These seven reproductions show the face of the sixteenth century, revealing how men and women looked in the Netherlands, Germany, and England when Europe was being torn apart by dynastic wars and the Reformation and Counter-Reformation.

Hans Holbein the Younger

(GERMAN, 1497–1543)

182   EDWARD VI AS A CHILD

This panel, painted soon after Holbein's second arrival in England, was given to Henry VIII on New Year's Day, 1539. It is listed in the Royal Inventory as "By Hanse Holbyne a table of the pictour of the p'nce [Prince's] grace." The King was undoubtedly pleased with the likeness, for according to the same document, he gave "To Hanse Holbyne, paynter, a gilte cruse [a type of cup] wt a cover Cornelis weing X oz. quarter."

The poem at the bottom of the picture was written by Cardinal Morison, an influential figure of the Church and Court. It urges Edward to emulate his illustrious father in every way, presumably in matrimony as in other matters. Healthy as the young Prince seems in this portrait, fate did not give him time to marry even once, for he died at the age of fifteen.

The English were easily pleased in matters of art. Since the monkish illuminators of the Middle Ages they had never produced or imported a painter of the first rank. Therefore when Holbein arrived from Switzerland his popularity was enormous. He was particularly admired for his ability to ennoble his sitters. Here, commissioned to paint a portrait of a child not yet two years old, he manages to convey rank and majesty. The future monarch of England is dressed in courtly clothes of gold and velvet; he holds his rattle as though it were a scepter, and he raises his right hand in a gesture of royal magnanimity. Thus an effigy becomes a symbol rather than a portrait. Holbein has presented the quintessence of royalty, the embodiment of the princely infant.

Collections: English Royal Collection; Arundel (where engraved in 1650); Provincial Museum, Hanover (from the Royal and Ducal Hanoverian Collections). *Andrew W. Mellon Collection*, 1937. Painted presumably in 1538. Wood, 22⅜ x 17⅜" (57 x 44 cm.).

PARVVLE PATRISSA, PATRIÆ VIRTVTIS ET HÆRES
    ESTO, NIHIL MAIVS MAXIMVS ORBIS HABET.
GNATVM VIX POSSVNT COELVM ET NATVRA DEDISSE,
    HVIVS QVEM PATRIS, VICTVS HONORET HONOS.
ÆQVATO TANTVM, TANTI TV FACTA PARENTIS,
    VOTA HOMINVM, VIX QVO PROGRFDIANTVR, HABENT
VINCITO, VICISTI. QVOT REGES PRISCVS ADORAT
    ORBIS, NEC TE QVI VINCERE POSSIT, ERIT.

200

Raphael's effortless achievement is at the core of what we call Classicism. Of the paintings reproduced here, *The Flagellation of Christ* (plate 197) and *Putti with a Wine Press* (plate 201) are so close to the master's style that they were formerly ascribed to him. The other artists whose work is shown, Andrea del Sarto, Bacchiacca, and Aspertini, were completely under his influence. The *Portrait of a Man* (plate 200) has traditionally been identified as Baldassare Castiglione, who knew Raphael at the court of Urbino, and whose handbook, *The Courtier*, describes the *beau idéal* of social intercourse.

201

202

Raphael

(UMBRIAN, 1483-1520)

203 THE SMALL COWPER MADONNA

The Small Cowper Madonna was purchased in Italy in the eighteenth century by that remarkable Earl Cowper who is referred to frequently in Horace Walpole's correspondence with Sir Horace Mann, and the painting hung for over a century in Lord Cowper's country estate of Panshanger. A great connoisseur with an instinctive sympathy for the Renaissance, Lord Cowper was so drawn to Italy that he spent most of his life in Florence and became a prince of the Holy Roman Empire. Horace Walpole wrote scathingly of this eighteenth-century expatriate, "He has the awkward dignity of a temporary representative of nominal power."

Although Walpole might despise Lord Cowper's choice of titles, he could not but envy his choice of pictures. For this eccentric English Earl was the only collector of his time who could show the span of Raphael's development during his Florentine period. The two Madonnas, which were in his collection and which are now both in the National Gallery of Art (see plate 204), reveal the quintessence of Raphael's early and best manner of painting on panel. Giovanni Morelli, the founder of the system on which the modern attribution of Italian painting is based, considered *The Small Cowper Madonna* to be "perhaps the most lovely of all Raphael's Madonnas . . . [It] sets the young artist before our eyes in the full blaze of his independence." In the half-century that has elapsed since Morelli made this statement, no serious critic has questioned either his evaluation or his placing of the picture in Raphael's development. There has been general agreement among critics that *The Small Cowper Madonna* was probably painted sometime in the year 1505, shortly after Raphael achieved his mature style in Florence. Our Lady's expression still retains the dry, tired wistfulness we find in the Madonnas and saints painted by his master, Perugino, but the figures are drawn with more certainty, their forms modeled with more solidity, than in any work of the Umbrian period. The buildings in the background, however, seem quite definitely to be the convent and church of San Bernardino on the outskirts of Urbino. Thus even though the picture may have been painted in Florence, it was probably commissioned by an Umbrian patron.

Collections: Purchased in Florence by Lord Cowper about 1780, the present painting remained in the possession of his family at Panshanger, Hertfordshire, until 1913. *Widener Collection*, 1942. Painted probably c. 1505. Wood, 23⅜ x 17⅜" (59.5 x 44 cm.).

Raphael

(UMBRIAN, 1483-1520)

204 THE NICCOLINI-COWPER MADONNA

Signed and dated 1508, *The Niccolini-Cowper Madonna* was probably one of the first pictures Raphael painted in Rome, at the end of his Florentine period. It was a work for which he must have made innumerable studies. There is a drawing for the head of the child in the Lille Museum, and another drawing of heads in the British Museum in London. The latter study bears a close relation to the painting reproduced here, though it has also been connected with other works. A master of composition, Raphael never achieved a more intricately and satisfactorily balanced design of two figures.

The early history of the painting is unknown. It is first recorded in the Casa Niccolini in 1677. It seems to have been bought from the Niccolini family by the painter and art dealer Johann Zoffany shortly after his arrival in Florence in 1772. He had been commissioned by Queen Charlotte of England to paint a view of the Tribuna, the room in the Uffizi which housed many of the greatest art treasures of the Grand Dukes of Tuscany. In many ways a precursor of Lord Duveen, Zoffany did not hesitate to get as much publicity as possible from his *Tribuna*. In the painting (which is now at Windsor), he has shown himself offering for sale the *Casa Niccolini Madonna* to Earl Cowper and to the other English cognoscenti sojourning in Florence. In 1826 the *Literary Gazette* ran an amusing account of Zoffany's dealings. "He was wont to ask all English comers to Florence, 'Have you seen my Raffael?—Ah! den you must see it.' . . . His lordship [Lord Cowper] paid down a certain liberal sum [five hundred guineas according to the Panshanger papers], and granted, by way of residue, an annuity of a hundred pounds, which the fortunate painter (who lived, as is said and pretty generally believed, to be between ninety and a hundred) enjoyed to the last. Hence this 'Madonna', perhaps, whatever may be its merits, is the dearest Raffael that ever was purchased, even by a traveling English lord!"

Actually, Zoffany lived to be only seventy-seven. He had originally asked five thousand guineas for his Raphael and, in spite of his long life, did not quite realize this figure. Lord Cowper in turn tried to sell the *Madonna* to George III at a very low price, hoping this bargain would cause him to be made a Knight of the Garter. Fortunately for the National Gallery of Art, the King did not accept the offer and Lord Cowper never got the Garter. The painting was finally sold by his heirs through Duveen Brothers to Andrew Mellon. In the end, Zoffany's *Madonna* brought 170,000 guineas, thirty-four times his original asking price.

Collections: Casa Niccolini, Florence (as early as 1677); Johann Zoffany; Earl Cowper and his heirs, Panshanger, Hertfordshire, until 1928. *Andrew W. Mellon Collection*, 1937. Signed with initials, and dated 1508. Wood, 31¾ x 22⅝" (81 x 57 cm.).

214

215

The afterglow of Florentine art produced several painters of genius, among whom Pontormo was the most original and accomplished. As Raphael's work is the supreme expression of Renaissance Classicism, so Pontormo's paintings offer the most beautiful examples of early Mannerism. This style, which flourished in the second half of the sixteenth century, has three major characteristics: the chiaroscuro of Leonardo, the contours of Raphael, and the exaggerated *contrapposto* and restless compositions of Michelangelo. To these is later added an element of distortion, of elongation, which reaches its climax in the work of El Greco.

216

217

218

214 **Pontormo** (Florentine, 1494–1556/57): *The Holy Family.* c. 1525. Wood, 39⅞ x 31″ (101 x 79 cm.). Samuel H. Kress Collection

215 **Pontormo:** *Portrait of a Young Woman.* c. 1535. Wood, 22 x 17″ (56 x 43 cm.). Widener Collection

216 **Pontormo:** *Ugolino Martelli.* c. 1545/50. Wood, 36 x 26¾″ (91 x 68 cm.). Samuel H. Kress Collection

217 **Pontormo:** *Monsignor della Casa.* Probably 1541/44. Wood, 40⅛ x 31″ (102.1 x 78.8 cm.). Samuel H. Kress Collection

218 **Federico Barocci** (Roman, 1535–1612): *Quintilia Fischieri.* Probably c. 1600. Canvas, 48¾ x 37½″ (124 x 95 cm.). Samuel H. Kress Collection

219 **Domenico Beccafumi** (Sienese, c. 1485–1551): *The Holy Family with Angels.* c. 1545/50. Wood, 32 x 24¼″ (81 x 62 cm.). Samuel H. Kress Collection

219

Lorenzo Lotto

(VENETIAN, c. 1480-1556)

220   ALLEGORY

In July 1505, Lorenzo Lotto completed a portrait of Bernardo Rossi, who was Bishop of Treviso from 1499 to 1527. This painting is now one of the masterpieces of the Naples museum. Some years ago the picture reproduced here was discovered, and on the back of the panel was an inscription identifying it as the cover for Rossi's portrait. As further identification, propped against the tree is his coat-of-arms, showing a lion rampant on a blue shield, which also appears on his signet ring in the Naples portrait. Such covers were often hinged, thus forming with the portrait itself a diptych. Their purpose remains obscure: perhaps the sitter wished his likeness to be seen only by intimate friends; perhaps he wished to protect the portrait itself; or perhaps he welcomed the opportunity that this additional panel offered for a further symbolic interpretation of his character or his life. This latter allegorical intention seems to have motivated Bernardo Rossi. That he was interested in allegory is indicated by his portrait medal, which is also in the National Gallery of Art. This has on the reverse a female figure in tunic and mantle, holding a sunflower and standing in a car drawn by an eagle and a winged dragon (see plates 221, 222).

The meaning of Lotto's *Allegory* is less baffling than its medallic counterpart. The painted cover seems to present in figurative terms the desirability of choosing virtue instead of vice. On the left, a naked child bathed in sunlight is picking up instruments—a compass, a carpenter's square, a flute, a scroll—symbols of cultural pursuits and thus, for the Renaissance man, symbols of the virtuous life. The right side of the picture is devoted to an allegory of vice. The light has gone, and in the umbrageous gloom a drunken satyr sprawls among overturned vessels, while in the distance a ship founders in the storm. Lotto tactfully indicates that his sitter has triumphed over passion and won his way to virtue. Rossi's winged spirit is shown climbing rapidly upward on a steep and stony path toward the summit of a mountain where the sky is clearing.

Collections: Probably Garden Palace of the Farnese, Parma (seventeenth century); Antonio Bertioli, Parma; Giacomo Gritti, Bergamo. *Samuel H. Kress Collection*, 1939. Painted 1505. Wood, 22¼ x 16⅝" (56 x 42.2 cm.).

189

249

250

246 **Vittore Carpaccio** (Venetian, c. 1460/65–
1523/26): *The Flight into Egypt.* c. 1500. Wood, 28¼ x
43⅞″ (72 x 111.5 cm.). Andrew W. Mellon Collection

247 **Vittore Carpaccio:** *Madonna and Child.* c. 1505.
Wood, 33⅜ x 26⅞″ (84.8 x 68.3 cm.). Samuel H. Kress
Collection

248 **Vittore Carpaccio:** *The Virgin Reading.* c. 1505.
Wood, 30¾ x 20″ (78 x 51 cm.). Samuel H. Kress Collection

249 **Giovanni Bellini** (Venetian, c. 1430–1516): *Madonna and Child with Saints.* c. 1490. Wood, 29¼ x 20″
(76 x 51 cm.). Samuel H. Kress Collection

250 **Giovanni Bellini:** *Madonna and Child.* c. 1480.
Wood, 28¼ x 20⅞″ (72 x 53.2 cm.). Ralph and Mary
Booth Collection

251 **Giovanni Bellini:** *The Infant Bacchus.* Probably
1505/10. Wood, 18⅞ x 14½″ (48 x 36.8 cm.). Samuel
H. Kress Collection

251

Titian

(VENETIAN, c. 1477–1576)

252 DOGE ANDREA GRITTI

The seal of Charles I of England and a label reading, "Bought for his Majesty in Italy, 1626," are still preserved on the back of the canvas of this stupendous portrait, more recently in the Czernin Collection in Vienna. The royal catalogue also listed it: "Duke Grettie, of Venice, with his right hand holding his robes. Bought by the King, half figures so big as the life, in a black wooden gilded frame." Perhaps Charles saw in the stern, implacable face of the Venetian Doge those traits of character he himself lacked. Titian has dowered Gritti with a grim, ruthless personality and made him a symbol of the power of the galleys that, under the patronage of St. Mark, caused Venice to be honored and feared along the trade routes of the world. But Gritti was also a patron of the arts. At his order, a considerable number of Titian's large religious, historical, and allegorical pictures, now mostly lost, were painted.

The hand with which the Doge grasps his flowing cape may be based upon the hand of Moses in the famous statue by Michelangelo in Rome. A Venetian sculptor, Jacopo Sansovino, is believed to have brought a cast of this hand to Venice, where Titian probably studied its massive power to help him create an image of uncompromising majesty, the archetype of the imperious ruler moving forward in a ceremonial procession.

Collections: King Charles I of England; Wenzel Anton, Prince von Kaunitz-Rietburg, Chancellor of Empress Maria Theresa; Count Johann Rudolf Czernin von Chudenitz, Vienna; Czernin Gallery, Vienna. *Samuel H. Kress Collection*, 1961. Signed. Painted probably between 1535 and 1540. Canvas, 52½ x 40⅝" (133.6 x 103.2 cm.).

205

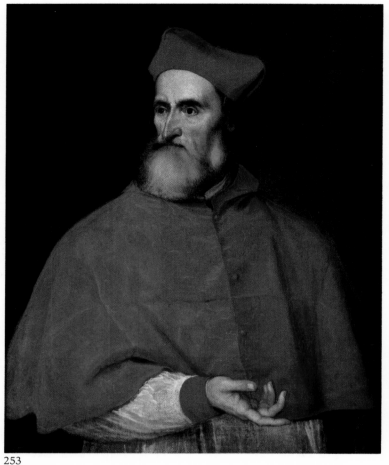

253

254

253 **Titian** (Venetian, c. 1477–1576): *Cardinal Pietro Bembo*. c. 1540. Canvas, 37⅛ x 30⅛″ (94.5 x 76.5 cm.). Samuel H. Kress Collection

254 **Titian**: *Ranuccio Farnese*. Signed. 1542. Canvas, 35¼ x 29″ (89.7 x 73.6 cm.). Samuel H. Kress Collection

255 **Titian**: *Vincenzo Capello*. c. 1540. Canvas, 55½ x 46½″ (141 x 118 cm.). Samuel H. Kress Collection

256 **Sebastiano del Piombo** (Venetian, c. 1485–1547): *Portrait of a Young Woman as a Wise Virgin*. c. 1510. Wood, 21 x 18⅛″ (53.4 x 46.2 cm.). Samuel H. Kress Collection

257 **Sebastiano del Piombo**: *Portrait of a Humanist*. c.1520. Wood mounted on Masonite, 53 x 39¾″ (134.7 x 101 cm.). Samuel H. Kress Collection

258 **Sebastiano del Piombo**: *Cardinal Bandinello Sauli, His Secretary and Two Geographers*. Dated 1516. Wood, 47⅞ x 59″ (121.6 x 149.8 cm.). Samuel H. Kress Collection

255

256

Like Andrea Gritti, Vincenzo Capello, his contemporary and the admiral of the Venetian fleet, looks as though he might have spoken those impressive lines from *Othello*: ''I have done the state some service, and they know't.'' All three of Titian's sitters have been dowered with an enlargement of personality that distinguishes the work of the greatest portraitists. Sebastiano del Piombo reduces his models to a more human scale. The Cardinal (plate 258), about to be incarcerated for conspiring to poison the Pope, becomes a pathetic terrorist, and the humanist (plate 257) a neurotic scholar.

257

258

Titian

(VENETIAN, c. 1477–1576)

259 VENUS WITH A MIRROR

Titian, more than any other Renaissance artist, understood the spirit of classical art. Yet he was nearly seventy when he went to Rome and had his first opportunity to visit the capital of the ancient world and to see the great works of art accumulated there. When he was not executing his many important missions at the Vatican and among the Roman nobility, he was, as he said, "learning from the marvelous, ancient stones." Although he regretted that he had not received this inspiration earlier, still it came at a time when he was about to enter upon his period of supreme achievement, which lasted until he was well into his nineties. Under the influence of classical art his late nudes gained an amplitude of form, a heavy magnificence which suggests Greek sculpture of the Golden Age.

From his earliest masterpieces like the Bacchanals, painted for the Duke of Ferrara, to canvases like this, painted when he was over seventy, Titian repeatedly celebrated the goddess of love. All these pictures are permeated with a sensuality which deepens with age, growing always more impersonal. In his final work he expresses the indwelling power of feminine beauty, a quality which transcends the loveliness of any individual woman. These pictures are his final homage to Venus, as moving in their way as the late love poems of Yeats.

But Titian's amatory tribute was not arrived at suddenly. From data revealed by recent X-rays it appears that the canvas was used previously for two other compositions, which Titian abandoned in succession. The first was a horizontal composition of a man and a woman standing together, possibly an allegory of marriage with the bride and groom in the roles of Venus and Mars. The second was a vertical composition representing a Venus with two cupids; the head and pose of the Venus were retained in the final picture.

Having found the composition he wanted, Titian painted several further variations on this theme, and still others were produced by followers and imitators, but this particular canvas he kept for himself, feeling for it perhaps some special affection. After his death it was sold by his son Pomponio to the Barbarigo family, and remained in their possession until it was purchased by Nicholas I for the Hermitage Gallery, Leningrad.

Collections: Pomponio Vecellio, Venice; Barbarigo family, Venice; Hermitage Gallery, Leningrad. *Andrew W. Mellon Collection*, 1937. Painted c. 1555. Canvas, 49 x 41½" (124.5 x 105.5 cm.).

276

272 **Correggio** (School of Parma, 1489/94–1534): *The Mystic Marriage of St. Catherine*. c. 1510/15. Wood, 10⅞ x 8⅜″ (27.7 x 21.3 cm.). Samuel H. Kress Collection

273 **Correggio**: *Salvator Mundi*. c. 1515. Wood, 16¾ x 13⅛″ (42.6 x 33.3 cm.). Samuel H. Kress Collection

274 **Jacopo Bassano** (Venetian, c. 1515–1592): *The Annunciation to the Shepherds*. Probably c. 1555/60. Canvas, 41¾ x 32½″ (106 x 83 cm.). Samuel H. Kress Collection

275 **Bartolommeo Veneto** (Lombard-Venetian, active 1502–1546): *Portrait of a Gentleman*. c. 1520. Transferred from wood to canvas, 30¼ x 23″ (77 x 58 cm.). Samuel H. Kress Collection

276 **Paris Bordone** (Venetian, 1500–1571): *The Baptism of Christ*. c. 1535/40. Canvas, 51 x 52″ (129.5 x 132 cm.). Widener Collection

277 **Marco Basaiti** (Venetian, active 1496–1530): *Madonna Adoring the Child*. Signed. c. 1520. Wood, 8⅛ x 6½″ (21 x 17 cm.). Samuel H. Kress Collection

278 **Sodoma** (Sienese, 1477–1549): *Madonna and Child with the Infant Saint John*. c. 1505. Wood, 31 x 25½″ (79 x 65 cm.).Samuel H. Kress Collection

277

278

Giovanni Battista Moroni

(BRESCIAN, c. 1520–1578)

279   A GENTLEMAN IN ADORATION BEFORE THE MADONNA

Little is known of Moroni's life except that he was active in the provincial town of Bergamo. His portraits, in which he revealed his true ability, his sensitive under- standing of character, recall the work of his master, Moretto, who was active in nearby Brescia. The mood he creates is the same wistful melancholy that we find in Moretto's style. The figures in Moroni's portraits seem to implore our sympathy with a shy, solemn insistence. This elusive note of diffident sadness, so often to be found in provincial portraiture, is the opposite of the mood created by Titian, Veronese, and Tintoretto, in whose portraits we have a feeling of inner strength, a sense that the men and women they portray were destined by some ineluctable right to dominate, to possess the world.

Probably Moroni's provincial patrons lacked the self-assurance which is so con- spicuous in the people who sat for the Venetian masters. Or perhaps this lack was in the artist himself, for Moroni never mastered the *gusto grande*, the grand man- ner, which was fashionable in his day. He never learned that art of ennobling, or amplifying, the personalities of his sitters. He painted his subjects as he saw them; he delineated with touching fidelity the commoners and the petty nobility of a pro- vincial town, men and women who were close to their peasants, who often helped in the vineyards and fields, and were not above menial tasks. His canvases mirror, perhaps better than the work of any other artist, the personalities of a small town in the sixteenth century.

In the painting *A Gentleman in Adoration before the Madonna* Moroni was confronted with a subject common enough in Venetian art, a miraculous appari- tion. Titian, for instance, has often created such scenes with his easy invention, his great imaginative power, but Moroni, devoid of all visionary feeling, was para- lyzed, as Berenson has said, the moment he was separated from the model. Thus in portraying the Madonna and Child he dared not trust his own creative genius. He turned instead to an engraving by Albrecht Dürer for his model. Yet the amazing fact remains that his painting triumphs over such naive imitation. Moroni's sensi- tive and poetic treatment of the kneeling man gives his picture a mood of intimate devotion, an atmosphere of fervent piety, which seems an echo from a simpler, more innocent world.

Collection: Casa Grimani, Venice. *Samuel H. Kress Collection*, 1939. Painted c. 1560. Canvas, 23½ x 25½" (60 x 65 cm.).

The Venetian paintings so far reproduced indicate that
the leadership of the Italian Schools was gradually
passing from Florence to Venice, whose suzerainty at
the beginning of the sixteenth century extended from
the head of the Adriatic to Lake Como. In Venice's expansion over this wide territory a number of city-states
were overrun, each of which had developed its own
school of painting. Although the artists of these North
Italian towns accepted the preeminence of the great
Venetian masters, their styles remained local and
idiomatic. Thus the paintings of Savoldo and Moretto
are marked by a religious feeling hard to find in Venice
itself after the death of Giovanni Bellini.

281

280

282

283

284

280 **Giovanni Girolamo Savoldo** (Brescian, active 1508–1548): *Elijah Fed by the Raven*. c. 1510. Transferred from wood to canvas, 66⅛ x 53⅜" (168 x 135.6 cm.). Samuel H. Kress Collection

281 **Giovanni Girolamo Savoldo**: *Portrait of a Knight*. c. 1525. Canvas, 34¾ x 28⅞" (88.3 x 73.4 cm.). Samuel H. Kress Collection

282 **Moretto da Brescia** (Brescian, c. 1498–1554): *Pietà*. 1520s. Wood, 69⅛ x 38¼" (175.8 x 98.5 cm.). Samuel H. Kress Collection

283 **Giovanni Battista Moroni** (Brescian, c. 1520–1578): "*Titian's Schoolmaster*." c. 1575. Canvas, 38⅛ x 29¼" (97 x 74 cm.). Widener Collection

284 **Giovanni Battista Moroni**: *Gian Federico Madruzzo*. c. 1560. Canvas, 79½ x 46" (201.9 x 116.8 cm.). Timken Collection

285 **Northern Follower of Titian** (probably mid-XVI century): *Alessandro Alberti with a Page*. Canvas, 48⅞ x 40⅜" (124.2 x 102.7 cm.). Samuel H. Kress Foundation

285

François Clouet

(FRENCH, c. 1510–1572)

286   "DIANE DE POITIERS"

François Clouet's work is an example of the wide dissemination in the sixteenth century of the Italian style. This is one of three portraits he signed. In the nineteenth century the sitter was considered to be Diane de Poitiers, and the portrait retained this title for many years. The children in the painting were supposed to be the offspring of her lover Henri II and Catherine de' Medici. We know they were placed in her care. The unicorn embroidered on a chair back or firescreen was thought to be a reference to the unicorn horn purchased by Diane to preserve the health of the royal children through its supposed therapeutic properties.

More recently the date of the picture has been placed much later, toward the end of Clouet's life. The lady's coiffure, for example, resembles that of Clouet's portrait of Elizabeth of Austria, a drawing for which is dated 1571. As Diane died in 1566, scholars have gone in search of some other royal favorite. Gabrielle d'Estrées, mistress of Henri IV, and Marie Touchet, mistress of Charles IX, have had their advocates but have yet to gain general acceptance. In 1966 Roger Trinquet published the most fascinating suggestion of all. He believes the lady to be Mary Queen of Scots and the painting to have been done with satirical intent for some Huguenot patron, possibly François, Maréchal de Montmorency.

Although the lady's face is highly idealized, a beautiful feminine mask, there is no doubt that she resembles accepted portraits of the tragic Scottish queen, particularly a drawing in white mourning attire attributed to François Clouet. If this identification is correct, then the infant is her son and the crossed black bands on his swaddling clothes an allusion to the Cross of St. Andrew and possibly also to the death of Darnley, the baby's father. The same child at four or five would then be the boy reaching for the fruit, a symbol of his grasping for the crown of Scotland. There is also the supporting evidence that the unicorn and the grapes appear in emblematic devices of Mary Stuart; and Colin Eisler, who is inclined to accept this identification, has pointed out that the bather's cap "is closer to English than to French fashion."

The setting may seem unusual, but judging by the numerous copies of this picture in the sixteenth century and the variations on the theme of a lady in her bath, which continued into the seventeenth century, Clouet's painting made bathing portraits extremely fashionable. Trinquet claims that a lady shown in her bath must be

(continued)

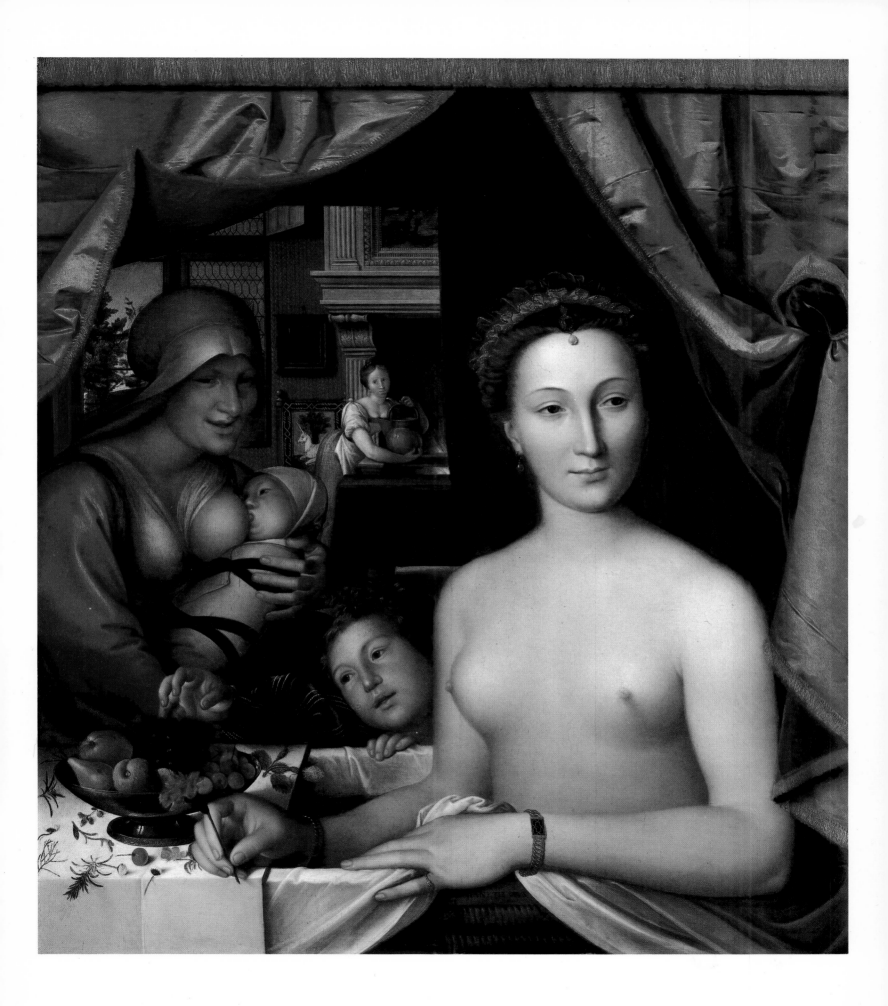

287

French painting came under the spell of the most famous artist ever to visit France, Leonardo da Vinci. Leonardo spent the last three years of his life at Amboise, where he died in 1519. His influence, which is particularly apparent in Clouet's portrait (plate 286), was ubiquitous in France. His personality was so overwhelming that it also dominated the School of Milan, where he stayed from 1482 to 1499. We see, for example, the Leonardesque modeling in Boltraffio's Youth and the Mona Lisa smile in Luini's Magdalen.

288

(continued)

a lady of questionable virtue. If so, judging by the popularity of this setting, many sixteenth-century ladies were delighted to have their virtue questioned. If the bather is Mary Stuart, must Clouet's painting be considered satirical? May not some French admirer have wanted a portrait that would convey the fatal sexual attraction of this woman for whom so many men died or were imprisoned? Is this perhaps the finest portrait in existence of the most fascinating queen in history?

Collections: Sir Richard Frederick, Burwood Park; Cook, Doughty House, Richmond, Surrey. *Samuel H. Kress Collection*, 1961. Painted probably c. 1571. Wood, 36¼ x 32″ (92.1 x 81.3 cm.).

289

290

291

287 French School (XVI century): *Prince Hercule-François, Duc d'Alencon.* Dated 1572. Canvas, 74½ x 40¼″ (188.6 x 102.2 cm.). Samuel H. Kress Collection

288 Bernardino Luini (Milanese, c. 1480–1532): *The Magdalen.* c. 1525. Wood, 23⅛ x 18⅞″ (58.8 x 47.8 cm.). Samuel H. Kress Collection

289 Bernardino Luini: *Venus.* c. 1530. Wood, 42 x 53½″ (107 x 136 cm.). Samuel H. Kress Collection

290 Giovanni Antonio Boltraffio (Milanese, 1467–1516): *Portrait of a Youth.* Shortly before 1500. Wood, 18⅜ x 13¾″ (46.7 x 35 cm.). Ralph and Mary Booth Collection

291 French School (XVI century): *Portrait of a Nobleman.* c. 1570. Wood, 12¾ x 9¼″ (32.5 x 23.5 cm.). Gift of Chester Dale

292 Jacopo Tintoretto (Venetian, 1518–1594): *Susanna.* c. 1575. Canvas, 59⅛ x 40⅜″ (150 x 103 cm.). Samuel H. Kress Collection

292

Jacopo Tintoretto

293   CHRIST AT THE SEA OF GALILEE

Ask a contemporary painter to name the greatest of the Venetian artists, and the chances are he will choose Tintoretto. There are many reasons for this choice, but in the painting reproduced one is especially evident: Tintoretto's emotional intensity. In *Christ at the Sea of Galilee*, the event illustrated is described in John 21:7. Our Lord, standing on the shore, reveals himself to his disciples who are fishing: "Now when Simon Peter heard that it was the Lord, he girt his fisher's coat unto him (for he was naked), and did cast himself into the sea." Here almost for the first time nature becomes an actor in the drama. The driven clouds, the storm-tossed waves, the "light that never was, on sea or land," all heighten the terrible intensity of the moment of ecstatic union when man is irresistibly drawn to His Lord and Saviour. How marvelously Tintoretto conveys the towering majesty of Christ and the yearning desire of the disciple who flings himself into the sea to reach his Master!

It is interesting to note that Hans Tietze, one of the most astute authorities on Venetian painting, always believed this picture to be by El Greco. The elongation of Christ, the color and modeling of the waves, and the emotional intensity of the scene suggest the Spanish painter. But it is hard to place the picture in the chronology of El Greco's works, and the touch in the smaller figures and the painting of the sky seem typical of Tintoretto's style.

Collections: Count J. Galotti; Arthur Sachs, New York. *Samuel H. Kress Collection*, 1952. Painted c. 1575/80. Canvas, 46 x 66¼" (117 x 168.5 cm.).

294

294

Jacopo Tintoretto (Venetian, 1518–1594)

294 *Doge Alvise Mocenigo and Family Before the Madonna and Child.* Probably 1573. Canvas, 85⅛ x 164" (216.1 x 416.5 cm.). Samuel H. Kress Collection

295 *A Procurator of St. Mark's.* c. 1575/85. Canvas, 54½ x 39⅞" (138.7 x 101.3 cm.). Samuel H. Kress Collection

296 *The Worship of the Golden Calf.* c. 1560. Canvas, 62⅝ x 107" (159 x 272 cm.). Samuel H. Kress Collection

297 *The Conversion of St. Paul.* c. 1545. Canvas, 60 x 92⅞" (152.4 x 236.2 cm.). Samuel H. Kress Collection

298 *Summer.* c. 1555. Canvas, 41⅝ x 76" (105.7 x 193 cm.). Samuel H. Kress Collection

299 *The Madonna of the Stars.* 2nd half of XVI century. Canvas, 36½ x 28⅝" (92.7 x 72.7 cm.). Ralph and Mary Booth Collection

300 Guercino (Bolognese, 1591–1666): *Cardinal Francesco Cennini.* c. 1625. Canvas, 46¼ x 37⅞" (117.4 x 96.2 cm.). Samuel H. Kress Collection

301 Domenico Fetti (Roman, c. 1589–1623): *The Veil of Veronica.* c. 1615. Wood, 32⅛ x 26½" (81.5 x 67.5 cm.). Samuel H. Kress Collection

295

296

309

310

El Greco (Spanish, 1541–1614)

307 *St. Martin and the Beggar.* 1597/99. Canvas, 76⅛ x 40½" (193.5 x 103 cm.). Widener Collection

308 *St. Ildefonso.* c. 1600/1605. Canvas, 44¼ x 25¾" (112 x 65 cm.). Andrew W. Mellon Collection

309 *St. Jerome.* c. 1610/14. Canvas, 66¼ x 43½" (168 x 110.5 cm.). Gift of Chester Dale

310 *St. Martin and the Beggar.* 1604/14. Canvas, 41 x 23⅝" (104 x 60 cm.). Andrew W. Mellon Collection

311 *The Holy Family.* Probably c. 1590. Canvas, 20⅞ x 13½" (53.2 x 34.4 cm.). Samuel H. Kress Collection

311

El Greco

(SPANISH, 1541–1614)

312 MADONNA AND CHILD WITH ST. MARTINA AND ST. AGNES

Among the Old Masters, the true prophet of modern art is El Greco. His work foreshadows the abandonment three hundred years later of naturalism for Expressionism, of proportions determined by nature for proportions determined by emotion. Academic critics fighting this trend used to assert that El Greco distorted the human form because his eyesight was defective. We now believe that astigmatism affected him less, if at all, than the stylization of Byzantine icons and mosaics he had seen as a young man on his native island of Crete. But the fashion initiated by Parmigianino, that vogue for tall, slender figures with small heads, which became modish in European painting of the late sixteenth century, also played its part and prepared the public to accept the exaggerated elongations El Greco found suitable for his highly emotional style.

El Greco, however, was not merely a precursor of many contemporary artists; he also expressed, through the flamelike forms he created, the spirit of his own time, that ardent and mystical piety which followed the newly launched Counter Reformation. The *Madonna and Child with St. Martina and St. Agnes*, once in the chapel of San José in Toledo, the Spanish town which became El Greco's final home, is a summit of such visionary painting. What more marvelous rendering of substance at once tangible and intangible, corporeal and incorporeal, than the cherubim who surround the Virgin? They seem modeled in ectoplasm, formed of some emanation of thought. Even the artist's signature, the initials of his Greek name (Domenikos Theotokópoulos) traced on the forehead of St. Martina's lion, seems to have taken on symbolic significance. The whole scene illustrates, so far as this is possible, the experiences described by El Greco's contemporary, St. John of the Cross, and other mystics.

But if El Greco himself was a mystic, he was a very practical one. We know that he was an efficient painter, ran a profitable shop, and was ready to repeat his pictures as many times as the market required. Even his distortions did not diminish his popularity, for his paintings apparently gave concrete and convincing form to visions that many pious people in Spain had seen or hoped to see.

Collection: Chapel of San José, Toledo (until 1906). *Widener Collection*, 1942. Signed with initials. Painted 1597–99. Canvas, 76⅛ x 40½" (193.5 x 103 cm.).

El Greco

(SPANISH, 1541–1614)

313   LAOCOÖN

The story of Laocoön is told by Arctinus of Miletus and repeated with some variations by Vergil. Laocoön was a priest of Poseidon who warned his fellow Trojans not to carry into their city the wooden horse left behind by the invading Greeks. But his famous words, "Fools, trust not the Greeks, even when bearing gifts," went unheeded. In despair he hurled his spear against the horse, a gesture of sacrilege against Minerva, to whom the wooden statue had been dedicated. The deities, perhaps portrayed on the right of the canvas, avenged this desecration by causing sea serpents to kill Laocoön and his two sons. Their deaths were interpreted by the Trojans as a sign of the anger of the gods, and the horse was brought inside the city walls. At night Greek soldiers concealed inside its belly crept out and opened the city gates, thus bringing about the fall of Troy and ending the Trojan War. In the middle distance the wooden horse can be seen, and in place of Troy is a view of Toledo, El Greco's adopted home.

Although El Greco was, as his name implies, Greek, he ignored the mythology and the history of his fatherland except for this one subject. In the inventory of his possessions made in 1614 three Laocoöns are listed, one of which is similar in measurements to the painting reproduced here. El Greco may have been working on this particular version when he died, for a recent cleaning suggests that the three figures on the right remained unfinished.

Why was the story of Laocoön of such exceptional interest to a painter whose work, apart from portraits, was almost entirely religious? Some scholars explain this by arguing that the Greek myth bears a relationship to Christianity, E. W. Palm going so far as to identify the figures on the right as Adam and Eve. (The third head is presumably a *pentimento*.) It is true that the legend of Laocoön and the beginning of Genesis both illustrate divine retribution for transgression, the serpent playing an important role in the classical and Biblical stories.

But El Greco's motivation, one feels, had little to do with Judeo-Hellenic parallels. He was more probably impelled to paint this subject by an artistic challenge, the desire to surpass the most famous of all statuary groups, the *Laocoön* of the Vatican discovered in 1506, which he must have scrutinized when he visited Rome in 1570. El Greco, one may presume, wished to show how much more effectively this legendary theme of suffering could be treated in paint than in marble; and with his masterpiece of twisting, contorted figures he has offered a strong argument for the pictorial as opposed to the sculptural.

Collections: Probably the large painting of Laocoön listed in the inventory of El Greco's estate in Toledo; Duke of Montpensier, Palace of San Telmo, Seville; Infante Don Antonio d'Orléans, Sanlúcar de Barrameda; E. Fischer, Charlottenburg; Prince Paul of Yugoslavia, Belgrade. *Samuel H. Kress Collection*, 1946. Painted c. 1610. Canvas, 54⅛ x 67⅞" (137.5 x 172.5 cm.).

241

Diego Velázquez

(SPANISH, 1599–1660)

314   THE NEEDLEWOMAN

The few pictures Velázquez painted to please himself are among his finest and most original achievements. In such paintings as the two views of the garden of the Villa Medici in the Prado and *The Needlewoman* in the National Gallery of Art, he appears a precursor of Corot, revealing a similar simplicity of treatment joined to a penetrating power of observation.

It would seem at first as though this study of a woman sewing were never finished. The left hand is merely blocked in, and the fingers of the right barely indicated. But this device of adumbrating rather than defining shapes was used by Velázquez in a number of late works to suggest motion. In the painting of Innocent X in the Palazzo Doria in Rome (for which the painting reproduced in plate 320 is a sketch) the outlines of the fingers are blurred, an indistinction which makes them seem to twitch with nervous energy. Again there is the hand of the boy with his foot on the dog in *Las Meninas*, where a flickering movement is given by making the contours seem faltering or indiscernible; and in *Las Hilanderas* if one looks at the hand of the woman in the foreground one sees what appear to be successive positions of her fingers as she winds her yarn. In all these pictures the vibrating effect of shifting planes of light conveys a sense of motion in a way that is new in art. Similarly *The Needlewoman* may not be an incomplete work but rather an experiment on the road leading to Impressionism.

A. Mayer identifies the sitter with the painter's daughter Francisca, who married his pupil Juan Bautista del Mazo; and Sánchez Cantón suggests that this painting may be a *Head of a Woman Sewing* mentioned in the inventory of Velázquez' effects at the time of his death.

Collections: Amédée, Marquis de Gouvello de Keriaval, Château de Kerlevenant, Sarzeau, Morbihan, Brittany; Mme Christiane de Polès, Paris. *Andrew W. Mellon Collection*, 1937. Painted c. 1640. Canvas, 29⅛ x 23⅝" (74 x 60 cm.).

243

Bartolomé Esteban Murillo

(SPANISH, 1617–1682)

315   A GIRL AND HER DUENNA

All the paintings we have reproduced so far have been either devotional pictures, allegorical or mythological scenes, or portraits. In the seventeenth century scenes of daily life—genre subjects—came into fashion. In the past such material was to be found with rare exception only in the cheaper media of woodcut and engraving. This double portrait is essentially a genre picture. A young girl and her duenna stare boldly at the spectator, much as Murillo must have seen such women gazing from the high windows in the narrow streets of Seville. The painting was popularly known as *Las Gallegas*, the Galicians, referring to the tradition that it represents two notorious courtesans of Seville who originally came from the province of Galicia. Murillo was an artist of the people: genial, commonplace in outlook, with an easy eloquence. In religious painting his sentiment was torrential, and his immense popularity finally wore away a technical ability which was second only to that of Velázquez. Disconcertingly uneven as was his achievement, he occasionally created a masterpiece like the present picture. Here he has avoided the sticky sentimentality and trite picturesqueness which spoil so much of his work. He presents these two women with that detached observation which is the hallmark of the best Spanish painting.

What Northern artist would have treated the subject with such subtle restraint? Rembrandt alone would have had the insight to eliminate the extraneous and focus attention, as Murillo has done, on the young girl so beautifully placed in the window, so plastically rendered. But not even Frans Hals would have had sufficient alertness of vision to suggest the smile of the older woman, witty, sardonic, yet expressed by the eyes and cheek alone.

Collections: Duque de Almodóvar, Madrid; Lord Heytesbury, Heytesbury House, Wiltshire. *Widener Collection*, 1942. Painted c. 1670. Canvas, 50¼ x 41¾″ (127.7 x 106.1 cm.).

245

316

317

Spanish painting of the seventeenth century is evidence of the erratic emergence of genius. In the sixteenth century all the painters of significance in Spain were foreigners. Then suddenly, for no apparent reason, five major native artists appeared: Velázquez, Murillo, Zurbarán, Ribera, and Valdés Leal. With their deaths foreigners took over again until, unexpectedly, Goya arrived on the scene. Then a period of sterility followed until once more three great masters, all exiled Spaniards, emerged: Picasso, Juan Gris, and Miró. After them a new aridity seems probable, though no one knows.

318

319

320

321

316 **Juan de Valdés Leal** (Spanish, 1622–1690): *The Assumption of the Virgin.* Signed. c. 1670. Canvas, 84⅝ x 61½" (215.1 x 156.3 cm.). Samuel H. Kress Collection

317 **Juan van der Hamen y Leon** (Spanish, 1596–1631): *Still Life.* Signed, and dated 1627. Canvas, 33⅛ x 44⅜" (84.2 x 112.8 cm.). Samuel H. Kress Collection

318 **Francisco de Zurbarán** (Spanish, 1598–1664): *St. Jerome with St. Paula and St. Eustochium.* c. 1640. Canvas, 96½ x 68⅛" (245.1 x 173 cm.). Samuel H. Kress Collection

319 **Francisco de Zurbarán**: *Santa Lucia.* c. 1625. Canvas, 41 x 30⅜" (104.1 x 77.2 cm.). Gift of Chester Dale

320 **Diego Velázquez** (Spanish, 1599–1660): *Pope Innocent X.* c. 1650. Canvas, 19½ x 16¼" (49 x 42 cm.). Andrew W. Mellon Collection

321 **Circle of Velázquez** (Spanish, XVII century): *Portrait of a Young Man.* Canvas, 23¼ x 18⅞" (59 x 48 cm.). Andrew W. Mellon Collection

322 **Bartolomé Esteban Murillo** (Spanish, 1617–1682): *The Return of the Prodigal Son.* 1670/74. Canvas, 93 x 102¾" (236.6 x 261 cm.). Gift of the Avalon Foundation

322

247

Flemish &
Dutch Schools

XVII CENTURY

Peter Paul Rubens

(FLEMISH, 1577–1640)

323   DANIEL IN THE LIONS' DEN

The rarest of paintings by an Old Master is one with a testimony of authenticity from the artist himself. In a letter of 1618 to Sir Dudley Carleton, the British Ambassador at The Hague, Rubens describes the picture reproduced here as "Daniel among many lions, taken from life. Original entirely by my hand, 8 x 12 ft." This document was involved in a sale being negotiated between Rubens and the Ambassador. The British diplomat had made a collection of antique marbles while *en poste* in Venice, and these marbles Rubens coveted. After several weeks of negotiations an agreement was worked out whereby Rubens would pay two thousand florins and give four thousand florins' worth of his own work, in exchange for which Carleton would let him have the classical sculpture he so ardently desired.

Carleton, though an ambassador, was also engaged in forming the art collection of the Prince of Wales, who was later to become Charles I, and whom Rubens called "le prince le plus amateur de la peinture qui soit au monde." It is probable that having been created Viscount Dorchester in 1628 and Secretary of State soon after, Carleton in gratitude presented the *Daniel* to his royal master. For some reason the painting was subsequently given by Charles to the Duke of Hamilton, and it remained in the Hamilton Collection, with one short interruption, until 1919.

In the 1960s it was put up for sale at a small London auction house. The owner was unaware that he possessed one of Rubens' greatest masterpieces. All the British art dealers, however, knew, and were waiting for the auction, ready to bid £100,000 to £200,000; but an American dealer living in London made an offer of less than a thousand pounds just before the day fixed for the sale, saying that he would be away when the auction was to take place and that he had a client named Daniel who collected such pictures. Informed by the auctioneer, the owner was delighted to be offered anything for a painting he considered worthless, and immediately accepted. His folly handed the American the chance for one of the greatest art coups of all time. Since the picture had fetched less than a thousand pounds, it could be exported legally without an examination by the British museum authorities. Taken by surprise, and helpless, they have since stated they would certainly have stopped one of their greatest works by Rubens from leaving the country had this been possible. If the American dealer had paid a shilling over a thousand pounds, a British museum might have robbed him of his fantastic profit by buying the picture in at the same price.

Collections: Sir Dudley Carleton; Charles I of England; the Marquess of Hamilton (at Hamilton Palace, with one brief interruption, until 1919); by inheritance, third Viscount Cowdray. *Ailsa Mellon Bruce Fund*, 1965. Painted c. 1615. Canvas, 88¼ x 130⅛" (224.3 x 330.4 cm.).

324

325

324 **Peter Paul Rubens** (Flemish, 1577–1640): *The Assumption of the Virgin*. c. 1626. Wood, 49⅜ x 37⅛″ (125.4 x 94.2 cm.). Samuel H. Kress Collection

325 **Peter Paul Rubens**: *The Meeting of Abraham and Melchizedek*. c. 1625. Wood, 26 x 32½″ (66 x 82.5 cm.). Gift of Syma Busiel

326 **Peter Paul Rubens**: *Decius Mus Addressing the Legions*. Probably 1617. Wood, 31¾ x 33¼″ (80.7 x 84.5 cm.). Samuel H. Kress Collection

327 **Peter Paul Rubens**: *Tiberius and Agrippina*. c. 1614. Wood, 26¼ x 22½″ (66.6 x 57.1 cm.). Andrew W. Mellon Fund

328 **Sir Anthony van Dyck** (Flemish, 1599–1641): *The Assumption of the Virgin*. c. 1627. Canvas, 46½ x 40¼″ (118 x 102 cm.). Widener Collection

326

The special qualities of Rubens' genius can be seen in the paintings reproduced here. These stylistic characteristics are: a spiritual exuberance we associate with the Counter Reformation; a sustained rhythm of twisting, turning forms; the transformation of pigment into flesh, fur, silk, and steel while remaining paint, a miraculous change which Rubens could work as no other artist; and a sumptuousness which was the goal of all Baroque decorators, among whom Rubens was supreme.

327

328

Peter Paul Rubens

(FLEMISH, 1577–1640)

329   **DEBORAH KIP, WIFE OF SIR BALTHASAR GERBIER,**
         AND HER CHILDREN

The mood of introspection of the Gerbier family is puzzling, particularly as it is virtually unique in Rubens' work. Why does Lady Gerbier appear so withdrawn, as though meditating on some inner problem, which her elder son, looking at her almost beseechingly, seems to share? The two daughters gaze appraisingly and joylessly at the spectator. Only the baby is unaffected by this atmosphere of somber contemplation, which somehow suggests unhappiness, an air of foreboding.

How easy it is to invent the psychology of others, especially in paintings! There is nonetheless in this case reason to believe that Lady Gerbier had many problems which might well have made her pensive, if not melancholy. She was married to a scoundrel, and perhaps Rubens saw reflected in her face the tragedies—debts, frauds, even murder—which were to plague her life.

We can identify these sitters because the group portrait in the National Gallery of Art has been repeated on a much larger canvas, with the additions of Gerbier, five more children, and a coat of arms. George Vertue knew both pictures and discussed them in his unpublished letters in the British Museum. In 1749 he was asked to examine a sketch, sent from Flanders, of a painting offered to the Prince of Wales purporting to be a portrait of Sir Balthazar Arundel and his family. Vertue soon established that no one of that name had ever existed. Nevertheless the picture was bought for the Prince, and Vertue was called in again. In examining the purchase he found a half-erased inscription, "La Famille de Balthasar Gerbiere Chevaliere," and he identified the Gerbier coat of arms. The Prince was shocked. "How shall I come off of this?" he said to Vertue, "I have for this month past told many persons of quality that I have purchased a family peece of the Sheffield ancestor to the late Duke of Buckingham . . . as I was assured it (was) . . . be said the truth that dealers in pictures are like false moneyers." The picture the "false moneyers" sold the Prince is now in the Rubens Room at Windsor Castle, labeled correctly *Sir Balthazar Gerbier and His Family*. It is a rather poor copy in its central part of the National Gallery of Art painting. The latter, according to Vertue, "was sold at Lord Radnor's in St. James Square, there I saw Lord Burlington bid five hundred pounds for it, and Mr. Scowen bought it. . . . many years afterwards Mr. Scowen being obliged to sell it . . . it was bot by a Gent of the Law, who lately sold it to Mr. Gideon, the Jew." One of Gideon's descendants married into the Fremantle family, and the painting was owned by the family until it was acquired by the National Gallery.

Collections: Balthazar Gerbier; First Earl of Radnor; Thomas Scowen; Sampson Gideon and descendants; Baron Eardley; Sir Culling Eardley; Mrs. W. H. Fremantle; Colonel F. E. Fremantle; E. V. Fremantle, Esq., Belvedere, Kent. *Andrew W. Mellon Fund, 1971*. Painted 1629–30. Canvas, 64¼ x 70" (165.8 x 177.8 cm.).

255

Sir Anthony van Dyck

(FLEMISH, 1599–1641)

330   ISABELLA BRANT

In spite of the smiling face of the sitter there is about this portrait an elusive sadness. Isabella Brant was Rubens' first wife. They were married for fifteen years. She
was painted by her husband many times, and also by his pupil van Dyck. These
portraits reveal the gradual change from a buxom girl to a sick, middle-aged
woman. The last of the series may be the portrait reproduced here, which shows a
face drawn and pinched by illness, though still with a courageous if somewhat wistful smile. In the background is the ornamental gateway which formed a part of the
garden of Rubens' house in Antwerp, an entrance into what was once for Isabella
her desirable life. But now her melancholy eyes seem to meditate on something else.
Perhaps on the transience of beauty. Rubens seems to have loved her dearly. Shortly after her death he wrote a friend, "Such a loss seems to me worthy of deep grief. I
must, no doubt, hope that the daughter of Time, Oblivion, who cures all sorrows,
will grant me relief." His hope apparently was granted, for four years later he married the young and beautiful Hélène Fourment, with whom he lived happily the rest
of his life.

In the eighteenth century this portrait was in the famous Crozat Collection,
where Watteau and many of his contemporaries learned to paint by copying Rubens, van Dyck, and other artists. It was bought subsequently by Catherine the
Great for the Hermitage Gallery in Leningrad. For many years this painting was attributed to Rubens, but more recent scholars have ascribed it to van Dyck. They
tend to identify it with the picture which Félibien, writing in 1666, says van Dyck
gave to his master on leaving his studio, as a token of gratitude.

Collections: Crozat, Paris; Catherine II, Empress of Russia; Hermitage Gallery, Leningrad. *Andrew W.
Mellon Collection*, 1937. Painted c. 1621, the year Isabella died. Canvas, 60¼ x 47¼" (153 x 120 cm.).

331

333

332

Antonis Mor was the outstanding portraitist of an international school whose work was based on that of Titian. Since sitters of various nationalities in the sixteenth century wore similar clothes, it is difficult to tell from any portrait whether Mor was executing one of his Flemish, Italian, Portuguese, Spanish, or English commissions. The conventional stiffness of Mor's portraits is seen also in Rubens' earliest work, when he was painting in Italy (see plate 333), but it soon disappeared. *The Portrait of a Man* (plate 336) seems at first glance typical of Rubens' mature style, and the painting was long ascribed to him. With remarkable connoisseurship, Professor Michael Jaffé saw evidence pointing to Jordaens, and subsequent examination in 1969 with infrared light revealed this artist's abbreviated signature. Many Flemish portraits of the time present similar problems of attribution.

331 Antonis Mor (Flemish-Dutch, Probably 1517–1576/77): *Portrait of a Gentleman*. Signed, and dated 1569. Transferred from wood to canvas, 47⅛ x 34¾" (119.7 x 88.3 cm.). Andrew W. Mellon Collection

332 Sir Anthony van Dyck (Flemish, 1599–1641): *Portrait of a Flemish Lady*. 1618/21. Canvas, 48⅜ x 35½" (123 x 90 cm.). Andrew W. Mellon Collection

333 Peter Paul Rubens (Flemish, 1577–1640): *Marchesa Brigida Spinola Doria*. c. 1606. Canvas, 60 x 38⅞" (152.2 x 98.7 cm.). Samuel H. Kress Collection

334 Sir Anthony van Dyck: *Susanna Fourment and Her Daughter*. c. 1620. Canvas, 68 x 46¼" (173 x 117 cm.). Andrew W. Mellon Collection

335 Sir Anthony van Dyck: *Doña Polyxena Spinola Guzmán de Leganés*. Early 1630s. Canvas, 43⅛ x 38⅛" (109.7 x 97 cm.). Samuel H. Kress Collection

336 Jacob Jordaens (Flemish, 1593–1678): *Portrait of a Man*. c. 1624. Wood, 41½ x 29" (105.5 x 73.5 cm.). Ailsa Mellon Bruce Fund

335

334

336

259

Sir Anthony van Dyck

(FLEMISH, 1599–1641)

337   MARCHESA ELENA GRIMALDI,
WIFE OF MARCHESE NICOLA CATTANEO

Paintings have their vicissitudes, as do human beings. Van Dyck's portrait of the Marchesa Elena Grimaldi has experienced the mutability of fortune. It was probably painted in 1623, when the artist was a young man, still at the height of his vigor. He had left his native Flanders and settled temporarily in Genoa, where he became overnight the fashionable portraitist of the patrician families. There he created on canvas a race of supermen and superwomen, richly dressed, of lofty stature and aloof expression. However, of all the Genoese who sat for him, van Dyck has given to none so dignified, so majestic a pose as to the wife of the Marchese Cattaneo. He has also favored her with perhaps his most brilliant design. How skillfully the parasol is used to heighten still further the Marchesa's tallness, "towering in her pride of place" as she advances across her terrace and casts at the spectator, far below, an appraising glance! This is the ultimate in the grand manner in portraiture.

The failure of their trade and the decline of their independence, however, brought the great families of Genoa close to destitution. English collectors cast covetous eyes on their works of art, and especially on the Marchesa Grimaldi's portrait. Sir David Wilkie in 1828 wrote Sir Robert Peel saying he had heard from his agent that in the palace of Nicola Cattaneo there was a picture of "a Young Lady, with a Black Servant holding a Curious Parasol over her head," which he tried to buy. The family would not sell, but should he try once more? Apparently the later efforts of Wilkie's agent were equally unavailing, for early in this century, when the van Dyck scholar Lionel Cust gained admission to the Cattaneo palace, he was ushered into a room where he halted spellbound. "From every wall, as it seemed, Van Dyck looked down, and on one there stood and gazed at me a haughty dame, over whose head a negro-page held a scarlet parasol. All, however, spoke of dust and neglect, and when I left the palace, it was with a feeling of regret that such treasures of painting should be left to moulder on the walls." Van Dyck's masterworks were not to crumble away much longer; they had in fact reached the nadir of their fortune. A dealer bought all the Cattaneo paintings shortly before World War I, and eventually P. A. B. Widener acquired the most important of the lot, the portrait of the Marchesa Grimaldi and the portraits of her two children (overleaf). These he gave with the rest of his collection to the nation.

Collection: Palazzo Cattaneo, Genoa. *Widener Collection*, 1942. Painted probably 1623. Canvas, 97 x 68" (246 x 173 cm.).

353

354

355

356

Frans Hals was one of the first artists in Europe to paint *alla prima* (i.e., directly on the canvas without preliminary underpainting). This rapid technique is the one normally used by modern painters. It is especially adapted to catching momentary expressions and gestures, as one can see in these reproductions. The comment about the superficiality of Hals' interpretation of his sitters in the discussion of *Balthasar Coymans* (plate 349) must be modified by saying that at the end of his life he showed a far deeper insight into character (see plate 355).

Rembrandt van Ryn

(DUTCH, 1606–1669)

357   SELF-PORTRAIT

Rembrandt was a much more profound artist than Frans Hals. Few autobiographies are as searching as his self-portraits. The one reproduced here was signed and dated 1659, ten years before his death. In 1656 he had been declared bankrupt and during the next two years everything he owned was sold. His son and his mistress were shortly to make themselves custodians even of his still-unpainted pictures. Once more he looked in a mirror to take stock of himself, to analyze the problem of his personality. He saw reflected a face lined with age and misfortune. He saw eyes which had searched more profoundly into the human soul than those of any other artist. He saw a mouth and a chin weak, infirm of purpose, manifesting that flaw in his character which had ruined his life. His hands are grasped as though in anguish at the spectacle of a self-ruined man. There exists no painting more pitiless in its analysis or more pitiful in its implications.

Collection: Duke of Buccleuch, London. *Andrew W. Mellon Collection*, 1937. Signed, and dated 1659. Canvas, 33¼ x 26" (84 x 66 cm.).

Rembrandt in his self-portraits does not always reveal his weaknesses. Many reflect the mask he held up before the world. In the *Self-Portrait* of 1650 (plate 360), in spite of reverses he had suffered, he still appears proud, self-confident, challenging. Here one sees the look of the man Saskia van Uilenburgh (see plate 358) married in 1634. Her death seven years later was an affliction which altered Rembrandt's life. Without her practicality and influence, wealth, with its concomitant compromises with the taste of his middle-class patrons, eluded him, but achievement at a far higher level followed.

358

359

360

361

362

REMBRANDT VAN RYN (Dutch, 1606–1669)

358 *Saskia van Uilenburgh, the Wife of the Artist.*
Probably 1633. Wood, 23¾ x 19¼" (60.5 x 49 cm.).
Widener Collection

359 *A Polish Nobleman.* Signed, and dated 1637.
Wood, 38⅛ x 26" (97 x 66 cm.). Andrew W. Mellon
Collection

360 *Self-Portrait.* Signed, and dated 1650. Canvas,
36¼ x 29¾" (92 x 75.5 cm.). Widener Collection

361 *A Girl with a Broom.* Signed, and dated 1651.
Canvas, 42¼ x 36" (107 x 91 cm.). Andrew W. Mellon
Collection

362 *The Philosopher.* c. 1650. Wood, 24¼ x 19½"
(61.5 x 49.5 cm.). Widener Collection

363 *A Turk.* c. 1630/35. Canvas, 38¾ x 29⅛" (98 x
74 cm.). Andrew W. Mellon Collection

363

Rembrandt van Ryn

(DUTCH, 1606–1669)

364   THE MILL

The Mill is Rembrandt's supreme achievement in landscape painting. It is usually dated about 1650, when he was still at the height of his fame. John Constable judged it "sufficient to form an epoch in the art . . . the first picture in which a sentiment has been expressed by chiaroscuro only, all details being excluded." And this melancholy sentiment, this mood of sublime sadness, which Rembrandt conveys through the stark simplicity of a windmill silhouetted in the fading light against the mist-filled sky, is indescribably moving. As Roger Fry has said, "It is surely the most complete expression of the dramatic mood in landscape that has ever been achieved in Western art."

Probably no single canvas has so strongly affected English painting. Turner admired it, and the notes in his sketchbook show that it was the basis of his conception of Rembrandt's handling of light. Sir Joshua Reynolds painted a free adaptation of it; and it was engraved by Charles Turner for his *Gems of Art*, a book to be found in the studio of nearly every nineteenth-century English painter.

In his autobiography, Peter Widener, the son and grandson of the founders of the collection, says that when Wilhelm von Bode, director of the Kaiser Friedrich Museum and an authority on Rembrandt, came to Lynnewood Hall to see the collection, he sat for half an hour contemplating *The Mill*. Finally he turned to Joseph Widener, who was waiting for his opinion, and said, "This is the greatest picture in the world. The greatest picture by any artist."

Collections: Duc d'Orléans, Paris; William Smith, London; Marquess of Lansdowne, Bowood Hall, Wiltshire. *Widener Collection*, 1942. Painted c. 1650. Canvas, 34½ x 41½" (87.5 x 105.5 cm.).

Rembrandt van Ryn

(DUTCH, 1606–1669)

365   PORTRAIT OF A LADY WITH AN OSTRICH-FEATHER FAN

Were I asked to select the greatest portrait of a woman ever painted, my choice would be the *Lady with an Ostrich-Feather Fan*. Like Isabella Brant (plate 330), her looks, once beautiful, seem faded by illness. She is a woman to me infinitely sad and endlessly fascinating. I am always entranced by the simplicity of her pose, by her mood of stillness and serenity, by her seeming acceptance of life with all its richness of experience, its sorrows, and its joys.

What a strange history her portrait was to have. It hung for many years in the Yousupoff Palace, where it looked down on carnivals and balls, on the gaiety of the Ancien Régime under the shadow of the Revolution; even on Rasputin and his murderers—perhaps in the very hall where the great hulking monk himself staggered, bleeding and poisoned. Then, after the Revolution, it was smuggled out of Russia, concealed under an amateurish landscape hastily painted by the fleeing Prince.

Still to come was the adventure of one of the most famous lawsuits in the history of collecting. After having sold the painting and its pendant (plate 366) to Joseph Widener, Prince Yousupoff tried to reclaim them, asserting that they were only the collateral for a loan. His motives are easily explained. Calouste Gulbenkian had offered him the largest price ever paid up to that time for works by Rembrandt. Everything seemingly depended on a telegram from Yousupoff to Widener acknowledging the sale, and this could never be found, though an exhaustive search was made of the Widener offices, their files, and their home, Lynnewood Hall. Without being able to produce the cable, the Widener lawyers nonetheless convinced the jury of its existence and won the suit. When Lynnewood Hall was being dismantled and the works of art shipped to the National Gallery, the missing telegram fell out of an old stud book, which Joseph Widener, many years before, must have been consulting in connection with his racing stable.

Collection: Prince Yousupoff, Leningrad. *Widener Collection*, 1942. Signed; date partially effaced. Painted c. 1660. Canvas, 39⅛ x 32½" (99.5 x 82.5 cm.).

366

367

368

REMBRANDT VAN RYN (Dutch, 1606–1669)

366 *Portrait of a Gentleman with a Tall Hat and Gloves*. c. 1660. Canvas, 39⅛ x 32½" (99.5 x 82.5 cm.). Widener Collection

367 *A Woman Holding a Pink*. Signed, and dated 1656. Canvas, 40⅜ x 33¾" (103 x 86 cm.). Andrew W. Mellon Collection

368 *An Old Lady with a Book*. Signed, and dated (164)7. Andrew W. Mellon Collection

369 *A Young Man Seated at a Table*. Signed, and dated 1662 (or 1663). Canvas, 43¼ x 35¼" (110 x 90 cm.). Andrew W. Mellon Collection

370 *Portrait of a Man in a Tall Hat*. c. 1662. Canvas, 47¾ x 37" (121 x 94 cm.). Widener Collection

370

369

Plate 366 is the companion piece to plate 365. This unknown gentleman's face is pale and shadowed, the skin almost translucent in contrast to the strong black and white of his garments. All the portraits reproduced here bring out a quality in Rembrandt's art that has been insufficiently stressed; his mastery of volume, of three-dimensional form. The apples in *A Woman Holding a Pink*, for example, are as solid and weighty in their suggestion of specific gravity as any painted by Cézanne. The same feeling for substance is evident throughout Rembrandt's work.

Rembrandt van Ryn

(DUTCH, 1606–1669)

371   JOSEPH ACCUSED BY POTIPHAR'S WIFE

This picture is a calmer, more monumental version of the subject treated in another picture by Rembrandt in the Berlin Museum, which is also dated 1655. Joseph is falsely accused by Phraxanor, the wife of Potiphar, of trying to seduce her. The reverse is actually the case, as the story is told in Genesis 39. The scene was one which Baroque artists delighted in representing. Usually Joseph is shown fleeing from his would-be seductress, who leaps from her bed and grabs at his coat, here shown on the bedpost. But Rembrandt has interpreted the legend at the level of the highest tragedy. The aging beauty, the beautiful youth, the puzzled husband, all seem bemused by passions beyond their comprehension. One senses Rembrandt's deep compassion for each of the actors in this archetypal domestic drama, which has been the subject of many books and poems. Yet in literature there has been nothing to equal Rembrandt's insight and profundity until our own time and Thomas Mann's great novel *Joseph and His Brothers*, for which this seems an illustration. Of the many masterpieces in the collection of Catherine the Great, this painting may have had a special significance for the Empress, for she, like Phraxanor, knew the anguish of love by command.

Collections: Catherine II, Empress of Russia; Hermitage Gallery, Leningrad. *Andrew W. Mellon Collection*, 1937. Signed, and dated 1655. Canvas, 41⅝ x 38½" (106 x 98 cm.).

372

373

Of all the artists who have ever lived, Rembrandt was the greatest illustrator of the Bible. Where in art can one find the tenderness, the yearning faith, and at the same time the troubled puzzlement one sees in the face of Joseph of Arimethea, who grasps the body of Our Lord as He is lowered from the Cross? What painter has expressed pure, intense thought more clearly than Rembrandt does in the face and posture of St. Paul as he meditates on the letter he is about to write to his brothers in Christ? Rembrandt was drawn also to Roman history and legend, to which he brought his unique sense of theater. *Lucretia* (plate 375) would have been the envy of Sarah Bernhardt, or of any great actress, as she totters forward, dagger in hand, seeming to try to push away the dark fate that forces her to choose death over a life of dishonor.

374

REMBRANDT VAN RYN (Dutch 1606–1669)

372 *The Descent from the Cross.* Signed, and dated 165(1). Canvas, 56¼ x 43¾″ (143 x 111 cm.). Widener Collection

373 *The Circumcision.* Signed, and dated 1661. Canvas, 22¼ x 29½″ (56.5 x 75 cm.). Widener Collection

374 *The Apostle Paul.* Signed. Probably 1657. Canvas, 50¾ x 40⅛″ (129 x 102 cm.). Widener Collection.

375 *Lucretia.* Signed, and dated 1664. Canvas, 47¼ x 39¾″ (120 x 101 cm.). Andrew W. Mellon Collection

376 *Philemon and Baucis.* Signed, and dated 1658. Wood, 21½ x 27″ (54.5 x 68.5 cm.). Widener Collection

376

Gerard ter Borch

(DUTCH, 1617–1681)

377   THE SUITOR'S VISIT

The easel picture, the kind of picture we are accustomed to hang in our homes, flourished in the seventeenth century, especially in Calvinistic Holland. Here a new secular style replaced the timeless dramas of Christian art, which had occupied painters in the past; and instead momentary glimpses of everyday life became the fashion. Of such genre pieces *The Suitor's Visit* is typical. We watch, as though through an open window, the suitor in all his finery forever approaching his pensive fiancée; while her father from behind looks on appraisingly and her sister or friend with self-conscious concentration strums on a theorbo. As sometimes happens in the movies, the film seems to have caught, the actors suddenly to have become immobile. Everyone, even the dog, questions the future which cannot begin while the enchanted stillness lasts. Here is a different kind of timelessness, one described by Goethe when he said to Eckermann, "Every situation—nay, every moment—is of infinite worth; for it is the representative of a whole eternity."

This new search in painting for the permanent in the ephemeral led to a more realistic transcription of appearance. The achievement of this necessitates a careful adjustment of tones and values. In the present picture the figure of the suitor, the friend, and the father are mutually consistent, but the figure of the fiancée is out of key. The highlights on her white dress and coral bodice are too bright to be justified by the apparent illumination of the room. This overemphasis on certain passages, especially of white silk, repeatedly upsets the balance of ter Borch's colors. Yet paradoxically his fame rests on this flaw in the actuality of his scenes, for the popularity of his canvases is due largely to his handling of satin, to his rendering of texture, which, skillful as it is, at the same time affects the reality of his paintings.

Collections: Charles-Auguste-Louis-Joseph, Duc de Morny, Paris; Marqués de Salamanca, Madrid; Adolphe de Rothschild, Paris; Maurice de Rothschild, Paris. *Andrew W. Mellon Collection*, 1937. Painted c. 1658. Canvas, 31½ x 29⅝" (80 x 75 cm.).

378

379

Rembrandt, Hals, and Vermeer tower high above the
other Dutch painters, but there were scores of artists
ready to satisfy the demands of the Dutch burghers for
portraits of themselves, their countryside, and their
way of life. And what a pleasant life it must have been!
Avercamp's skating scene almost makes one long en-
viously for the cold Northern winter; the Flemish artist
David Teniers depicts the festive Twelfth Night feast;
and Metsu shows an amusing and delightful flirtation,
even if it has been temporarily frustrated.

380

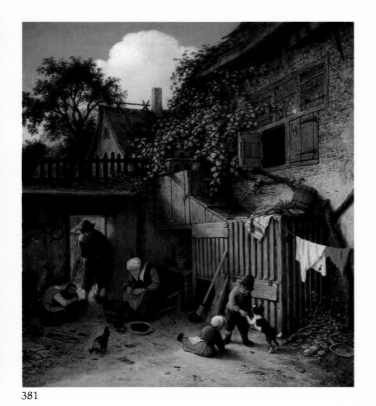

381

382

378 Hendrick Avercamp (Dutch, 1585–1634): *A Scene on the Ice.* c. 1625. Wood, 15½ x 30⅜″ (39.3 x 77.1 cm.). Ailsa Mellon Bruce Fund

379 Gabriel Metsu (Dutch, 1629–1667): *The Intruder.* Signed. c. 1660. Wood, 26¼ x 23½″ (67 x 60 cm.). Andrew W. Mellon Collection

380 Nicolas Maes (Dutch, 1632–1693): *An Old Woman Dozing over a Book.* c. 1655. Canvas, 32⅜ x 26⅜″ (82 x 67 cm.). Andrew W. Mellon Collection

381 Adriaen van Ostade (Dutch, 1610–1685): *The Cottage Dooryard.* Signed, and dated 1673. Canvas, 17⅜ x 15⅝″ (44 x 39.5 cm.). Widener Collection

382 Judith Leyster (Dutch, c. 1609–1660): *Self-Portrait.* c. 1635. Canvas, 29⅜ x 25⅝″ (72.3 x 65.3 cm.). Gift of Mr. and Mrs. Robert Woods Bliss

383 David Teniers II (Flemish, 1610–1690): *Peasants Celebrating Twelfth Night.* Signed, and dated 1635. Wood, 18⅝ x 27½″ (47.2 x 69.9 cm.). Ailsa Mellon Bruce Fund

383

Pieter de Hooch

(DUTCH, 1629–c.1683)

384   A DUTCH COURTYARD

Paul Claudel, the French poet, has analyzed with wonderful penetration the charm of Dutch scenes of everyday life such as the picture reproduced here. He points out that these canvases make us conscious of time. "They are the reservoir of evanescent feelings. We do not merely glance at a painting by . . . de Hooch with condescending approval; we are immediately within it, we live there." Thus, as in paintings by Vermeer and ter Borch, we share an ephemeral moment which is given an enchanted permanence.

Beyond the wall of de Hooch's courtyard is the Nieuwe Kerk in Delft. This picture was probably painted, therefore, when during the 1650s and early '60s de Hooch was living in the native city of the greatest of the Dutch genre painters, Jan Vermeer. During several years under the inspiration of Vermeer, he painted, along with his more usual interiors, an occasional scene out-of-doors. In these he catches in a web of almost invisible brushstrokes the texture of crumbling brick and mortar, the undulations of old paving, the gleam of metals, and the transparency of liquids. Masterpieces of a true visual effect, such canvases conjure up a domestic paradise of eternal sun-drenched felicity. The best painters in Holland, with the exception of Rembrandt, were in varying degrees scientific investigators of such images which the eye conveys to the mind. It is significant in this connection that the Dutch are also credited with the practical discovery of both the compound microscope and the telescope, one in 1590 and the other in 1608.

Collections: Possibly Samuel A. Koopman, Utrecht; Baron Lionel Nathan de Rothschild; Alfred Charles de Rothschild; Countess of Carnarvon, Newbury, England. *Andrew W. Mellon Collection*, 1937. Painted c. 1660. Another version, lacking the cavalier holding the beer jug, is in the Mauritshuis, The Hague (formerly Ten Cate Collection). Canvas, 26¾ x 23" (68 x 59 cm.).

289

Jan Vermeer

(DUTCH, 1632-1675)

406   A WOMAN WEIGHING GOLD

Jan Vermeer of Delft was a master of stillness, of those moments of life when all action has ceased, held by an ephemeral adjustment of forces. This canvas conveys a sense of dynamic quiescence; it is in fact an allegory of balances. The unmoving figure weighing gold balances in her scales her earthly treasure, while Christ, in the Last Judgment in the background, in His divine knowledge weighs human guilt. The woman is absorbed, wrapped in the serene and mysterious thought of approaching maternity; and her pregnant body half concealing the painting hung behind her suggests a further equation, as though, as in Santayana's phrase, "The truth of life could be seen only in the shadow of death; living and dying were simultaneous and inseparable."

Such symbolic profundity is rare among Dutch painters of the seventeenth century and only intermittent in Vermeer's own work. The quality for which his paintings are always distinguished is form rather than content. For Vermeer among all Dutch artists is unrivaled in his mastery of optical reality. In his paintings just so much detail is included as can be seen from a normal distance, not by focusing the eye successively on different objects, or in an instant of time, but with a steady gaze. Similarly in his treatment of tone relations, there is a perfect consistency with what we actually see. No other painter has been able to maintain such subtle distinctions of color in different planes of light, or to extend this organization of tone into such depths of shadow.

Symmetry and balance in design, consistent selection of detail, proportional organization of tone relations, these are difficult to achieve, and Vermeer must have labored long and hard over each painting. Recently a Dutchman, van Meegeren, painted a series of religious pictures in the manner of Vermeer; but of these forgeries only one, *Supper at Emmaus*, is worthy of exhibition. The rest are so poor in quality that nothing but the chaos of the years of World War II could explain their temporary success. For Vermeer's mastery of optical truth cannot be imitated by the forger and is lost to some extent in the most faithful color reproduction.

Collections: Possibly in the collection of Jac. Abrahamsz. Dissius, Amsterdam; Nieuhof, Amsterdam; van der Bogaerd, Amsterdam; King of Bavaria, Munich; Duke of Caraman, Vienna and Paris; Casimir Périer; Comtesse de Ségur (née Périer) Paris. *Widener Collection*, 1942. Painted c. 1664. Canvas, 16¾ x 15" (42.5 x 38 cm.).

303

Jan Vermeer

(DUTCH, 1632–1675)

408   YOUNG GIRL WITH A FLUTE

407 **Jan Vermeer** (Dutch, 1632–1675): *The Girl with a Red Hat.* c. 1665/67. Wood, 9⅛ x 7⅛" (23 x 18 cm.). Andrew W. Mellon Collection

Of the pictures now generally attributed to Vermeer, two of the most beautiful are *The Girl with a Red Hat* and *Young Girl with a Flute.* These two paintings, which Vermeer must have intended to hang together since the same tapestried background and the same chair appear in both, were separated in the seventeenth century, only to be reunited in the twentieth, when Andrew Mellon gave one to the National Gallery and Joseph Widener the other.

Both pictures are superb examples of Vermeer's characteristic technique, which is most evident in works like these when he used wood as a support. Here one sees clearly how much more vitreous the surface is than in other Dutch paintings, with the pigments seemingly fused in a glassy medium. It has been suggested that this is the result of painting from images reflected in a mirror. But the hat of the Young Girl, calling to mind a Chinese origin, implies another explanation. Delft, where Vermeer worked, was closely in contact with the Orient because of its famous china. The paintings on Chinese porcelains have a vitreous look, and craftsmen in Delft studied how to imitate this effect. Is it not possible that Vermeer was seeking to achieve on wood and canvas something of the surface texture of Chinese porcelain painting? The only other artist, so far as I know, who gained a similar effect in his pictures is the English painter George Stubbs. And we know Stubbs worked for a famous porcelain manufacturer, Josiah Wedgwood. This may be a coincidence, but if not, it would seem to throw some light on the mystery of Vermeer's technical method.

Collections: Possibly Jac. Abrahamsz. Dissius, Amsterdam; Jan Mahie van Boxtel en Liempde; s-Hertogenbosch, Holland; de Grez family, Brussels; August Janssen, Amsterdam. *Widener Collection,* 1942. Painted c. 1665/67. Wood, 7⅞ x 7" (20 x 18 cm.).

French &
Italian Schools

XVII AND XVIII CENTURY

Georges de La Tour

(FRENCH, 1593–1652)

409   THE REPENTANT MAGDALEN

Jan Vermeer and Georges de La Tour were born only a generation apart. Although of different nationalities, they had much in common. For several centuries both virtually disappeared as artists and existed only as names in obscure archives. Both were finally resurrected by modern art historians. Their pictures also are equally rare—we can find fewer than forty by either, a meager number by comparison with the oeuvre of other painters. But their most significant resemblance is their preoccupation with the realistic rendering of light: Vermeer with the appearance of daylight; La Tour, more and more, with the effects of chiaroscuro and the diffusion of artificial illumination.

To discover those few pictures which can be ascribed to La Tour has been relatively simple, because a number are signed and the rest stamped with a distinctive style, but to unearth biographical material has proved nearly impossible. We know he was born at Vic-sur-Seille, a village about twenty kilometers from Nancy, and spent most of his life in Lunéville in the Duchy of Lorraine. In 1639, when the Duchy was absorbed by France, he was named *peintre du roi*, a high honor. For stylistic reasons it seems likely that he went to Rome and saw the work of Caravaggio and his followers. These *tenebristi*, as they were called, may have turned his attention to night scenes with their strong contrasts of light and shadow. He could, however, have learned the same lesson in Holland from Caravaggio's Northern disciple, Gerard Honthorst. His travels outside France, if they exist, are purely conjectural.

But wherever he journeyed, though he would have seen many penitent Magdalens, none would have been as beautiful as those he was to paint in Lunéville. For him this subject, which he treated at least four times, may have had some special significance. But it was in any case a popular scene, one greatly encouraged by the Church, which during the Counter Reformation emphasized penance and absolution in contrast to the Calvinistic doctrine of predestination.

Is there really forgiveness, the young girl's eyes seem to ask as they stare introspectively beyond the mirror with its reflection of the skull? Her sensitive fingers caress the brain's empty case, while the concentrated power of her thought seems a kinetic force, which, like a current of air, bends the candle flame, the only source of light. Few paintings exist of greater psychological and spiritual intensity.

Collections: Marquise de Caulaincourt; her sister, Comtesse d'Andigné: André Fabius, Paris. *Ailsa Mellon Bruce Fund*, 1974. Painted c. 1640. Canvas, 44½ x 36½" (113 x 92.7 cm.).

Claude Lorrain

(FRENCH, 1600–1682)

410   THE JUDGMENT OF PARIS

Unknown masterpieces still come to light. One day in 1966 a lady brought to Sotheby's, the London auction house, a dirty painting which she believed to be by the eighteenth-century English landscapist Richard Wilson. It was destined for a small sale, an unillustrated item in the catalogue, when one of the Sotheby partners noticed barely visible sheep in the foreground and realized that they looked like the sheep Claude often drew. The auctioneers, uncertain whether they were selling a copy, called in Marcel Röthlisberger, the greatest living authority on Claude Lorrain. With remarkable perspicacity he recognized under yellowed varnish and accumulated grime the touch of the master. When the landscape was sold, instead of a few thousand dollars it brought $480,000. The lady was indeed fortunate, and so was the dealer who bought the painting, for though its condition was scarcely discernible, when cleaned it proved to be excellently preserved.

It is, as Röthlisberger has said, "one of the most beautiful examples of classical landscape." Reproduced in Claude's *Liber Veritatis*, the book of drawings he made to authenticate his oeuvre, it contains figures larger than those of any other painting by him of like dimensions. They are considered entirely autograph, which cannot be said of the figures in many of his canvases, for in the words of Baldinucci, a contemporary, "he took no displeasure in having the figures in his landscapes or sea pieces added by another hand."

But it is not the figures, fine as these are, which entrance the viewer of this glorious landscape. It is the vista enframed on the right by one of the most magnificent trees Claude ever painted and balanced on the left by a steep, shadowy embankment. Here, in the far distance and in the middle ground, Claude enchants us, entraps our spirit in his Arcadian world. From the sweep of space in his paintings, from the way the eye glides to distant mountains and headlands, clear in shape but impalpable in substance, comes a curious psychological release, which both Dostoevski and Nietzsche have noted—an emotion difficult to describe but one which makes Claude, for some of us, the most satisfactory of all landscape painters.

Collections: Probably Marquis de Fontenay, Rome; recorded at auction sales in Paris, 1748, and London, 1819 and 1820; Miss V. Price, London. *Ailsa Mellon Bruce Fund*, 1969. Painted 1645/46. Canvas, 44¼ x 58⅞" (112 x 149.5 cm.).

411

Contemporary biographers state that Annibale Carracci painted and sketched landscapes for his own amusement and as a form of relaxation from the arduous work of filling his many commissions for figure painting. It was not until the time of Claude, who was familiar with Annibale's rare landscapes, that connoisseurs accepted and valued pictures of classical scenery. Nevertheless, except in Holland, landscapists held an inferior place in the hierarchy of artists until well into the nineteenth century.

412

413

414

411 **Simon Vouet** (French, 1590–1649): *The Muses Urania and Calliope*. c. 1634. Wood, 31⅛ x 49⅜" (79.8 x 125 cm.). Samuel H. Kress Collection

412 **Simon Vouet**: *Saint Jerome and the Angel*. c. 1625. Canvas, 57 x 70¾" (144.8 x 179.8 cm.). Samuel H. Kress Collection

413 **Annibale Carracci** (Bolognese, 1560–1609): *Landscape*. Probably c. 1590. Canvas, 34¾ x 58¼" (88.5 x 148.2 cm.). Samuel H. Kress Collection

414 **Annibale Carracci**: *Venus Adorned by the Graces*. c. 1595. Transferred from wood to canvas, 52⅜ x 67⅛" (133 x 170.6 cm.). Samuel H. Kress Collection

415 **Claude Lorrain** (French, 1600–1682): *Landscape with Merchants*. Signed. c. 1630. Canvas, 38¼ x 56½" (97.2 x 143.6 cm.). Samuel H. Kress Collection

416 **Claude Lorrain**: *The Herdsman*. Signed. c. 1635. Canvas, 47¾ x 63⅛" (121.5 x 160.5 cm.). Samuel H. Kress Collection

415

416

Nicolas Poussin

(FRENCH, 1594–1665)

417 THE ASSUMPTION OF THE VIRGIN

This early work by Poussin is dependent on the past and predicts the future. On the one hand, it is strongly influenced by several paintings done a century earlier: Titian's *Assumption of the Virgin* and his Pesaro Altarpiece, both in the Church of the Frari in Venice, and his *Venus Worship*, now in the Prado but at that time in the Villa Aldobrandini in Frascati. On the other hand, it anticipates the freedom of brushwork and general exuberance which characterize the French Rococo. There are passages, especially in the painting of the chubby, rosy children, which might have been done by Fragonard.

It is difficult to imagine a more joyous Assumption than this. Three cherubs fill Our Lady's grave with flowers to take the place of her risen body. Accompanied aloft by swarms of other children who need no wings for their levitation, she looks upward in ecstasy while two of her entourage pull back the clouds as though they were draperies concealing Heaven. Poussin has achieved a miracle of movement, of twisting, turning *putti* that lead the eye toward a divine vision kept just out of sight. All this turbulence is controlled in turn by the verticals of two stately columns enframing the central scene and by the horizontals of the geometric sarcophagus in the foreground.

Such superb compositions are not easily arrived at. Poussin planned them carefully, often attaining his final design by placing on a miniature stage small figures which he moved around until he achieved the perfect balance of thrust and counterthrust. His intellectual approach to painting has made his work an inspiration to some of the best painters of our time. Picasso was greatly influenced by him, and the Cubists adopted many of his ideas on art, especially his emphasis on harmony, clarity, and, above all, reason.

But there is another side of Poussin as well. He could convey the sensuality of Titian and the great Venetians, a tradition continued in the eighteenth century in the work of Watteau, Fragonard, Boucher, and others, and in the nineteenth century in many artists from Delacroix to Renoir. It is an oversimplification to see the French School as a constant battle between the advocates of Rubens and the supporters of Raphael. Many of the greatest French artists, like Poussin, combined the richness of color and the fluency of brushwork of the one and the probity of draftsmanship and firmness of design of the other.

Collections: The Marquis of Exeter, Burghley House, at least as early as 1794, where it is said to have come from the Palazzo Soderini, Rome. *Ailsa Mellon Bruce Fund*, 1963. Painted c. 1626. Canvas, 52⅞ x 38⅝" (134.4 x 97.8 cm.).

Nicolas Poussin

(FRENCH, 1594–1665)

418   HOLY FAMILY ON THE STEPS

Poussin defined the grand manner of painting as consisting of four elements, which he declared were "subject matter or theme, thought, structure, and style. The first thing that, as the foundation of all others, is required," he said, "is that the subject matter shall be grand, as are battles, heroic actions, and divine things. . . . Those who elect mean subjects take refuge in them because of the weakness of their talents."

The *Holy Family on the Steps* perfectly illustrates Poussin's theory. It is of a divine subject; the theme is lofty; the structure is skillfully arranged; and the style shows Poussin's particular gift, his mastery of design. There is also a subtle allegory of the relative values of the intellectual and the spiritual life. St. Joseph with his compass and T-square is shown as a mathematical philosopher, symbolizing the human intellect; but he is placed in the shadow of Our Lady and her Son, who represent religion, or the life of the spirit. Note, however, that Poussin did not place St. Joseph entirely in shadow. For aesthetic reasons his foot is shown in brilliant light, which attracts the eye to the far right of the picture and thus balances the large mass of St. Elizabeth, nearer the central axis. The asymmetrical placing of the bowl, the jar, and the box balance the composition in a similar way. (As proof, try to imagine St. Joseph's foot in the same darkness as his body, or any of the vessels moved in either direction or changed in value, and the equilibrium vanishes.) This is one of the most beautiful compositions in art—a challenge to Raphael, with a complex richness of form in the relation between the pyramidal group of figures and the geometrical shapes of the architecture that Raphael rarely attempted in his easel pictures and only surpassed in the frescoes of the *Stanze* in the Vatican. Anthony Blunt has admirably described the *Holy Family on the Steps* as "one of Poussin's most compellingly beautiful pictures, one in which he has attained the aim of the classical artist that nothing could be added to it or taken away from it but for the worse. It has a finality rare in classical art."

Collections: Probably Nicolas Hennequin de Fresne, Master of the Royal Hunt; probably Jacques Amelot du Quaillou, Marquis de Mauregard; probably Marquis de Lassay, Paris; Abbé Le Blanc, Paris; Comte de Vaudreuil, Paris; M. de La Reynière, Paris; Duke of Sutherland, Stafford House, London. *Samuel H. Kress Collection,* 1952. Painted 1648, for Nicolas Hennequin de Fresne, according to Félibien, who saw the picture in the Hôtel de Guise, Paris, sometime between 1666 and 1688. Canvas, 27 x 38½" (68.6 x 97.8 cm.).

419

420

421

Lodovico Carracci, with other members of his family, helped to found in Bologna the most celebrated Academy in Europe. The style taught was an amalgam of Classicism and the painting of the High Renaissance. Sébastien Bourdon was one of the founding members of the French Academy, established a little later. French artists were instructed to paint with precision, detachment, and logic. *Omer Talon* by Philippe- de Champagne (plate 424) shows the dignified and impressive treatment required in official portraits.

422

423

424

419 Lodovico Carracci (Bolognese, 1555–1619): *The Dream of St. Catherine of Alexandria.* c. 1590. Canvas, 54⅝ x 43½" (138.8 x 110.5 cm.). Samuel H. Kress Collection

420 Nicolas Poussin (French, 1594–1665): *The Feeding of the Child Jupiter.* c. 1640. Canvas, 46⅛ x 61⅛" (117.4 x 155.3 cm.). Samuel H. Kress Collection

421 Nicolas Poussin: *The Baptism of Christ.* 1641/42. Canvas, 37⅝ x 47⅝" (95.5 x 121 cm.). Samuel H. Kress Collection

422 Sébastien Bourdon (French, 1616–1671): *Countess Ebba Sparre.* Probably 1653. Canvas, 41¾ x 35½" (106.1 x 90.2 cm.). Samuel H. Kress Collection

423 Sébastien Bourdon: *The Finding of Moses.* Probably c. 1650. Canvas, 47 x 68" (119.6 x 172.8 cm.). Samuel H. Kress Collection

424 Philippe de Champagne (French, 1602–1674): *Omer Talon.* Signed, and dated 1649. Canvas, 88½ x 63⅝" (225 x 161.6 cm.). Samuel H. Kress Collection

Louis Le Nain

(FRENCH, c. 1593–1648)

425 LANDSCAPE WITH PEASANTS

Louis Le Nain has caught the exact tone of that gray wintry light so characteristic of the countryside near the Belgian border. This feeling for a particular place gives his picture a modern quality. The painting reproduced here also resembles, in the seemingly informal yet carefully staged arrangement of isolated figures, the work of certain twentieth-century Neo-Romantic artists, like Eugene Berman.

The three Le Nain brothers, all painters, were apparently trained by a Dutch artist. Their work represented a reaction against the academic style, discussed in connection with Poussin's *Holy Family* (plate 418). Poussin seems to have had them in mind when he said, "Those who elect mean subjects take refuge in them because of the weakness of their talents." It is evident that the Le Nain brothers were disliked by the official court painters led by Poussin, who were occupied with religious themes or scenes of history or mythology. But there was a demand among middle-class patrons for glimpses of rural life, a demand which the three brothers helped satisfy with the canvases they exhibited and sold at popular fairs, such as those at St. Germain-des-Prés.

In the eighteenth century the same interest in everyday life appears in the work of Chardin, a style totally different from the art popular at the French court. This difference becomes especially evident when the picture reproduced here is contrasted with those by Boucher (plates 447–51). A painting by Le Nain is also reproduced in plate 427, beside one by Chardin, to show the continuity of this French tradition of unadorned realism.

This picture is the canvas listed in an exhibition catalogue of 1829, in which it is said to be by "Le Nain, a favourite of Gainsborough and was twice in his collection." The sweep of landscape, with its strongly emphasized receding planes, was exactly what Gainsborough sought in his early work, usually thought to be entirely under Dutch influence. Actually this continual recession, neither interrupted by detail nor broken up by bands of light and shade, is rare in Dutch art; and Gainsborough in his handling of distance in landscape seems also to owe a debt to France, which should not be ignored.

Collections: Thomas Gainsborough, London; Dr. Didbin; Joseph Neeld, London; Sir Audley Neeld, Chippenham, Wiltshire. *Samuel H. Kress Collection*, 1946. Painted c. 1640. Canvas, 18⅜ x 22½" (46.5 x 57 cm.).

321

Jean-Baptiste-Siméon Chardin

(FRENCH, 1699–1779)

426   THE ATTENTIVE NURSE

Chardin was the favorite painter of Diderot, whereas Boucher was the favorite, as we shall see, of Mme de Pompadour. The editor of the Encyclopedia had different taste from that popular at Versailles. He wished to see on canvas the virtues of domesticity rather than the enticements of femininity. In the long run, however, feminine charm is more tedious than domestic virtue, especially when this virtue is interpreted by Chardin's brush, which gilds with poetic light the everyday life of the middle class in eighteenth-century France.

For it was Chardin's talent to find plastic poetry in a bowl of fruit, a blue-and-white pitcher, or a nurse preparing a meal for her convalescent patient. In the picture reproduced here the painter conveys, with his exquisite sensibility, emotions of love and tenderness, sincere feelings springing from the charity in his heart but difficult to express without banality and triteness. Nothing could be further from the sometimes delicious and always glittering artificiality preferred at Versailles. Chardin was a product of Paris—the city of merchants and bankers, of traders and shopkeepers, of encyclopedists and bluestockings. His art is an affirmation of their independently developed taste, which at its best has a great appeal. But it was also a taste in which was latent that germ of sentimentality which a hundred years later became a plague that almost destroyed French painting.

Chardin's canvases also had considerable charm for the aristocracy. *The Attentive Nurse* was purchased from the artist by the Prince of Liechtenstein when he was Austrian Ambassador to France. It was one of the few works by Chardin that were not engraved before being sold, and it has been assumed that the Prince was so enamored of the picture, when it was displayed in the Salon of 1747, that he took it immediately to Vienna. Apart from a sketch which was probably the basis for Jules de Goncourt's etching, there are no other versions, which is unusual in Chardin's genre compositions of this type.

Collections: The Princes of Liechtenstein. *Samuel H. Kress Collection*, 1952. Signed. Painted probably 1738, the date which appears on its pendant, *The Governess*, in the National Gallery of Canada, Ottawa. Canvas, 18⅛ x 14½" (46.2 x 37 cm.).

427

A painting by Louis Le Nain is included with those of Chardin, who was born a century later, to show how a tradition of Realism continued in French painting. In spite of the dominance in the Academy of the Classicists, the new middle class was not interested in reminders of spiritual values and the glorious pages of history. They wanted instead the subjects Chardin provided: a girl being instructed, a child playing cards, a glimpse of a kitchen, scenes of everyday life with which they were familiar. Through the purity and beauty of his handling of the paintbrush, Chardin transforms these commonplace subjects into enduring works of art.

429

428

430

427 Louis Le Nain (French, c. 1593–1648): *A French Interior.* c. 1645. Canvas, 21⅞ x 25⅜" (55.6 x 64.7 cm.). Samuel H. Kress Collection

428 Jean-Baptiste-Siméon Chardin (French, 1699–1779): *The House of Cards.* Signed. c. 1735. Canvas, 32⅜ x 26" (82 x 66 cm.). Andrew W. Mellon Collection

429 Jean-Baptiste-Siméon Chardin: *The Kitchen Maid.* Signed, and dated 1738. Canvas, 18⅛ x 14¾" (46.2 x 37.5 cm.). Samuel H. Kress Collection

430 Jean-Baptiste-Siméon Chardin: *The Young Governess.* Signed. c. 1739. Canvas, 22⅞ x 29⅛" (58.3 x 74 cm.). Andrew W. Mellon Collection

431 Jean-Baptiste-Siméon Chardin: *Soap Bubbles.* Signed. c. 1745. Canvas, 36⅝ x 29⅜" (93 x 74.6 cm.). Gift of Mrs. John W. Simpson

432 Jean-Baptiste-Siméon Chardin: *Still Life.* Signed. c. 1760/65. Canvas, 19½ x 23⅜" (49.6 x 59.4 cm.). Samuel H. Kress Collection

431

432

Nicolas de Largillière

(FRENCH, 1656–1746)

433 ELIZABETH THROCKMORTON

Nicolas de Largillière, who lived to be ninety, was the John Singer Sargent of the age of Louis XIV. Everyone in society wanted to be painted by him. As a young man he had traveled to London to become a pupil of Lely, and while there attracted the attention of Charles II, who wished to keep him in his service. But the anti-Catholic feeling in England was so strong that he feared for his life and returned to Paris, where he spent his remaining years except for a short stay in England during the reign of James II.

While in London he had come to know the Catholic families who under Charles II and James II had enjoyed a brief respite from their disabilities. Among these families were the Throckmortons, staunch supporters of the Pope and the Stuarts. Like other recusants, numerous Throckmortons resided in France. The ladies of the family were almost invariably educated in Paris and usually by the Blue Nuns, whose Reverend Mother, Anne Throckmorton, was Elizabeth's aunt. Letters are preserved from Anne to her brother in London telling about the childhood of Elizabeth, who seems to have been very delicate and to have recovered with difficulty from smallpox. Her aunt was of sufficient distinction to be able to take her niece to tea with the royal children at Versailles, the summit of social prestige.

In 1714, at the age of twenty, Elizabeth took vows in the convent of the Augustinian Blue Sisters. She was elected Mother Superior twice, from 1736 to 1744 and from 1752 to 1760. Because of her delicate health, however, she was released from many of the austerities of the Order.

Neither the scars of smallpox nor later signs of ill health appear in Largillière's portrait. He has shown a ravishingly attractive nun whose radiant beauty, had she not spent her life in a convent, might have brought her, in those dissolute days, many lovers. When she was painted, according to an inscription on the back of the canvas, she was thirty-five years of age. Looking at her one realizes that life in a convent must have preserved feminine beauty more successfully than any method devised in the secular world. Little wonder that in the eighteenth century men often fell in love with nuns.

Collections: Family of the sitter, Coughton Court, Warwickshire. *Ailsa Mellon Bruce Fund*, 1964. Painted 1729. Canvas, 32 x 25⅞" (81.3 x 65.7 cm.).

ELIZABETH DAUGHTER OF Sᴿ ROBᵀ THROCKMORTON BARᵀ.

434

436

435

434 Maurice-Quentin de La Tour (French, 1704–1788): *Claude Dupouch*. Probably 1739. Pastel on paper, 23⅜ x 19⅜″ (59.4 x 49.4 cm.). Samuel H. Kress Collection

435 Jean-Marc Nattier (French, 1685–1766): *Joseph Bonnier de la Mosson*. Signed, and dated 1745. Canvas, 54¼ x 41½″ (137.9 x 105.4 cm.). Samuel H. Kress Collection

436 Nicolas de Largillière (French, 1656–1746): *A Young Man with His Tutor*. Signed, and dated 1685. Canvas, 57½ x 45⅛″ (146 x 114.8 cm.). Samuel H. Kress Collection

437 François-Hubert Drouais (French, 1727–1775): *Group Portrait*. Signed, and dated *ce. 1 avril. 1756*. Canvas, 96 x 76⅝″ (244 x 195 cm.). Samuel H. Kress Collection

438 Attributed to François-Hubert Drouais: *Marquis d'Ossun*. Probably 1762. Canvas, 85⅞ x 64⅝″ (218 x 164.1 cm.). Gift of Mrs. Albert J. Beveridge in memory of her aunt Delia Spencer Field

439 Hubert Drouais (French, 1699–1767): *Portrait of a Lady*. c. 1750. Canvas, 46½ x 37½″ (118 x 95 cm.). Gift of Chester Dale

French eighteenth-century portraitists were subtle analysts of character, much more so than their English contemporaries. One of the most percipient representations in art of upper-class family life is Drouais' *Group Portrait* (plate 437). The father leans forward tenderly and smiles equivocally. He doubtless has a mistress, but his wife's complacency makes one imagine that he might also be a cuckold. Only the child seems innocent, and this condition, one feels, will not last long. The painting is appropriately inscribed "First of April 1756"—April Fools' Day!

438

437

439

329

Antoine Watteau

(FRENCH, 1684–1721)

440   CERES (SUMMER)

Born in Valenciennes, a part of Flanders then recently acquired by France, Watteau during his brief life established French Rococo painting. *Ceres*, or *An Allegory of Summer*, shows the characteristics of this new style: its essential derivation from Rubens and the Venetians, in this case Paolo Veronese; its slighter rhythms and more delicate phrasing; and its somewhat enervated sensuality. In Watteau's work, however, the inevitable animation and somewhat affected charm of the Rococo is kept from monotony by an overtone of sadness, autumnal and pensive.

Watteau came to Paris at the age of eighteen. For a time he produced religious and popular pictures. Finally he gained access to the Louvre, where he scrutinized the paintings by Rubens in the Maria de' Medici Gallery. But, much more important, he was invited to live with Pierre Crozat, the greatest collector in France, whose drawings and paintings by Raphael, Rubens, van Dyck, Giorgione, Titian, and Veronese he was able to study. These were the artists who formed his style and taught him what he could never have learned from his contemporaries. Among the paintings he must have seen were Raphael's *St. George and the Dragon* (plate 196) and van Dyck's *Isabella Brant* (plate 330).

It was while he was living in the Crozat palace in the Rue de Richelieu that his patron asked him to decorate his dining room with allegories of the Four Seasons, one of which is the painting reproduced here. These he completed sometime between 1712 and 1716.

When Crozat died, his palace was inherited through his great-niece by the Duc de Choiseul, the most powerful man in France. Choiseul ran through his fortune, however, and on his death in 1786 his property was sold to pay his immense debts. The National Gallery painting and the *Allegory of Winter* were in the sale. The other two, *Spring* and *Autumn*, also known from engravings, had disappeared at an earlier date. *Spring* was rediscovered and identified in an English collection as recently as 1963, but three years later it was burned during a robbery. *Autumn* and *Winter* are still missing; perhaps a fortunate connoisseur will one day bring them to light. If the Crozat decorations could be reassembled, they would challenge many of the decorative cycles of G. B. Tiepolo and indicate that Watteau was capable of more than his characteristic *Fêtes Galantes*, entrancing as they are with their curious blend of gaiety and melancholy.

Collections: Pierre Crozat; Louis-François Crozat, Marquis du Châtel; Duchesse de Gontaut-Biron; Duc and Duchesse de Choiseul; Alphonse Roehn, Paris; possibly H.A.J. Munro of Novar; Lionel Phillips, Tylney Hall, Winchfield; H. Michel-Lévy, Paris; Léon Michel-Lévy, Paris; Charles-Louis Dreyfus, Paris. *Samuel H. Kress Collection*, 1961. Painted c. 1712. Canvas, oval, 56¾ x 45¾" (142 x 115.7 cm.).

462 Jean-Honoré Fragonard (French, 1732–1806): *A Game of Hot Cockles*. 1767/73. Canvas, 45½ x 36" (115.5 x 91.5 cm.). Samuel H. Kress Collection

463 Jean-Honoré Fragonard: *The Visit to the Nursery*. Before 1784. Canvas, 28¾ x 36¼" (73 x 92 cm.). Samuel H. Kress Collection

464 Jean-Honoré Fragonard: *The Happy Family*. After 1769. Canvas, oval, 21¼ x 25⅝" (53.9 x 65.1 cm.). Timken Collection

465 Hubert Robert (French, 1733–1808): *The Old Bridge*. Probably c. 1775. Canvas, 35⅞ x 47⅝" (91.3 x 121 cm.). Samuel H. Kress Collection

466 Elisabeth Vigée-Lebrun (French, 1755–1842): *The Marquise de Pezé and the Marquise de Rouget with Her Two Children*. 1787. Canvas, 48⅝ x 61⅜" (123.4 x 155.9 cm.). Gift of the Bay Foundation in memory of Josephine Bay Paul and Ambassador Charles Ulrick Bay

467 Elizabeth Vigée-Lebrun: *Portrait of a Lady*. Signed, and dated 1789. Wood, 42⅛ x 32¾" (107 x 83 cm.). Samuel H. Kress Collection

468 Jean-Marc Nattier (French, 1685–1766): *Madame de Caumartin as Hebe*. Signed, and dated 1753. Canvas, 40⅜ x 32" (102.5 x 81.5 cm.). Samuel H. Kress Collection

466

468

467

Giovanni Battista Tiepolo

(VENETIAN, 1696–1770)

469 QUEEN ZENOBIA ADDRESSING HER SOLDIERS

The subject of this picture has for a long time mystified some of the best scholars of classical history and of Venetian painting. Lionello Venturi thought it might represent the founding of Rome, illustrating an episode in the Aeneid when Venus appeared to Aeneas and his followers to encourage them on their landing in Latium. But it is hard to recognize in this helmeted Amazon the Goddess of Love. Wilhelm Suida suggested that she was, instead, an allegorical figure of Rome urging all the legionaries to unite. This would explain the gesture of her left hand making a ring, the sign of unity.

My own preference has been for the theory put forth by Dr. Kezia Knauer, that the subject is "Agrippina Addressing the Legionaries." This is based on a passage in Tacitus: "Gaius Plinius . . . relates how she took her stand at the head of the bridge, bestowing praise and thanks on the returning legions . . . and in the most artless manner conceivable paraded the General's son about the camp in the dress of a private soldier, delighting to hear him called by the appellation of *Little Caesar in Boots.*" "Little Caesar in boots" would then be the young boy about to mount the podium. This interpretation explains a figure to whom Tiepolo has given considerable importance.

However, a fourth interpretation, first proposed by Erwin Panofsky, has now been accepted and further documented by Dr. Fern Rusk Shapley in her catalogue *Paintings from the Samuel H. Kress Collection* (1973), and the National Gallery has accordingly changed the title of the painting from *A Scene from Roman History* to the more specific one given here.

Queen Zenobia's story is retold in Gibbon's *Decline and Fall of the Roman Empire* from an ancient source. She ruled Palmyra in the third century A.D. and attained such power in the East that she could defy Rome. It would appear that the painting reproduced here formed a decorative scheme with at least three others: *A Hunter on Horseback* and *A Hunter with a Stag*, probably references to Zenobia's passion for hunting, both now in the Crespi Collection, Milan; and Tiepolo's well-known *Triumph of Aurelian*, now in the Galleria Sabauda, Turin, and undoubtedly a pendant to the National Gallery painting. It is intriguing to speculate that these paintings may have been commissioned by the Zenobio family of Venice, because of the resemblance of their name to that of the famous queen. Certainly it is known that Tiepolo did decorate a room in the Zenobio palace, which still stands in Venice, sometime before 1732.

Collections: Possibly Ca' Zenobio, Venice; Villa Grimani-Valmarana, Noventa Padovana; Count Dino Barozzi, Venice; C. Ledyard Blair, New Jersey. *Samuel H. Kress Collection*, 1961. Painted c. 1730. Canvas, 102⅞ x 144" (261.4 x 365.8 cm.).

470

470 Giuseppe Maria Crespi (Bolognese, 1665–1747): *Lucretia Threatened by Tarquin*. c. 1700. Canvas, 76¾ x 67⅝" (195 x 172 cm.). Samuel H. Kress Collection

471 Alessandro Magnasco (Genoese, 1667–1749): *Christ at the Sea of Galilee*. c. 1740. Canvas, 46½ x 57¾" (118 x 147 cm.). Samuel H. Kress Collection

472 Alessandro Magnasco: *The Baptism of Christ*. c. 1740. Canvas, 46¼ x 57¾" (117 x 147 cm.). Samuel H. Kress Collection

473 Donato Creti (Bolognese, 1671–1749): *The Quarrel*. c. 1705. Canvas, 51⅛ x 38" (129.9 x 96.5 cm.). Samuel H. Kress Collection

474 Giovanni Battista Piazzetta (Venetian, 1682–1754): *Elijah Taken Up in a Chariot of Fire*. c. 1745. Canvas, 68¾ x 104¼" (174.6 x 264.8 cm.). Samuel H. Kress Collection

The richness of the National Gallery in eighteenth-century Italian works is indicated by these paintings. The first generation of these artists who died about 1750 is represented by Crespi, Magnasco, Sebastiano Ricci, and Piazzetta. Their dashing brushwork and dramatic gestures reach a climax in Piazzetta's *Elijah* (plate 474), where the figures look as if they are being tossed by a whirlwind of flame, and in the two paintings by Magnasco, whose lightning-like streaks of paint lend his pictures an electric vibrancy. Tiepolo, who belongs to the next generation, was the greatest decorator of the eighteenth century. *The World Pays Homage to Spain* (plate 477) is typical of the models for ceiling designs with which he provided his patrons, in this case the King of Spain.

471

472

474

473

476

475

475 Giovanni Battista Tiepolo (Venetian, 1696–1770): *Timocleia and the Thracian Commander.* c. 1750. Canvas, 55¼ x 43⅛″ (140.3 x 109.3 cm.). Samuel H. Kress Collection

476 Sebastiano Ricci and Marco Ricci (Venetian, 1659–1734 and 1676–1730): *Memorial to Admiral Sir Clowdisley Shovell.* Signed. c. 1725. Canvas, 87½ x 62½″ (222.3 x 158.5 cm.). Samuel H. Kress Collection

477

478

The Italians of the eighteenth century, like the Dutch of
the seventeenth, wanted portraits of places and
buildings. No artist has rivaled Panini as a portrayer of
interiors; nor has anyone equaled Canaletto as a painter
of cityscapes. He delineated the palaces and canals of
Venice so vividly that the sightseer in that city, after
having looked at many of Canaletto's paintings, will
sometimes, when admiring a view, find himself almost
reaching out to touch a canvas before he realizes that he
is not looking at a picture, but is himself part of the
scene. Canaletto's nephew Bellotto does much the same
for Northern cities. Guardi, by contrast, gives poetic
and impressionistic visions of this aqueous Venetian
scenery, enchanting views of the most beautiful city in
the world.

479

480

482

481

483

484

485

484 Canaletto (Venetian, 1697–1768): *Venice, the Quay of the Piazzetta.* Signed. Early 1730s. Canvas, 45⅛ x 60⅜" (115.2 x 153.6 cm.). Gift of Mrs. Barbara Hutton

485 Francesco Guardi (Venetian, 1712–1793): *View of the Rialto.* Probably c. 1780. Canvas, 27 x 36" (68.5 x 91.5 cm.). Widener Collection

486 Gian Antonio Guardi and Francesco Guardi (Venetian, 1699–1760 and 1712–1793): *Carlo and Ubaldo Resisting the Enchantments of Armida's Nymphs.* 1750/55. Canvas, 98½ x 181" (250.2 x 459.8 cm.). Ailsa Mellon Bruce Fund

487 Gian Antonio Guardi and Francesco Guardi: *Erminia and the Shepherds.* 1750/55. Canvas, 99 x 174⅛" (251.5 x 442.2 cm.). Ailsa Mellon Bruce Fund

488 Francesco Guardi: *A Seaport and Classic Ruins in Italy.* 1730s. Canvas, 48 x 70" (122 x 178 cm.). Samuel H. Kress Collection

489 Francesco Guardi: *Campo San Zanipolo.* 1782. Canvas, 14¾ x 12⅜" (37.5 x 31.5 cm.). Samuel H. Kress Collection

490 Pietro Longhi (Venetian, 1702–1785): *The Simulated Faint.* c. 1745. Canvas, 19¼ x 24" (49 x 61 cm.). Samuel H. Kress Collection

486

487

489

488

490

491 Pietro Longhi (Venetian, 1702–1785): *Blind-man's Buff.* c. 1745. Canvas, 19¼ x 24" (49 x 61 cm.). Samuel H. Kress Collection

492 Bernardo Bellotto (Venetian, 1720–1780): *The Castle of Nymphenburg.* c. 1761. Canvas, 26⅞ x 47⅛" (68.4 x 119.8 cm.). Samuel H. Kress Collection

493 Bernardo Bellotto: *View of Munich.* c. 1761. Canvas, 27¼ x 47⅛" (69.3 x 119.8 cm.). Samuel H. Kress Collection

491

492

493

British &
American Schools

XVIII CENTURY

Thomas Gainsborough

(BRITISH, 1727–1788)

494 MRS. RICHARD BRINSLEY SHERIDAN

To understand this portrait, one must take into account its background in Whig society of the late eighteenth century—a society materialistic, rich, self-confident, yet with a love of learning and freedom and a special sensibility that sometimes verged on sentimentality. Mrs. Sheridan, the beautiful singer who married the wit, playwright, brilliant member of Parliament, and drunken favorite of Devonshire House, is a characteristic figure in that society. And this picture, at once charmingly pastoral (although nature is somewhat arranged, as the great Whig nobles liked it to be) and dashingly, artificially worldly, is a consummate expression of high Whig taste.

Gainsborough is known to have painted on occasion with brushes mounted on handles almost six feet long, in order to be the same distance from his model and his canvas. The consequent sketchiness of effect makes the certainty of each brushstroke still more remarkable. This feature of his style impressed Sir Joshua Reynolds, who wrote, "This chaos, this uncouth and shapeless appearance, by a kind of magic, at a certain distance assumes form, and all the parts seem to drop into their proper places; so that we can hardly refuse acknowledging the full effect of diligence, under the appearance of chance and hasty negligence."

Collections: Richard Brinsley Sheridan, Bath, England; Baron Nathaniel de Rothschild, Tring, Hertfordshire, and heirs, until sold by Lord Rothschild, London. *Andrew W. Mellon Collection*, 1937. Painted probably 1785/86. Canvas, 86½ x 60½" (220 x 154 cm.).

495

496

497

498

356

499

500

Thomas Gainsborough, more than any other British painter, delights the spectator with his technique in oil. Usually the surfaces of his pictures have the transparency of watercolor and the delicacy of pastel. His thinly brushed canvases have lasted better than those of his contemporaries who used a thicker pigmentation. Portraiture was Gainsborough's vocation, but his avocation was landscape. His visions of an imaginary countryside, however, were largely unsalable, and masterpieces like *Landscape with a Bridge* (plate 498) filled his studio at his death.

Thomas Gainsborough   (British, 1727–1788)

495   *Master John Heathcote*. c. 1770/74. Canvas, 50 x 39⅞" (127 x 101.2 cm.). Given in memory of Governor Alvan T. Fuller by the Fuller Foundation

496   *Georgiana, Duchess of Devonshire*. Probably 1783. Canvas, 92¾ x 57⅝" (235.6 x 146.5 cm.). Andrew W. Mellon Collection

497   *Miss Catherine Tatton*. Probably 1785. Canvas, 30 x 25" (76 x 64 cm.). Andrew W. Mellon Collection

498   *Landscape with a Bridge*. c. 1785. Canvas, 44½ x 52½" (113 x 133 cm.). Andrew W. Mellon Collection

499   *The Honorable Mrs. Graham*. Probably 1775. Canvas, 36 x 28" (89.5 x 69 cm.). Widener Collection

500   *The Earl of Darnley*. Probably 1785. Canvas, 30 x 25" (76 x 63.5 cm.). Widener Collection

501   *Seascape*. Probably 1781. Canvas, 40¼ x 50⅜" (102.2 x 127.9 cm.). Ailsa Mellon Bruce Collection

501

Sir Joshua Reynolds

(BRITISH, 1723–1792)

502   LADY CAROLINE HOWARD

In the portrait of Lady Caroline Howard, Reynolds has stressed a certain aspect of childhood, its innocence, its unstudied gracefulness. It does not matter that the portrait may not be a precise likeness of Lady Caroline, nor even that he used a similar pose and setting in other paintings of children, notably in *The Age of Innocence* in the National Gallery, London. For "the great aim of the art," as he said addressing the Royal Academy, "is to strike the imagination." In the portrait of Lady Caroline the mind is captured and converted to the romantic concept of childhood, "trailing clouds of glory," thirty years before Wordsworth's poem. Needless to say Reynolds himself was a bachelor!

Reynolds, in spite of the classical creed expounded in his *Discourses*, proves himself in many ways a precursor of the Romantics. This is manifest not only in his tendency to sentimentality but also in his faltering technique, in that uncertainty of craftsmanship which was the plague of Romantic painting. Thus many of his canvases, because of his constant technical experiments and his constant use of bitumen, have cracked and faded. *Lady Caroline Howard*, however, has lasted with its original brilliance and freshness; and for that reason it gives an idea of the luminosity of tone which must have characterized Reynolds' portraits when they left his studio, an impression hard to gain from many of his pictures in their present condition.

Collection: Earl of Carlisle, Castle Howard, England. *Andrew W. Mellon Collection*, 1937. Painted c. 1778. Canvas, 56¼ x 44½" (143 x 113 cm.).

Lady Caroline Howard
Lady Cawdor

359

503

505

504

Sir Joshua Reynolds was the first president of the Royal Academy, and his *Discourses*, comprising his annual lectures before that institution, were taken as the gospel of British painting for generations. They remain one of the most comprehensive, sensible, and persuasive aesthetic statements ever made. His portraits, though never reaching the level of his theories, are the supreme expression in the eighteenth century of the Grand Manner, which was introduced by van Dyck a century and a half earlier.

Sir Joshua Reynolds   (British, 1723–1792)

503   *Lady Betty Hamilton.* 1758. Canvas, 46 x 33″ (117 x 84 cm.). Widener Collection

504   *Lady Elizabeth Delmé and Her Children.* 1777–80. Canvas, 94 x 58⅛″ (239.2 x 147.8 cm.). Andrew W. Mellon Collection

505   *Squire Musters.* 1777/80. Canvas, 93⅞ x 58″ (238.5 x 147.3 cm.). Given in memory of Governor Alvan T. Fuller by the Fuller Foundation

506   *Lady Elizabeth Compton.* 1781. Canvas, 94½ x 58½″ (240 x 149 cm.). Andrew W. Mellon Collection

507   *Lady Cornewall.* c. 1785. Canvas, 50 x 40″ (127 x 101.5 cm.). Widener Collection

508   **Thomas Gainsborough** (British, 1727–1788): *Mrs. John Taylor.* Probably c. 1778. Canvas, oval, 30 x 25″ (76 x 64 cm.). Andrew W. Mellon Collection

506

507

508

George Romney

(BRITISH, 1734–1802)

509 MISS WILLOUGHBY

If there were only a divining rod to point out those artists destined to be the Old Masters of the future, we might enjoy portraits of ourselves or our children and at the same time count on our descendants being copiously enriched. Miss Willoughby's parents in 1784 paid Romney less than one-thousandth part of the price his picture brought when it was acquired for the National Gallery of Art a few decades ago, and many families in Europe today owe their fortunes to the perspicacity with which their ancestors selected their portraitists.

But how can we tell what picture will gain in appreciation? Why has *Miss Willoughby*, for instance, come to be so highly treasured? It is merely the conventional and scarcely individualized portrait of a pretty child. Perhaps Romney was even bored with the commission, for he disliked portraiture, and the only sitter he seems to have taken pleasure in painting was Emma, Lady Hamilton, whose strange, restless magnetism enthralled and maddened him. When he painted other people his real interests lay in solving certain problems of color and design rather than in getting a likeness.

But then, who cares any longer what Miss Willoughby looked like? Her portrait is enjoyed today because of Romney's genius as a colorist and as a decorator. The harmonious tone of the picture is a lesson in the adroit use of a limited palette, in this case a palette of only three colors, red, yellow, and blue. The design is as simple as the color, but just as subtly ingenious. The gesture of the child seems spontaneous and unposed, but note the tilt of the head at just the right angle to suggest a diagonal movement crosscutting the diagonal of the sloping landscape in the background. Imagine it upright and the rhythm of the composition vanishes. And how satisfactory in scale is Miss Willoughby in relation to the canvas. These qualities of color and design, so frequently to be found in eighteenth-century English portraiture, are the antecedent facts which make it probable that a painting will continue to interest posterity.

Collection: Major Sir John Christopher Willoughby, fifth bart., Fulmer Hall, Slough, Buckinghamshire (sold 1906). *Andrew W. Mellon Collection*, 1937. Painted 1781–83. Canvas, 36⅛ x 28" (91 x 71 cm.).

510

511

George Romney was one of the most popular of British portraitists, but he loathed portrait painting. He was interested in historical subjects, especially if there was some classical association. Nevertheless, he had to make his living, and sitters were queuing up to be painted. He gave the ladies who came to his studio charm and grace, and they were delighted. But in the artist's heart and mind only one face was stamped—that of Emma, the beautiful wife of Sir William Hamilton and the mistress

512

513

George Romney (British, 1734–1802)

510 *Lady Broughton.* 1770/73. Canvas, 94 x 58" (239 x 147 cm.). Andrew W. Mellon Collection

511 *Mr. Forbes.* c. 1780/90. Canvas, 30 x 25" (76.4 x 63.5 cm.). Gift of Pauline Sabin Davis

512 *Sir William Hamilton.* Probably 1783. Canvas, 30¼ x 25⅝" (76.8 x 65.1 cm.). Ailsa Mellon Bruce Collection

513 *Mrs. Blair.* 1787–89. Canvas, 50 x 40" (127 x 101.5 cm.). Widener Collection

514 *Sir Archibald Campbell.* Probably 1792. Canvas, 60⅜ x 48¾" (153.4 x 123.9 cm.). Timken Collection

515 *Mrs. Davenport.* 1782–84. Canvas, 30⅛ x 25⅛" (76.5 x 64 cm.). Andrew W. Mellon Collection

516 *Lady Arabella Ward.* 1783–88. Canvas, 30 x 25" (76 x 64 cm.). Widener Collection

of Britain's naval hero Lord Nelson. (Romney's painting of Sir William is reproduced in plate 512.) Romney painted some fifty portraits of Lady Hamilton; she provoked him with her coquetry and tantalizing loveliness until his health, never strong, broke under the emotional strain and he withdrew to Kendal in the north of England. His wife faithfully nursed him until he died.

514

515

516

Sir Henry Raeburn

(BRITISH, 1756–1823)

517   MISS ELEANOR URQUHART

Flaubert's admonition to artists, "Be regular and ordinary in your life, like a bourgeois, so that you can be violent and original in your work," might serve as a description of Sir Henry Raeburn. Art was a business to this most distinguished of Scottish painters, and from nine to five-thirty it kept him regularly in his studio, where he painted a succession of three to four sitters a day. When he left his easel, it was to speculate in real estate or to play golf. But conventional as was his life, there was nothing conventional about his portraiture.

As a young man Raeburn decided to record only what he saw in front of him and never to trust his memory even when painting a subordinate part of the picture. This practice, common today, was contrary to the regular procedure of eighteenth-century portraitists. They used instead a preestablished tone for flesh, a traditional arrangement of highlights and shadows, and other fixed conventions. Raeburn, relying on actual observation and not on a memorized formula, developed a style which foreshadows contemporary painting.

For while he anticipates the goal of modern portraitists, seizing in his best works on the salient features of the sitter and rendering them in the moment of conception, his technical performance at times goes beyond the attainments of any contemporary artist. It is amazing that in portraying Miss Urquhart, for example, he did not have to change a single brushstroke. Success in direct painting of this type depends on the swiftness and certainty of the artist's hand. The moment he falters, renders a false shadow, fails to find the correct contour, misses the right color, the passage must be repainted and the freshness is gone.

Raeburn himself failed more often than he succeeded, and his work frequently suffers from the same faults that plague modern portraitists: either the pigment is thick from reworking, or the shadows too black, or the colors dull. *Miss Urquhart* is an exception; and it is easy to imagine that on this occasion, fascinated by the beauty of his sitter, the artist forgot all hesitations and afterthoughts and put down *à premier coup* the image of an aristocratic and charming woman, creating spontaneously one of his supreme masterpieces.

Collection: Captain Michael Pollard-Urquhart, Craigston, Scotland. *Andrew W. Mellon Collection,* 1937. Painted c. 1793. Canvas, 29⅜ x 24¼" (75 x 62 cm.).

543

544

540 **Charles Willson Peale** (American, 1741–1827): *Benjamin and Eleanor Ridgely Laming*. 1788. Canvas, 42 x 60¼" (106.6 x 152.9 cm.). Gift of Morris Schapiro

541 **Rembrandt Peale** (American, 1778–1860): *George Washington*. c. 1850. Canvas, 35⅞ x 28⅞" (91.1 x 73.3 cm.). Gift of Mr. and Mrs. George W. Davison

542 **Mather Brown** (American, 1761–1831): *William Vans Murray*. Signed, and dated 1787. Canvas, 30⅛ x 25" (77 x 64 cm.). Andrew W. Mellon Collection

543 **Benjamin West** (American, 1738–1820): *Self-Portrait*. Probably c. 1770. Canvas, 30¼ x 25⅜" (77.3 x 64.4 cm.). Andrew W. Mellon Collection

544 **Jeremiah Theus** (American, 1719–1774): *Mrs. Cuthbert*. c. 1765. Canvas, 29¾ x 24⅞" (75.4 x 63.1 cm.). Gift of Edgar William and Bernice Chrysler Garbisch

545 **Matthew Pratt** (American, 1734–1805): *The Duke of Portland*. Probably 1774 or later. Canvas, 30 x 25" (76.7 x 64 cm.). Gift of Clarence Van Dyke Tiers

545

Gilbert Stuart

(AMERICAN, 1755–1828)

546   THE SKATER

In two hundred years America has produced several great painters, and among these at least one innovator of genius, Gilbert Stuart. Stuart, who arrived in London in 1775, a penniless young student, was trained by his compatriot Benjamin West. In West's studio he was taught accepted methods of eighteenth-century portraiture: a general tint for flesh, certain fixed places for highlights and deep shadows, and, often to improve the appearance of the sitter, touches of carmine in the nostrils and the corners of the eyes.

The Skater, a portrait of William Grant of Congalton, was Gilbert Stuart's first of major importance. It was painted in London while he was still working in West's studio. At the time it was said that he had learned to make "a tolerable likeness of the face, but as to the figure he could not get below the fifth button." Possibly it was to overcome such criticism that he determined his portrait of William Grant should be full-length. The sittings were arranged, and one wintry day Grant remarked that the weather seemed more suitable for skating than for painting. Stuart agreed, and both went to skate in Hyde Park. The ice cracked, however, and they were forced to return. It was then that Stuart had an inspiration. He decided to portray his sitter on skates.

When *The Skater* was sent to the Royal Academy in 1782, according to Stuart's account it caused a sensation. Grant went there dressed in his skating costume, and Stuart described how the crowd followed him so closely he was compelled to make his retreat, for everyone was exclaiming, "That is he! That is the gentleman!" Although Stuart was apt to exaggerate, it is true the portrait was much admired.

Nearly a century later the unsigned *Skater* was again exhibited at the Royal Academy. Controversy over its authorship raged. The *Daily Telegraph* attributed it to Romney, but the *Times* said it was too good for that artist and suggested Hoppner or Raeburn. The *Art Journal* reported, "A more graceful and manly figure was surely never painted by an English artist, and if Gainsborough were that artist, this is unquestionably his masterpiece." This was the most logical assumption, as the sketchy landscape in the background, showing Westminster Abbey in the distance, is rendered very much in the manner of Gainsborough.

Again, for half a century, *The Skater* vanished from public attention. Fortunately, however, it was located and purchased by the National Gallery of Art. It remains uniquely important in Stuart's career, for as he observed to Josiah Quincy it is rare for an artist to be "suddenly lifted into fame by a single picture."

Collections: Inherited by William Grant's granddaughter, through whose marriage it came into the Pelham-Clinton family, Moor Park, Stroud, Gloucestershire, and London. *Andrew W. Mellon Collection,* 1950. Painted 1782. Canvas, 96⅝ x 58⅛" (245.3 x 147.6 cm.).

547

548

Gilbert Stuart (American, 1755–1828)

547 *Lady Liston.* 1800. Canvas, 29⅛ x 24⅛" (74 x 61.3 cm.). Gift of Chester Dale

548 *Sir Robert Liston.* 1800. Canvas, 29¼ x 24⅛" (74.3 x 61.3 cm.). Gift of Chester Dale

549 *Sir Joshua Reynolds.* 1784. Canvas, 36 x 30" (95 x 76 cm.). Andrew W. Mellon Collection

550 *Commodore Thomas Macdonough.* Probably 1818. Wood, 28½ x 23" (72.3 x 58 cm.). Andrew W. Mellon Collection

551 *Mrs. Lawrence Lewis.* 1804/5. Canvas, 29 x 24¼" (73.7 x 61.6 cm.). Loan and partial gift of H. H. Walker Lewis in memory of his parents, Mr. and Mrs. Edwin A. S. Lewis

552 *John Bill Ricketts.* 1793/99. Canvas, 29⅝ x 24¼" (75.1 x 61.6 cm.). Gift of Mrs. Robert B. Noyes in memory of Elisha Riggs

549

550

551

552

Gilbert Stuart was one of the most original of eighteenth-century painters. His late portraits, such as *Commodore Thomas Macdonough* (plate 550), have the indistinctness of unfocused vision, with the planes of the face adumbrated rather than defined, that we find in Velázquez. Stuart said, "In the commencement of all portraits the first idea is an indistinct mass of light and shadows, or the character of the person as seen in the heel of the evening, in the grey of the morning, or at a distance too great to distinguish features with exactness." An earlier, very beautiful portrait is that of Mrs. Lewis (plate 551), who was Nellie Custis, granddaughter of Martha Washington.

Gilbert Stuart

(AMERICAN, 1755–1828)

553   MRS. RICHARD YATES

To quote a contemporary, Dunlap, soon after painting *The Skater* Stuart had "his full share of the best business in London, and prices equal to any, except Sir Joshua Reynolds and Gainsborough." But his earnings could not keep pace with his expenditures. Deeply in debt, he returned to America and spent the rest of his life painting the heroes of the new Republic and the increasingly wealthy merchants and their families.

He once said, "I want to find out what nature is for myself, and see her with my own eyes." Such freshness of vision was easier to achieve in the Colonies than in the mother country, for in America no formula for painting had yet been established. Patrons like Mrs. Yates, the wife of a New York merchant, wanted to see themselves as they really were, and they were perfectly willing that an artist should make technical experiments if these led to a more accurate portrayal. Thus, after his return to America in 1793, Stuart's power of observation increased, and he noted, among other facts of vision, that "good flesh coloring partook of all colors, not mixed, so as to be combined in one tint, but shining through each other, like the blood through the natural skin." Had there been the artists and the tradition of painting in America that there were in France, these innovations of Stuart's might have caused Impressionism to appear in the New World generations before it revolutionized art in Europe.

Collections: Carlisle Pollock II, grandson of the sitter, New Orleans; and by descent to Mrs. Louise Chiapella Formento; Dr. Isaac M. Cline, New Orleans; Thomas B. Clarke, New York. *Andrew W. Mellon Collection*, 1940. Painted 1793/94. Canvas, 30¼ x 25" (77 x 63 cm.).

554

555

556

554 Edward Savage (American, 1761–1817): *The Washington Family*. 1796. Canvas, 84⅜ × 111⅞" (213.6 × 284.2 cm.). Andrew W. Mellon Collection

Gilbert Stuart (American, 1755–1828)

555 *Benjamin Tappan*. 1814. Wood, 28⅝ × 23¼" (72.8 × 59 cm.). Gift of Lady Vereker

556 *John Randolph*. 1805. Canvas, 29⅛ × 24⅛" (74 × 61 cm.). Andrew W. Mellon Collection

557 *George Washington (Vaughan Portrait)*. 1795. Canvas, 29 × 23¾" (73.5 × 60.5 cm.). Andrew W. Mellon Collection

558 *Mrs. John Adams*. 1815. Canvas, 29 × 23¾" (73.7 × 60.5 cm.). Gift of Mrs. Robert Homans

559 *John Adams*. 1815. Canvas, 29 × 24" (73.7 × 61.3 cm.). Gift of Mrs. Robert Homans

When in 1793 Stuart was swept back to America by an avalanche of debts, he told his creditors, "I hope to make a fortune by Washington alone." He did. His Washington portraits were numerous, and came to be known as Stuart's hundred-dollar bills, his charge for a replica. To have a portrait of the first president hanging on one's wall was a certificate of patriotism eagerly sought after by many former Tories. Edward Savage likewise became prosperous—by the sale of innumerable engravings after his *Washington Family* (plate 554), which was to become one of the most popular and famous of all American icons.

557

558

559

John Singleton Copley

(AMERICAN, 1738–1815)

560   THE COPLEY FAMILY

The career of John Singleton Copley, the greatest American artist of the eighteenth century, was the reverse of that of Stuart. Copley got his start in Boston and did not settle in London, where he spent the rest of his life, until 1775.

His wife's father, Richard Clarke, was a consignee of the famous shipment of tea which was sent to America contrary to the wishes of the Colonists, only to be thrown into the harbor in the Boston Tea Party. Consequently Clarke, a loyal Tory merchant, left the Colonies in high dudgeon and low repute, taking with him Copley's family. Copley, who had been studying in Italy for a year, soon joined his family in London. Shortly after his arrival he painted the group portrait reproduced here.

Mrs. Copley and her father sit in the foreground, surrounded by the little Copleys, while the artist looks out pensively from behind and clutches all that remains of his New England prosperity—a few sheets of drawings. Copley had reached a crossroads in his life. He was settled in England, faced with the necessity of making his way in an alien country where standards were very different from those he had left behind in Boston. He decided to change his whole approach to portraiture. *The Copley Family* shows, side by side, his old and his new styles. The painting of his father-in-law, especially his face and hands, and the charmingly rendered doll in the corner of the picture are the last echoes of that visual truth which characterized his early work. The painting of his wife, of the children, the composition of the picture, all are reminiscent of Reynolds, of West, of the "grand manner" of portraiture, which Copley forced himself to adopt. For a period he was successful and was elected a member of the Royal Academy, but he fell out of fashion. And though he painted more industriously than ever, he was unable to gain back his reputation. The end of his life was sad, for he was constantly menaced by debts and seems to have felt that he had betrayed his original gifts.

Collections: Copley family, London and Boston. *Andrew W. Mellon Fund*, 1961. Painted 1776/77. Canvas, 72½ x 90⅜″ (184.4 x 229.7 cm.).

561

Copley's style, before the Revolution drove him to England, is illustrated by plates 561–64. Note in the men's portraits how every wrinkle is accurately delineated. It must have taken Copley days on end to paint these sitters, and there are records of some protests, but on the whole, it was easy in the Colonies to persuade them to pose repeatedly. There was nothing more amusing to do! This willingness to give the painter time benefited Copley. As he wrote, "My pictures are almost always good in proportion to the time I give them provided I have a subject that is picturesk." Two more "picturesk" faces than those of Sargent and Tyng would be hard to find.

562

563

564

565

561 **John Singleton Copley** (American, 1738–1815): *Jane Browne.* Signed, and dated 1756. Canvas, 30⅛ x 25⅛″ (77 x 64.3 cm.). Andrew W. Mellon Collection

562 **John Singleton Copley**: *Epes Sargent.* c. 1760. Canvas, 49⅞ x 40″ (126.8 x 101.6 cm.). Gift of the Avalon Foundation

563 **John Singleton Copley**: *Eleazer Tyng.* Signed, and dated 1772. Canvas, 49¾ x 40⅛″ (126.5 x 101.2 cm.). Gift of the Avalon Foundation

564 **John Singleton Copley**: *Mrs. Metcalf Bowler.* c. 1763. Canvas, 50 x 40¼″ (127 x 102 cm.). Gift of Louise Alida Livingston

565 **Winthrop Chandler** (American, 1747–1790): *Mrs. Samuel Chandler.* c. 1780. Canvas, 54¾ x 47⅞″ (139.1 x 121.7 cm.). Gift of Edgar William and Bernice Chrysler Garbisch

566 **Winthrop Chandler**: *Captain Samuel Chandler.* c. 1780. Canvas, 54⅞ x 47⅞″ (139.5 x 121.7 cm.). Gift of Edgar William and Bernice Chrysler Garbisch

566

John Singleton Copley

(AMERICAN, 1738–1815)

567   WATSON AND THE SHARK

Watson and the Shark represents a horrible incident which occurred in 1749 when a young British sailor swimming in Havana Harbor was attacked by a shark. On the first strike all the flesh from his leg below the calf was torn away, on the second his foot was bitten off at the ankle, and a third assault is about to begin. It is a moment of terror. Will the youth be dead before the boathook stops the shark?

Actually, the mutilated swimmer, Brook Watson, was rescued. He stumped on his wooden leg through a successful life to become a prominent merchant, Commissary General to the British armies in America, a member of Parliament, and Lord Mayor of London. The picture was commissioned to commemorate his survival, and ultimately willed to Christ's Hospital, a boys' school, in order, as a long inscription on the frame states, "that it might serve a most usefull Lesson to Youth." One must suppose the lesson Watson had in mind is the folly of bathing in the Caribbean. It is difficult to find any other message.

At the Royal Academy in 1778 the success of the painting was immediate. The *St. James Chronicle* said, "We heartily congratulate our Countrymen [*sic*. The War of Independence was still being fought] on a Genius, who bids fair to rival the great Masters of the Ancient Italian Schools." The comparison to Italian art is an astute one, for the pyramidal composition with its apex the top of the uplifted boathook is typical of the High Renaissance. Also, Copley probably learned how to achieve the recession into the picture, by a series of zigzagging diagonals, from his study of Italian painting.

Watson and the Shark was studiously prepared. Though Copley had never seen Havana, he must have studied engravings and maps. He has depicted Moro Castle on the right with some accuracy. Of the city itself he has shown the dome of the Cathedral and the Convent towers, all recorded in a drawing of 1762 by R. Bishop. Five detailed drawings and one oil sketch of the figures have also been preserved, and probably more have vanished. Copley made a careful replica, now in the Museum of Fine Arts in Boston. This he kept in his studio the rest of his life, and in 1782 he painted a small vertical version, now in the Detroit Institute of Arts. It is not surprising that he valued the painting greatly, for just as Stuart, four years later, was to be "suddenly lifted into fame by a single picture," *The Skater* (plate 546), so *Watson and the Shark* drew Copley "from silent insignificance to the beam of general notice." Thereafter for many years his success in England was assured.

Collections: Sir Brook Watson, London; Christ's Hospital, London. *Ferdinand Lammot Belin Fund*, 1963. Signed, and dated 1778. Canvas, 71¾ x 90½" (182.1 x 229.7 cm.).

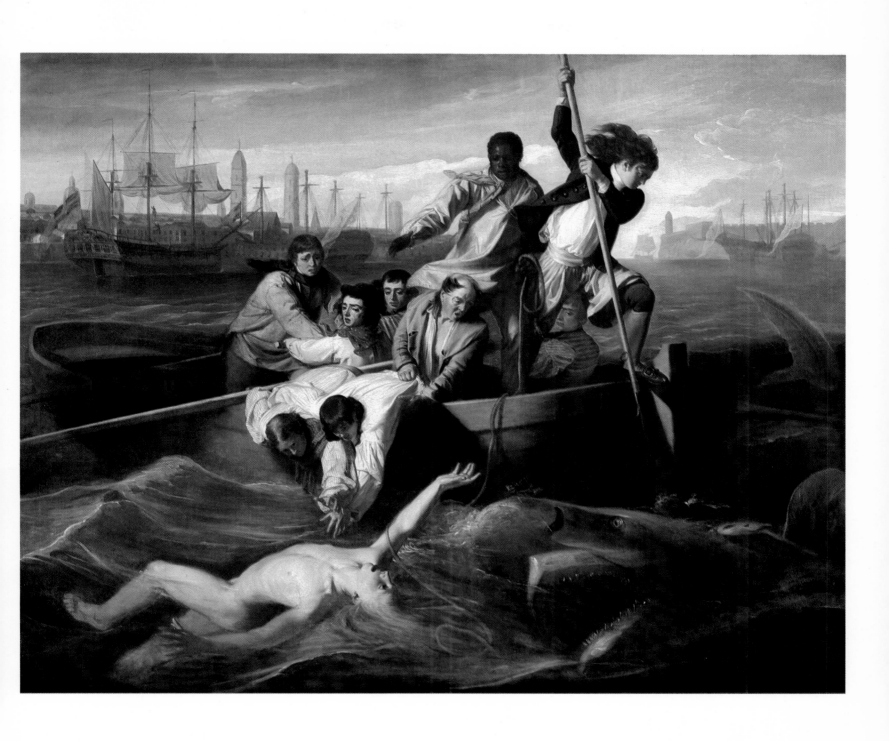

568 **John Singleton Copley** (American, 1738–1815): *The Death of the Earl of Chatham.* Signed, and dated 1779. Canvas, 20¾ x 25⅜″ (52.4 x 65 cm.). Gift of Mrs. Gordon Dexter

569 **John Singleton Copley**: *The Red Cross Knight.* 1793. Canvas, 84 x 107½″ (213.5 x 273 cm.). Gift of Mrs. Gordon Dexter

570 **John Singleton Copley**: *Baron Graham.* Signed. 1804. Canvas, 57¼ x 46⅞″ (145.3 x 118.9 cm.). Gift of Mrs. Gordon Dexter

571 **John Singleton Copley**: *Colonel Fitch and His Sisters.* 1800–1801. Canvas, 101½ x 134″ (259.1 x 340.2 cm.). Gift of Eleanor Lothrop, Gordon Abbott, and Katharine A. Batchelder

572 **Thomas Sully** (American, 1783–1872): *Lady with a Harp: Eliza Ridgely.* Signed (monogram), and dated 1818. Canvas, 84⅜ x 56⅛″ (214.6 x 142.6 cm.). Gift of Maude Monell Vetlesen

573 **Thomas Sully**: *Captain Charles Stewart.* 1811–12. Canvas, 93¼ x 58¾″ (237 x 149 cm.). Gift of Maude Monell Vetlesen

568

Copley's English period is exemplified by plates 568–71. In London the expatriated artist continued for a while to paint with the same observation of character which lends such distinction to his American portraits. But gradually he was forced to compromise, to adapt his style to the prevailing fashion of Reynolds, Gainsborough, and Lawrence. Often, he looked wistfully homeward, frequently inquiring whether it would be wise for him to return. Sully, by contrast, felt comfortable in the slick, English style, which became the vogue in America as sophistication increased.

569

570

571

572

573

John Trumbull

(AMERICAN, 1756–1843)

574   PATRICK TRACY

Detective work is one of the most amusing of curatorial activities, as I pointed out in the commentary to plate 245. The investigation of Trumbull's portrait of Captain Patrick Tracy is an example. It was once exhibited at the Museum of Fine Arts in Boston as by Copley. Then, in 1948, Theodore Sizer, the Trumbull authority, stumbled on the painter's own checklist. Under the year 1784 he found: "No. 15. Whole length of Mr. P. Tracy (father of Nat) leaning on an anchor—head copied—recd. 20 guineas." With this information the author of the portrait and the date it was begun were further established. But two curators of the Gallery were baffled by the words "head copied." Sizer had presumed that Trumbull had made a copy of the head, which, unless destroyed, should exist somewhere. A search for the picture, however, proved unavailing.

Then the detective work began in earnest. A family notebook was found with the entry: "Patrick Tracy, painted by John Trumbull. 20 gns. 1786." It was noted that the head was painted in the manner of Copley, whose work Trumbull at first imitated. Reynolds characterized this style as looking like "bent tin." Stung by this criticism, Trumbull changed almost overnight and began to paint more fluently. This occurred about 1785, a year after his arrival in London; and as Patrick Tracy's portrait reveals both methods, one in the head and the other in the body, it is logical to deduce that the painting was done over a period of time.

To understand the next deduction it is necessary to know something about the Tracy family in the eighteenth century. Patrick Tracy was a Massachusetts warehouse owner. His son, Nathaniel, Nat Tracy, as he was called, sailed on July 5, 1784, for England. But was his father also a passenger? Thomas Jefferson was on the boat on his way to his embassy in Paris, and in a letter to a friend shortly after his arrival he asks to be remembered to Nat, but no word of Patrick. Abigail Adams wrote at least seven letters in 1784 in which she speaks of seeing Nathaniel Tracy in London, but Patrick is never mentioned.

But if Patrick did not come to London, how then did he pose for Trumbull, who was in England during those years? The answer is that he did not. The mysterious words "head copied" probably mean that for Patrick Tracy's head Trumbull copied someone else's painting, perhaps a miniature brought to England by Nathaniel. "20 gns. 1786" indicates the painting was delivered that year. Thus Trumbull seems to have had the portrait in his studio for two years, which would explain the discrepancy in style between the head and the rest of the body. Like all denouements in good detective stories, the final explanation is simple.

Collections: Family of the sitter, Cambridge, Massachusetts. *Gift of Patrick T. Jackson*, 1964. Painted 1784–86. Canvas, 91½ x 52⅝" (232.5 x 133.7 cm.).

588

588 Attributed to Francisco de Goya (Spanish, c. 1827): *The Bullfight.* Canvas, 29 x 43¼" (73.9 x 109.9 cm.). Gift of Arthur Sachs

Francisco de Goya (Spanish, 1746–1828)

589 *The Bookseller's Wife.* Signed. c. 1805. Canvas, 43¼ x 30¾" (109.9 x 78.2 cm.). Gift of Mrs. P.H.B. Frelinghuysen

590 *The Duke of Wellington.* Probably 1812. Canvas, 41½ x 33" (105.5 x 83.7 cm.). Gift of Mrs. P.H.B. Frelinghuysen

591 *Don Bartolomé Sureda.* c. 1805. Canvas, 47⅛ x 31¼" (119.7 x 79.4 cm.). Gift of Mr. and Mrs. P.H.B. Frelinghuysen

592 *Señora Sabasa García.* c. 1806 or 1807. Canvas, 28 x 23" (71 x 58 cm.). Andrew W. Mellon Collection

589

590

591

592

The works reproduced here give some indication of the range of Goya's portraits. The Duke of Wellington has been transformed from an Englishman into a Spaniard, something he did not fancy. At the other end of the social scale is *The Bookseller's Wife* (plate 589), a handsome girl of the middle class, and a sitter more to Goya's taste. In between is Sabasa García, the niece of Spain's foreign minister. According to tradition, she entered Goya's studio while he was painting her uncle, and he was so struck by her dazzling beauty that he sent the foreign minister home and devoted himself to this portrait of a much more inspiring model.

John Constable

(BRITISH, 1776–1837)

593   WIVENHOE PARK, ESSEX

One function of art is to suggest a world perfectly attuned to human desires. During the Renaissance this earthly paradise was usually located in Greece, in a pastoral country known as Arcadia. Today the English countryside of a century or more ago has something of the same nostalgic appeal for us that the Hellenic world had for the humanists of the Renaissance. However, Arcadian shepherds are imaginary figures, whereas we know from a host of novelists how real was the English squirearchy, how actual its serene and stable environment.

"Arcadian realism" may seem a contradictory term, but it describes the charm of many of Constable's canvases. His scenes are filled with poetry, visions of the tranquil delight of an ideal rural existence. Yet, at the same time, they have an extraordinary reality, conveying as they do flashes of insight into the momentary moods of nature with that sensibility which is at the heart of modern landscape painting.

In a letter written in 1816 by Constable to his future wife, we sense how much owners of estates like Wivenhoe Park must have esteemed their possessions. "My dearest Love," Constable wrote, "I have been here since Monday and am as happy as I can be away from you. . . . I am going on very well with my pictures. The park is the most forward. The great difficulty has been to get so much in as they [the Rebows] wanted . . . so that my view comprehended too many degrees. But today I got over the difficulty and I begin to like it myself."

The wish of the owner to see as much as possible of his estate explains the unusually wide angle of the artist's view. But Constable, by the actuality he gives *Wivenhoe Park*, triumphs over this difficult composition and makes us agree with General Rebow that it would not be possible to see too much of so entrancing a scene. So there is no necessity for the twilight with which earlier landscapists gave a romantic aspect to their Arcadian scenery. Instead, Constable has found in a typical English day of scattered clouds and brilliant sunshine a new inspiration. He reveals "the infinite variety of natural appearances," and delights in the loveliness of flickering, sparkling light as it falls on leaves and grass and water. Painting was changed by such a fresh observation of landscape, just as poetry was changed at about the same time by Wordsworth's descriptions of nature.

Collection: Wivenhoe Park, Essex. *Widener Collection*, 1942. Painted 1816. Canvas, 22⅛ x 39⅞" (56.1 x 101.2 cm.).

594

594   **John Constable** (British, 1776–1837): *The White Horse*. Probably 1819. Canvas, 50 x 72" (127 x 183 cm.). Widener Collection

595   **John Constable**: *A View of Salisbury Cathedral*. Probably c. 1825. Canvas, 28¾ x 36" (73 x 91 cm.). Andrew W. Mellon Collection

596   **George Morland** (British, 1763–1804): *The End of the Hunt*. Signed. c. 1794. Canvas, 56 x 74" (142 x 188 cm.). Widener Collection

597   **John Ferneley** (British, 1782–1860): *In the Paddock*. c. 1830. Canvas, 36¼ x 60⅛" (92 x 152.6 cm.). Ailsa Mellon Bruce Collection

595

The White Horse, owned by the Frick Collection in New York City, is the first of the pictures Constable called his "six-footers." These canvases intended for the Royal Academy were preceded by paintings and drawings done directly from nature, followed by a full-scale sketch painted in the studio, and finally the picture to be exhibited—a procedure unusual if not unique among landscapists. Plate 594 reproduces the preliminary study for the Frick Collection painting. The final version was shown at the Academy in 1819 and bought by Archdeacon Fisher, the nephew of the Bishop of Salisbury and Constable's closest friend. Constable spent many weeks in the Bishop's palace painting his cathedral; one of the finest of these landscapes is plate 595.

596

597

Joseph Mallord William Turner

(BRITISH, 1775–1851)

598   MORTLAKE TERRACE

In 1827 Turner exhibited at the Royal Academy the picture reproduced here, which was titled *Mortlake Terrace, the Seat of William Moffatt, Esq.; Summer's Evening.* The preceding year he had exhibited the same site seen from the opposite direction and bathed in the light of an early summer morning, a picture now in the Frick Collection in New York. These two canvases were executed at a moment of significant change in Turner's style: a period when light and the rendering of a visible atmosphere were becoming his preoccupation, to the exclusion of his earlier interest in topography. Though he was doubtless fulfilling a commission in depicting Moffatt's garden terrace from opposite points and under contrasting illumination, Turner's whole effort was concentrated on the atmospheric envelope of the scene, on rendering the sun-filled mist of a hot afternoon. As one of the most astute of French critics, Théophile Thoré (W. Bürger), wrote in 1865, "Everything seems to be luminous with its own light and to throw its own rays and sparks. Claude, the master of luminosity, has never done anything so prodigious!"

How little Turner worried at this time about the design of his paintings is illustrated by the story of the dog on the parapet. The anecdote is recorded by Frederick Goodall, whose father engraved some of Turner's pictures. On Varnishing Day at the Royal Academy when Turner was out for lunch, Edwin Landseer, the animal painter, came in and noticed *Mortlake Terrace.* He saw at once that it needed an accent in the center, and so he cut out of paper a little dog and stuck it on the parapet. "When Turner returned," Goodall says, "he went up to the picture quite unconcernedly, never said a word, adjusted the little dog perfectly, and then varnished the paper and began painting it. And there it is to the present day." There is no doubt that the composition of the painting was saved by this accidental but highly successful collaboration, one of the most unusual in the history of art.

Collections: Perhaps William Moffatt, owner of Mortlake Terrace; Joseph Hamatt; Rev. Edward J. Daniel; Thomas Creswick, R.A.; E. B. Fripp; Samuel Ashton; Thomas Ashton; Mrs. Elizabeth Gair Ashton. *Andrew W. Mellon Collection,* 1937. Painted c. 1826. Canvas, 36¼ x 48⅛" (92 x 122.2 cm.).

599

Of these six pictures only *The Junction of the Thames and the Medway* belongs to Turner's first period. The change in his style over the years is extraordinary, and is well illustrated by the other reproductions. The somber colors of the early work are transformed into irridescent hues, the massive volumes of the waves to shimmering, glassy water, the dark, windswept clouds to dazzling light and translucent atmosphere. Turner in his paintings gradually transmutes the density of matter into the fluidity of air. His late pictures have been aptly described as "painted with tinted steam."

600

601

602

603

604

Joseph Mallord William Turner (British, 1775–1851)

599 *The Junction of the Thames and the Medway.* c. 1805/8. Canvas, 42¾ × 56½″ (108.8 × 143.7 cm.). Widener Collection

600 *Keelmen Heaving in Coals by Moonlight.* Signed with initials. Probably 1835. Canvas, 36¼ × 48¼″ (92.3 × 122.8 cm.). Widener Collection

601 *The Dogana and Santa Maria della Salute, Venice.* Signed with initials. Probably 1843. Canvas, 24⅜ × 36⅝″ (62 × 93 cm.). Given in memory of Governor Alvan T. Fuller by the Fuller Foundation

602 *Van Tromp's Shallop.* c. 1832. Canvas, 36⅜ × 48¼″ (92.3 × 122.5 cm.). Ailsa Mellon Bruce Collection

603 *Venice: Dogana and San Giorgio Maggiore.* Probably 1834. Canvas, 36 × 48″ (91.5 × 122 cm.). Widener Collection

604 *Approach to Venice.* c. 1843. Canvas, 24½ × 37″ (62 × 94 cm.). Andrew W. Mellon Collection

French School

XIX CENTURY

Jean-Baptiste-Camille Corot

(FRENCH, 1796–1875)

619 AGOSTINA

Time may prove Corot to have been the most important painter of the nineteenth century. Certainly the admiration he has aroused in other artists has been unceasing, and his influence even on contemporary artists like Picasso, immense. He was one of the few artists of recent times to excel not only in landscape but also in figure painting, of which *Agostina* is an outstanding example. Here he combines an alertness of vision with a profound knowledge of Renaissance style. This Italian peasant girl, who stands with unself-conscious detachment, evokes the heroic women of Piero della Francesca. But she is also of her own century, for she has been observed by the artist with an enamored and penetrating scrutiny which brings her much closer to actuality, to the living model, than her fifteenth-century forebears.

The plastic values which distinguish Corot's best landscapes are due in part to his constant study of human form. This is of importance in understanding his work. There is a profound difference in style between those landscape painters who are either incapable of drawing the human form, or draw it in a perfunctory way, and those whose art is based on a knowledge of the body. In one category we have artists like Perugino, Claude Lorrain, most of the Dutch landscape painters with the significant exception of Rembrandt, and, in the nineteenth century, Turner and Monet, among others. All these artists could draw the human figure after a fashion, but none of them was a figure painter of any consequence. In their landscapes we find that such effects as the sweep of distance and the play of light are stressed, but in the beautiful iridescent spaces they create, everything is insubstantial, intangible. The other category, those artists like Corot who have mastered the hollows and bosses of the human form, its plastic shape, seem able to translate this knowledge of mass and volume into hills and rocks and trees. Painters like Rubens, Poussin, Rembrandt, Cézanne, and, at his best, Corot are intent on rendering the plastic character of nature. They model trees and rocks with the same studious gravity they show toward the human body. They seem to be in search of the tendons and sinews of nature.

Collections: Breysse, Paris; Faure, Paris; Paton, Paris; Bernheim-Jeune, Paris. *Chester Dale Collection*, 1962. Signed. Painted probably 1866. Canvas, 52¼ x 38⅜″ (132.8 x 97.6 cm.).

620

621

622

Jean-Baptiste-Camille Corot (French, 1796–1875)

620 *Italian Peasant Boy.* Signed. 1825/26. Canvas, 10 x 12⅞" (25.4 x 32.6 cm.). Chester Dale Collection

621 *Gypsy Girl with Mandolin.* Signed. Probably c. 1870/75. Canvas, 25 x 20" (63.9 x 51 cm.). Gift of Count Cecil Pecci-Blunt

622 *The Artist's Studio.* Signed. c. 1855/60. Wood, 24⅜ x 15¾" (62 x 40 cm.). Widener Collection

623 *Portrait of a Young Girl.* Signed, and dated 1859. Canvas, 10¾ x 9⅛" (27.4 x 23.2 cm.). Chester Dale Collection

624 *Italian Girl.* Signed. c. 1871/72. Canvas, 25⅝ x 21⅝" (65.1 x 52.4 cm.). Gift of the Avalon Foundation

625 *Madame Stumpf and Her Daughter.* Signed. 1872. Canvas, 41¾ x 29¼" (106 x 74.2 cm.). Ailsa Mellon Bruce Collection

626 *River Scene with Bridge.* Signed, and dated 1834. Canvas, 9⅞ x 13⅜" (25 x 33.8 cm.). Ailsa Mellon Bruce Collection

623

624

Corot was extensively collected in the United States, and it is not surprising that the National Gallery's collection of his works is among the richest outside the Louvre. Looking at the pictures reproduced here offers an opportunity to measure Corot's monumentality and plasticity against the great Renaissance masters, and also to judge the precision of his observation of the subject, which, in the *Portrait of a Young Girl* (plate 623) and *The Artist's Studio* (plate 622), challenges Vermeer in faultless modeling and accurate rendering of light.

625

626

Jean-Baptiste-Camille Corot

(FRENCH, 1796–1875)

627   A VIEW NEAR VOLTERRA

A View near Volterra belongs to Corot's earlier style. It is dated 1838, four years after he had visited the Etruscan site of Volterra. It is therefore a *souvenir d'Italie*, an evocation of a mood the artist had felt when he entered that strange, wild country, that *pays magnifique*, as he described it in his sketchbook. But the painting itself was based on careful studies and sketches made at the time, and it seems to fulfill the profession of a faith which Corot expressed in his youth when he wrote, *"Il ne faut laisser d'indécision dans aucune chose."* Consequently, we feel in the scene itself the same sense of a vivid reality which the artist experienced as he sketched one day in the early summer sunlight, yet we also feel that the emotion conveyed is an "emotion recollected in tranquillity," a mood revived long after the event by some nostalgia, some longing for the olive greens and soft, luminous skies of Italy. This has given to the painting qualities both of timelessness and of actuality, qualities which Corot himself seems to have appreciated; for we find that he often returned in this way to scenes he had enjoyed on his early Italian journeys. Led by these recollections, he painted from memory again and again the sights of classical civilization, the world of Horace and Vergil, whose feelings for nature were so akin to his own.

It is curious, however, how little these superb paintings of Italy were appreciated during Corot's lifetime. He sent a *View of Volterra* to the Salon of 1838, doubtless the picture now in the Timken Art Gallery, San Diego, and the critics found it cold, timid in execution, without distinction or brilliance. Probably they would have been equally critical of the Chester Dale picture, which was painted the same year. They failed to see the real importance of these paintings: that they were remarkable revivals of the classical tradition, and that they illustrated what Cézanne had in mind when he is quoted as saying, *"Imaginez Poussin refait entièrement sur nature."* For Corot's landscapes of this period possess the formal beauty of Poussin's style without his artificiality, his declamatory effects, his suggestion of stage scenery. It was the blindness of the critics, year after year, which caused Corot to compromise and to give the classical style a sentimental interpretation. But as the familiar gray mist spread through his landscapes, his extraordinary gift for the rendering of plastic volume disappeared.

Collection: Baronne Thénard, Paris. *Chester Dale Collection*, 1962. Signed, and dated 1838. Canvas, 27⅜ x 37½" (69.5 x 95.2 cm.).

628

Jean-Baptiste-Camille Corot (French, 1796–1875)

628 *Forest of Fontainebleau.* Signed. c. 1830. Canvas, 69⅛ x 95½" (175.6 x 242.6 cm.). Chester Dale Collection

629 *The Eel Gatherers.* Signed. c. 1860/65. Canvas, 23¾ x 32" (60 x 81 cm.). Gift of Mr. and Mrs. P.H.B. Frelinghuysen in memory of her father and mother, Mr. and Mrs. H. O. Havemeyer

630 *The Forest of Coubron.* Signed, and dated 1872. Canvas, 37¾ x 30" (96 x 76 cm.). Widener Collection

631 *Rocks in the Forest of Fontainebleau.* Signed. 1860/65. Canvas, 18 x 23" (45.9 x 58.5 cm.). Chester Dale Collection

632 *View near Epernon.* Signed. 1850/60. Canvas, 12¾ x 21" (32.5 x 53.5 cm.). Widener Collection

633 *Ville d' Avray.* Signed. c. 1867/70. Canvas, 19⅜ x 25⅝" (49.2 x 65.3 cm.). Gift of Count Cecil Pecci-Blunt

634 *River View.* Signed. Probably c. 1870. Wood, 12⅝ x 16⅜" (32.3 x 41.8 cm.). Gift of R. Horace Gallatin

629

630

631

632

633

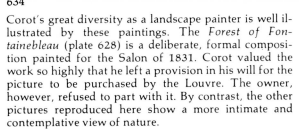

634

Corot's great diversity as a landscape painter is well illustrated by these paintings. The *Forest of Fontainebleau* (plate 628) is a deliberate, formal composition painted for the Salon of 1831. Corot valued the work so highly that he left a provision in his will for the picture to be purchased by the Louvre. The owner, however, refused to part with it. By contrast, the other pictures reproduced here show a more intimate and contemplative view of nature.

Honoré Daumier

(FRENCH, 1808–1879)

635   ADVICE TO A YOUNG ARTIST

Corot's figure style influenced the work of his close companion, Daumier. The two artists had much in common—both sought and found the true tradition of painting in the Italian masters. Balzac said of Daumier, "He is a man who has something of Michelangelo in his blood." But this great talent had to be lavished on caricatures for various periodicals. Poverty left Daumier little time for painting, and with failing eyesight he could not draw and sell his famous cartoons fast enough to pay his rent, even for the dilapidated cottage he occupied at Valmondois. But he was fortunate in one thing—in friendship. Corot secretly bought Daumier's house, and wrote him as follows: "My old comrade—I had a little house for which I had no use at Valmondois near the Isle-Adam. The idea came into my head of offering it to you, and as I think it is a good idea, I have placed it in your name at the notary's. It is not for you that I do this, it is merely to annoy your landlord." It was a simple gesture, and it gave Daumier a few serene and tranquil years. But it meant that Corot painted fewer Agostinas and more misty lakes, fewer masterpieces and more potboilers. In return for this sacrifice, a few paintings like this, which once belonged to Corot, were all that Daumier could give his old friend, but into their execution he poured all the brilliant genius that a lifetime of poverty could not destroy.

Collections: J.-B.-C. Corot, Paris; Adolphe A. Tavernier, Paris; Cronier, Paris; Goerg, Rheims. *Gift of Duncan Phillips*, 1941. Signed. Painted probably after 1860. Canvas, 16⅛ x 12⅞" (41 x 33 cm.).

636

637

638

Honoré Daumier (French, 1808–1879)

636 *The Beggars*. Signed. c. 1845. Canvas, 23½ x 29⅛″ (59.7 x 74 cm.). Chester Dale Collection

637 *French Theater*. Signed. c. 1857/60. Wood, 10¼ x 13¼″ (25.9 x 35 cm.). Chester Dale Collection

638 *Wandering Saltimbanques*. c. 1847/50. Wood, 12⅞ x 9¾″ (32.6 x 24.8 cm.). Chester Dale Collection

639 *In Church*. Probably c. 1860. Wood, 6 x 8⅝″ (15 x 22 cm.). Rosenwald Collection

Daumier was the greatest lithographer and social critic of the nineteenth century. He had a genius for gesture and facial expression. In *French Theater* he contrasts the restrained interest of the prosperous family in the foreground with the excited eagerness of those in the cheaper seats. In *The Beggars* and *Wandering Saltimbanques* he shows by the postures and movements of the figures the resigned weariness of these impoverished and exhausted members of society.

639

Jean-François Millet

(FRENCH, 1814-1875)

640   LECONTE DE LISLE

Artists' reputations are in a state of constant revision, but none has been more mutable than that of Jean-François Millet. Although he lived to see himself the most famous of the painters who worked at Barbizon, during much of his life he was on the verge of penury. As a result of privation, he was subject all his life to fearful headaches and pains in his eyes. But he never complained. "Art is no diversion," he told a friend; "it is a conflict in which one is crushed." Yet Millet was responsible for one of the most popular pictures of the nineteenth century, *The Angelus*, a painting underappreciated today.

Before he went to Barbizon and attained his vast popularity, Millet executed a few portraits. These were painted as potboilers, and there is no evidence that he especially valued them; but in recent years they have been more sought after than the paintings which gained him fame. In many ways they are better than his peasant subjects, and some even rank among the finest achievements of nineteenth-century painting. Since color is less important in portraiture than in figure painting or landscape, Millet's outstanding weakness is here less apparent. Also, while his portraits show his magnificent power of construction, they are free from his subjective sadness, from that "dark pleasure of a melancholy heart" upon which he was wont to be overinsistent.

Because of its subject, the painting reproduced here is the most interesting of the few portraits by Millet. It was a happy coincidence that brought together these two young men of genius, Millet and Leconte de Lisle, one an unknown artist, the other a still inexperienced poet. Leconte de Lisle was born in 1818 in the West Indies, the son of a plantation owner. His father sent him to Brittany to be educated. Between 1837 and 1843 he lived with his uncle at Dinan and attended the University of Rennes. During those years and before he returned to the West Indies he apparently met Millet, who was also in his twenties and who spent the summers in Brittany with his family. There is a letter in which Leconte de Lisle mentions sightseeing with "three landscapists from Paris." Whether Millet was one of these artists, or however they met, the young poet proved an attractive subject. He appears a romantic figure as he stands with one arm resting on a wall, which bears the proud inscription *F. Millet*. This is one of the earliest commissions Millet executed, and it is the first important portrait we have of Leconte de Lisle. Thus the painting is doubly precious, as a portrait of exceptional beauty and as the likeness of one of the geniuses of French literature, whose poem *Le Manchy* Baudelaire considered a masterpiece without an equal.

Collections: Henri Rouart; Ernest Rouart, Paris. *Chester Dale Collection*, 1962. Signed. Painted probably 1842. Canvas, 46⅛ x 32″ (117.1 x 81.2 cm.).

Eugène Boudin

(FRENCH, 1824–1898)

641 THE BEACH AT VILLERVILLE

In a short autobiographical piece Boudin stated, to the consternation of his admirers, that his principal object had been for many years "to please the sovereign public." During the 1860s he discovered a genre which did just that: seascapes of fashionable bathing places adorned with a frieze of small, modishly dressed figures. These canvases evoke an enchanting past, the world Proust was to describe a few decades later. In the painting reproduced here, it is a late summer day in 1864, and a group of men and women, who seem to have stepped without change of apparel from boulevard to beach, stroll about or sit on stiff chairs. They have wrapped themselves in coats and capes, for the days are drawing in and there is a cool breeze from the sea. Charming as we find this diminutive society, to Boudin it was merely a means to an end, a way to make his marvelous renderings of sea and sky more palatable to collectors, and in this he succeeded. As he wrote a friend in 1863, "My little ladies on the seashore are very popular. Some people even think there is a vein of gold in these subjects ready to be exploited."

But Boudin came to despise himself for its exploitation. The turning point was a trip to Brittany in 1867 to visit his wife's relations. On his return he wrote the same friend, "Having just passed a month among people who on black bread and water devote their lives to rude labor in the fields, one feels . . . ashamed to paint these idlers, this band of gilded parasites, who seem to have such a triumphant air." Although he continued to depict an occasional beach scene, his heart was not in it, and after 1870 he abandoned his "gilded parasites" altogether and devoted the rest of his life to views of harbors and shipping.

Unfortunately, when Boudin exchanged the idlers of the seashore for the toilers of the sea, he lost his vein of gold. The treasure he had found, though he did not realize it, had been aesthetic as well as commercial. For the poetry, the evocation in a canvas like *The Beach at Villerville* lies in the very incongruity of these fashionable people seen against the majestic setting of sea and sky. They suggest an audience come to the edge of the world to watch a drama of cosmic splendor, which in the end bores them with its magnificence. But our sympathies are touched, our hearts moved by these spectators. The infinite radiance of sky, streaked by the setting sun and hung with ominous clouds, lends a melancholy poetry to their transience. The tragedy is that the painter himself saw only "a hideous masquerade" where in reality he had expressed the poignancy of the transitory, the pathos of the evanescent. Boudin was a victim of social consciousness, perhaps the first but certainly not the last in the history of art.

Collections: Henry C. and Martha B. Angell, Boston; Museum of Fine Arts, Boston. *Chester Dale Collection*, 1962. Signed, and dated 1864. Canvas, 18 x 30"(45.7 x 76.3 cm.).

445

642

643

Return of the Terre-Neuvier depicts the unloading of a fishing schooner which has arrived in France from the Grand Banks. To facilitate the task of transporting the salted fish from the ship's hold to the carts, it was the practice to run the ship aground and unload when the tide receded. Here Boudin is painting the workers he admired. The other reproductions, except for plates 645 and 648, show the "gilded parasites" he despised.

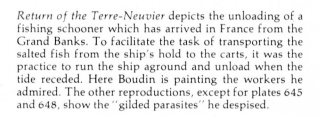

644   645

646

Eugène Boudin   (French, 1824–1898)

642   *Return of the Terre-Neuvier.* Signed, and dated 1875. Canvas, 29 x 39⅝″ (73.5 x 100.7 cm.). Chester Dale Collection

643   *The Beach.* Signed, and dated 1887. Wood, 4¼ x 10″ (10.9 x 25.4 cm.). Ailsa Mellon Bruce Collection

644   *On the Jetty.* 1869/70. Wood, 7¼ x 10¾″ (18.4 x 27.3 cm.). Ailsa Mellon Bruce Collection

645   *Washerwomen on the Beach of Étretat.* Signed, and dated 1894. Wood, 14⅝ x 21⅝″ (37.2 x 54.9 cm.). Ailsa Mellon Bruce Collection

646   *Beach at Trouville.* Signed. 1864/65. Wood, 10¼ x 18⅞″ (25.9 x 47.9 cm.). Ailsa Mellon Bruce Collection

647   *On the Beach, Trouville.* Signed, and dated 1887. Wood, 7½ x 12⅞″ (18.4 x 32.7 cm.). Chester Dale Collection

648   *Women on the Beach at Berck.* Signed, and dated 1881. Wood, 9¾ x 14¼″ (24.8 x 36.2 cm.). Ailsa Mellon Bruce Collection

649   *Yacht Basin at Trouville-Deauville.* Probably 1895/96. Wood, 18 x 14⅝″ (45.8 x 37.1 cm.). Ailsa Mellon Bruce Collection

647

648

649

650

651

Impressionism in its love of fugitive atmospheric
effects looks back to the out-of-door paintings of
Boudin, and in its absorption in the actuality of the
scene invokes the realism of Courbet. The landscapes
reproduced here show how carefully Courbet observed
a beach, a grotto, a forest. When working from a
human model, he painted with equal realism. There is
no idealization in the commonplace features of the
woman reading (plate 652) or in the oxlike stolidity of
Portrait of a Young Girl (plate 651).

652

653

654

655

Gustave Courbet (French, 1819–1877)

650 *The Stream.* Signed, and dated 1855. Canvas, 41 x 54″ (104.1 x 137.1 cm.). Gift of Mr. and Mrs. P.H.B. Frelinghuysen in memory of her father and mother, Mr. and Mrs. H.O. Havemeyer

651 *Portrait of a Young Girl.* Signed, and dated 1857. Canvas, 23¾ x 20⅝″ (60.4 x 52.4 cm.). Chester Dale Collection

652 *A Young Woman Reading.* Signed. 1868–72. Canvas, 23⅝ x 29¾″ (60 x 72.9 cm.). Chester Dale Collection

653 *La Grotte de la Loue.* Signed. c. 1865. Canvas, 38¾ x 51⅜″ (98.4 x 130.4 cm.). Gift of Charles L. Lindemann

654 *Beach in Normandy.* c. 1869. Canvas, 24⅛ x 35½″ (61.3 x 90.2 cm.). Chester Dale Collection

655 *Boats on a Beach, Étretat.* Signed. 1869. Canvas, 25½ x 36¼″ (64.9 x 92 cm.). Gift of the W. Averell Harriman Foundation in memory of Marie N. Harriman

656 *Landscape near the Banks of the Indre.* Signed, and dated 1856. Canvas, 24 x 28⅞″ (60.8 x 73.3 cm.). Gift of the W. Averell Harriman Foundation in memory of Marie N. Harriman

657 **Charles-François Daubigny** (French, 1817–1878): *The Farm.* Signed, and dated 1855. Canvas, 20¼ x 32″ (51.4 x 81.2 cm.). Chester Dale Collection

656

657

449

Edouard Manet

(FRENCH, 1832–1883)

658   THE OLD MUSICIAN

The principal pleasure to be gained from Manet comes from the beauty of his brushwork. He mixed on his palette the exact tone he needed and with swift and certain dexterity delineated on the canvas each area of light and shadow. In *The Old Musician* this virtuosity of handling can be seen most clearly in the trenchant strokes that define the folds in the shirt and trousers of the boy with the straw hat, or in the more caressing feather touch on the shawl of the girl holding the baby.

Manet's method of direct painting caused him to suppress the transitional tones of modeling which particularly suggest volume. Like Velázquez, who was also a master of brushwork, he chose an illumination which would flatten form as much as possible. Thus the light falls directly on the figures from behind the artist's head, and the shadows are reduced to a minimum. Through this arbitrary elimination of shadow Manet was able to state local color more freely. He attained, especially in such early works as *The Old Musician*, the most subtle harmonies of yellowish white and faded blue, here contrasted with warm browns and blacks and soft grays. This color scheme was as far as possible from the high intensities and broken colors of the Impressionists, which he adopted at the end of his life.

For Manet, in spite of a strong instinct for the traditional, became a leader of the Impressionists' revolt. The public attacked his pictures, as they attacked the other Impressionists, but less because of his method of painting than because of a certain outre quality in his subject matter. In *The Old Musician*, for instance, what is the meaning of the brooding octogenarian on the extreme right, who is bisected so unconventionally by the frame? Perhaps he was put there simply to balance the composition, for Théodore Duret, who knew Manet well, said he painted this troupe of beggars merely because it pleased him to preserve a record of them and for no other reason. And yet one senses a significance which just escapes, a hidden meaning which is baffling. In Manet's pictures these recurrent and tantalizing affectations infuriated his contemporaries and were in part the reason he never attained the popular admiration which he so desperately desired.

Collections: Manet family, Paris; Prince de Wagram, Paris; P. R. Pearson, Paris; Kunsthistorisches Museum, Vienna. *Chester Dale Collection*, 1962. Signed, and dated 1862. Canvas, 73¾ x 98" (187.5 x 249.1 cm.).

664

The still life by Manet reproduced in plate 665 cannot but stir the gastric juices of any oyster lover. If, on the other hand, one is a racing enthusiast, plate 664 will inevitably arouse the excitement of a close finish. Similarly, the viewer can almost smell the flowers in the vase in plate 667. Thus, in the originals of these reproductions, one experiences Manet's wonderful ability to create empathy between spectator and painting. But empathy is impossible for the spectator, as it was for the portraitist, confronted with the blank, bovine expression of Madame Michel-Lévy (plate 668). Here virtuosity in the use of pastel and paint together is the chief fascination.

666

665

667

Edouard Manet (French, 1832–1883)

664 *At the Races.* Signed. c. 1875. Wood, 5 x 8½"
(12.5 x 21.5 cm.). Widener Collection

665 *Oysters.* Signed. 1862. Canvas, 15⅜ x 18⅜"
(39.1 x 46.7 cm.). Gift of the Adele R. Levy Fund, Inc.

666 *Portrait of a Lady.* c. 1879. Wood, 5¾ x 4½" (15
x 11.5 cm.). Gift of Mrs. Charles S. Carstairs

667 *Flowers in a Crystal Vase.* Signed. c. 1882. Canvas, 12⅞ x 9⅝" (32.6 x 24.3 cm.). Ailsa Mellon Bruce
Collection

668 *Madame Michel-Lévy.* Signed, and dated 1882.
Pastel and oil on canvas, 29¼ x 20⅛" (74.4 x 51 cm.).
Chester Dale Collection

668

Edouard Manet

(FRENCH, 1832–1883)

669   GARE SAINT-LAZARE

Why does this painting convey such a sense of gaiety? There is, of course, the marvelous observation of the little sleeping dog, one of the most enchanting puppies in art. There is also the pretty Victorine Meurend, whose beauty is more familiar to us from pictures of ten years earlier, *Olympia* and *Le Déjeuner sur l'herbe*. Dressed or undressed she is a joy, delighting us with the wonderfully candid gaze of a woman to whom shyness is unknown. But the real source of our pleasure, the heroine of the picture, is the little girl, the daughter of Manet's friend Alphonse Hirsch. From the way she holds the railing, from the angle of her head, from the beautiful line made by the curve of her neck, we know the intensity of her scrutiny. We share the excitement we felt in childhood at seeing trains and steam and smoke. Manet knew better than anyone else how to catch the fugitive charm of everyday life. He was a master of the informal composition. He had a keen sense of the immediacy this type of design can convey. The *Gare Saint-Lazare* is a family snapshot. But this moment of time, made timeless, is held with a beauty and intensity far beyond the possibilities of photography.

The painting was admitted, somewhat unexpectedly, to the Salon of 1874, where it aroused more protests than praise. It was the first large canvas Manet had executed mostly out-of-doors, perhaps acknowledging thereby his association with the younger Impressionists, Monet and Renoir especially, who had for some time been working in the open air. Thus it carried into the citadel of the official Salon the banner of their revolt.

Collections: Jean-Baptiste Faure, Paris; Havemeyer family, New York. *Gift of Horace Havemeyer in memory of his mother, Louisine W. Havemeyer, 1956.* Signed, and dated 1873. Canvas, 36¾ x 45⅛" (93.3 x 114.5 cm.).

Berthe Morisot

(FRENCH, 1841–1895)

670   THE MOTHER AND SISTER OF THE ARTIST

The question is constantly asked, "How should my son [or daughter] learn to be a painter?" When Mme Morisot put this question to Guichard about her daughter, Berthe, then age fifteen, the painter answered, "The first thing to do, Madame, is to get your daughter permission to work in the Louvre, where I shall give my instruction in front of the masters." The answer was not surprising, for the Louvre was the traditional art school of all French painters of ability. There, as Ingres said, they sought to draw out from the Old Masters, *"le suc de la plante,"* that quintessential quality which is in all *great* art. This intelligent use of the Louvre explains to a large extent the superiority of French painting in the last century.

Berthe Morisot was an assiduous copyist. She began with the Old Masters and ended with Corot, whose work she had the advantage of discussing with the artist himself. In the Louvre she often saw Manet, the brother of her future husband. During the winter before the outbreak of the Franco-Prussian War, when she was just twenty-nine, she completed the portrait of her mother and sister and asked Manet to come to her studio to give her a criticism. He was delighted with the picture, but suggested a few changes and then seized the brush and spent the afternoon retouching it. His brushstrokes are still visible in the somewhat heavier touch around the eye and mouth of Mme Morisot and the thicker impasto of her dress. While Manet was working, the van to take the picture to the Salon arrived, and Berthe Morisot, though she was angry, could do nothing but send the painting as it was. Fortunately, the canvas was received with enthusiasm by many artists, especially by Fantin-Latour, and the painter herself became reconciled to the changes.

Among women Berthe Morisot's only peer was Mary Cassatt, and they had much in common. Both tried to fashion a modern style from a lifelong study of the masters of the past, one with the guidance of Manet, the other with the help of Degas. Berthe Morisot showed a piquant delicacy joined to a Parisian chic, Mary Cassatt a mastery of formal design combined with good taste. It is remarkable that the nineteenth century should have given us two women of such genius in art. How many, one wonders, will the twentieth century produce?

Collections: Mme Pontillon and Mme Forget (sister and niece of the artist), Paris. *Chester Dale Collection*, 1962. Painted during the winter of 1869–70. Canvas, 39¾ x 32¼" (101 x 82 cm.).

671

672

673

674

Until the twentieth century, the handicaps faced by a woman who wished to be a professional artist were nearly insurmountable. The whole social structure was against her. But as Berthe Morisot proves, there is a vision of the external world which is entirely feminine. These pictures could never have been painted by a man!

675

676

Berthe Morisot   (French, 1841–1895)

671   *The Sisters.* Signed. 1869. Canvas, 20½ x 32"
(52.1 x 81.3 cm.). Gift of Mrs. Charles S. Carstairs

672   *The Artist's Daughter with a Parakeet.* Signed.
1890. Canvas, 25¾ x 20⅝" (65.6 x 52.4 cm.). Chester
Dale Collection

673   *In the Dining Room.* Signed. 1886. Canvas, 24⅛
x 19¾" (61.3 x 50 cm.). Chester Dale Collection

674   *The Artist's Sister at a Window.* 1869. Canvas,
21⅝ x 18¼" (54.8 x 46.3 cm.). Ailsa Mellon Bruce
Collection

675   *The Harbor at Lorient.* Signed. 1869. Canvas,
17½ x 28¾" (43.5 x 73 cm.). Ailsa Mellon Bruce Collection

676   *Young Woman with a Straw Hat.* 1884. Canvas,
21⅞ x 18⅜" (55.5 x 46.7 cm.). Ailsa Mellon Bruce
Collection

677   *Girl in a Boat with Geese.* Signed. c. 1889. Canvas, 25¾ x 21½" (65.4 x 54.6 cm.). Ailsa Mellon Bruce
Collection

677

Auguste Renoir

(FRENCH, 1841–1919)

678   A GIRL WITH A WATERING CAN

A Girl with a Watering Can, painted in 1876, is one of the most popular pictures in the National Gallery. It is evocative of sunlight and childhood, springtime and the breath of flowers, images and sensations which are in themselves attractive. But these are not enough. To be great a painting must have more than charm of subject matter; it must have certain aesthetic values as well. In the case of *A Girl with a Watering Can*, these values consist largely in the relationship of figure and landscape, in the way the two are fused by ingenious repetition of colors and a consistent treatment of detail. The whole picture is made up of a web of brilliantly colored brushstrokes, which from a distance are seen to be a child, roses, grass, a garden path. The little girl seems to merge with her surroundings, to become one with the variegated tones of nature. This creates a mysterious sense of interrelations, as though one substance permeated humanity, vegetation, and earth.

The unity of figure and background Renoir extends to a psychological unity between himself and the child. The scene is depicted from the level of the little girl's own vision, so that her outlook on nature is suggested. Thus the garden becomes the world seen through her eyes, narrow and circumscribed. By accepting her scale of observation, Renoir evokes, in an almost unique way, memories of childhood. This mood, this "remembrance of things past," is intensified by the pleasure of the painter in his subject, by the spontaneity and gaiety of his treatment of the scene. Renoir, in canvases like this, seems almost a pagan Fra Angelico. "I arrange my subject as I want it," he once said, "and then I go ahead and paint it like a child." He loved bright colors, joyous and pretty human beings, and nature drenched in sunshine. He was a painter moved to lyrical ecstasy by the beauty of the everyday world. His great gift was to catch on canvas

> A strain of the earth's sweet being in the beginning . . .
> Innocent mind and Mayday in girl and boy.

Collections: Paul Bérard, Paris; A. Rosenberg, Paris; Prince de Wagram, Paris. *Chester Dale Collection*, 1962. Signed, and dated 1876. Canvas, 39½ x 28¾" (100 x 73 cm.).

679

680

681

Auguste Renoir   (French, 1841–1919)

679   *Mademoiselle Sicot.* Signed, and dated 1865. Canvas, 45¾ x 35¼" (116 x 89.5 cm.). Chester Dale Collection

680   *Woman with a Cat.* Signed. c. 1875. Canvas, 22 x 18¼" (56 x 46.4 cm.). Gift of Mr. and Mrs. Benjamin E. Levy

681   *The Dancer.* Signed, and dated 1874. Canvas, 56⅛ x 37⅛" (142.5 x 94.5 cm.). Widener Collection

682   *Madame Henriot.* Signed. c. 1876. Canvas, 26 x 19⅝" (65.9 x 49.8 cm.). Gift of the Adele R. Levy Fund, Inc.

683   *Marie Murer.* Signed. 1877. Canvas, oval, 26⅝ x 22½" (67.6 x 57.1 cm.). Chester Dale Collection

684   *Oarsmen at Chatou.* Signed, and dated 1879. Canvas, 32 x 39½" (81.3 x 100.3 cm.). Gift of Sam A. Lewisohn

685   *Caroline Rémy ("Séverine").* Signed. c. 1885. Pastel, 24½ x 20" (62.3 x 50.8 cm.). Chester Dale Collection

682

683

685

The important canvases by Renoir reproduced in this volume illustrate fully the artist's career, although they do not represent entirely the Renoir collection of the National Gallery of Art. Renoir was the most attractive of the Impressionist painters, and more of his work is to be seen in the United States than anywhere else in the world. The earliest of his pictures in Washington is the portrait of Mlle Sicot (plate 679). His training as a decorator of porcelain is evident in the delicate nuances of color in the flesh tones of the face. The sitter, an actress of the Comédie Francaise, was astute enough to recognize Renoir's genius when he was only twenty-four. The other portraits of women were also of friends: Marie Murer (plate 683), the half-sister of a pastry cook who owned a small, flourishing restaurant and was one of Renoir's chief backers while he was still unknown; Caroline Rémy ("Séverine") (plate 685), a writer and feminist who also supported his early endeavors; Madame Henriot (plate 682), another enchanting actress of the Comédie Francaise; and Madame Hagan (plate 689), the mistress of one of his first patrons, Caillebotte. All these women are beautiful and charming in different ways.

684

686

687

688

Auguste Renoir (French, 1841–1919)

686 *Girl with a Hoop.* Signed, and dated 1885. Canvas, 49½ x 30⅛" (125.7 x 76.6 cm.). Chester Dale Collection

687 *Young Woman Braiding Her Hair.* Signed, and dated 1876. Canvas, 21⅞ x 18¼" (55.6 x 46.4 cm.). Ailsa Mellon Bruce Collection

688 *Madame Monet and Her Son.* 1874. Canvas, 19⅞ x 26¾" (50.4 x 68 cm.). Ailsa Mellon Bruce Collection

689 *Madame Hagen.* Signed, and dated 1883. Canvas, 36¼ x 28¾" (92 x 73 cm.). Gift of Angelika Wertheim Frink

690 *Woman Standing by a Tree.* Signed with initials. 1866. Canvas, 9⅞ x 6¼" (25.2 x 15.9 cm.). Ailsa Mellon Bruce Collection

691 *Child with Brown Hair.* Signed. 1887/88. Canvas, 4⅝ x 4" (11.8 x 10.2 cm.). Ailsa Mellon Bruce Collection

692 *Woman in a Park.* Signed R. 1870. Canvas, 10¼ x 6⅜" (26.1 x 16.1 cm.). Ailsa Mellon Bruce Collection

689

690

691

692

710

Degas was the son of prosperous parents with some claim to aristocracy. Hence the occasional spelling of their name as de Gas, as it appears in the titles of plate 706 and an early work, *Achille de Gas in the Uniform of a Cadet* (plate 707). These family portraits reveal in their drawing and modeling the influence of Degas' hero, Ingres. But in the composition of his pictures Degas never emulated the great master of Classicism. The portrait of Degas' sister and her banker husband, Edmondo Morbilli (plate 709), shows, in the informal poses and the abrupt angle of the chair, a snapshot effect, a type of design which would have shocked Ingres. The picture was intentionally left unfinished; it is evident that any further detail would have spoilt it.

711

712

Edgar Degas

(FRENCH, 1834–1917)

713 FOUR DANCERS

Degas was the major exponent of a new type of design introduced by the Impressionists. Whereas earlier artists like Poussin had usually devised their compositions out of their imagination, Degas would watch the kaleidoscope of appearance, like a cat watching its prey, until this moving pattern would seem to resolve itself into a momentary significance. Such accidental, ready-made designs he would store up in his memory and use later for the compositions of his pictures. This pouncing upon the scene, holding an instantaneous pattern and giving it permanency, was the essence of Impressionism; but in return there was the necessary sacrifice of an enduring equilibrium, the structural design to be found in the compositions of the Old Masters.

Degas found a rich mine of casual yet perfectly balanced arrangements in the ballet, as one can see in the picture reproduced here. There is no question that he was helped to discover these ready-made compositions by Japanese prints. The Japanese printmakers sought to make their woodcuts a mirror of the passing world, and Impressionism had essentially the same goal. But the Impressionists, especially Degas, went far deeper into the study of appearance than the superficial actuality of Japanese prints. In a way that would have been inconceivable for Eastern artists, these French painters were scientists, intent upon analysis of vision. In his painting *Four Dancers* Degas is experimenting with effects of artificial illumination, with the appearance of these ballet dancers under beams of green and red spotlights, noting how flesh tones and drapery catch the mixture of these two lights, changing color either toward green tones or toward red tones.

Degas ranked this canvas among his finest achievements and would never part with it. It is one of his last large paintings in oil and shows the influence of his use of pastel, a medium which, because of failing eyesight, he employed for most of his later works.

Collections: Degas' atelier until 1918; Wilhelm Hansen, Copenhagen. *Chester Dale Collection*, 1962. Atelier stamp: Degas. Painted about 1899. Canvas, 59½ x 71" (151.1 x 180.2 cm.).

714

Edgar Degas (French, 1834–1917)

714 *Girl Drying Herself.* Signed, and dated 1885. Pastel, 31½ x 20⅛″ (80.1 x 51.2 cm.). Gift of the W. Averell Harriman Foundation in memory of Marie N. Harriman

715 *Before the Ballet.* Signed. 1888. Canvas, 15¾ x 35″ (40 x 89 cm.). Widener Collection

716 *Dancers at the Old Opera House.* Signed. c. 1877. Pastel, 8⅝ x 6¾″ (21.8 x 17.1 cm.). Ailsa Mellon Bruce Collection

717 *Ballet Dancers.* Signed. c. 1877. Pastel and gouache, 11¾ x 10⅝″ (29.7 x 26.9 cm.). Ailsa Mellon Bruce Collection

718 *Ballet Scene.* c. 1907. Pastel on cardboard, 30¼ x 43¾″ (76.8 x 111.2 cm.). Chester Dale Collection

719 *Dancers Backstage.* Signed. c. 1890. Canvas, 9½ x 7⅜″ (24.2 x 18.8 cm.). Ailsa Mellon Bruce Collection

Degas was a master at discovering beauty in the world around him. He particularly loved the opera and the ballet, but he loved them for professional reasons—for the fleeting gesture, the significance given to a passing moment. In the performance or the rehearsals of the ballerinas he found a kaleidoscope of shifting forms, which stimulated his sense of design. In the reproductions in this volume, especially in *Ballet Scene* (plate 718), a pastel painted in his last years, he reveals the plasticity of these young bodies and the motion of their complicated postures as no other artist has ever done.

715

716

717

718

719

483

Edgar Degas

(FRENCH, 1834-1917)

720   MADEMOISELLE MALO

Mlle Malo was a dancer, and with her Degas formed a close friendship. When he journeyed to New Orleans in 1872 to visit his uncle and brothers, who were in the cotton business, he corresponded with her. She puzzled him, and he communicated his bewilderment to a mutual friend. "I thanked her warmly for all her goodness to me. Why does she wish me more calmness in my ideas? Am I then an unusually excitable person?" When he returned to Paris he continued to see her, and during that period he painted the portrait reproduced here, which remained in his possession until he died.

Was there more than friendship in Degas' feeling for Mlle Malo? Probably not, for he seems never to have been in love. "This heart of mine has something artificial," he wrote. "The dancers have sewn it into a bag of pink satin, pink satin slightly faded, like their dancing shoes." His affections belonged not to a single ballerina but to the whole corps de ballet, not to an individual but to the *appearance* of all the performers at rest and at work.

Though Degas might deplore the artificiality of his heart, he could boast of the sincerity of his eye. And to the functioning of this organ, to its cold, analytical penetration, his personal life was sacrificed. From morning to night his single overwhelming passion was to record on paper or canvas what he had seen. But his vision had always been weak, and with incessant work he became almost blind. In the end he was a pathetic figure, wandering unkempt and careworn around Paris, unable to draw even with pastel, which he had come to use instead of oil as his eyesight faded.

He once advised Vollard to marry. "You do not realize how terrible it is to be alone as you grow old," he said. But, as for himself, he could not marry. "I could never bring myself to do it. I would have been in mortal misery all my life for fear my wife might say, 'That's a pretty little thing,' after I had finished a picture."

Degas never painted a "pretty" picture. Austere, detached, aristocratic, his art reembodies the high ideals of the Renaissance. He himself stood aloof from the fashion of his time. He believed "one should work for a few people, as for the others it is quite immaterial." If in his blindness he was lonely, he was also proud. Like Yeats he had "cast a cold eye on life, on death"; and the record of his observations gave him a deep sense of accomplishment. He knew that his detached, analytical vision, while it lasted, had enabled him to change the course of art, to introduce a new goal for painting: the realization of the essential gesture.

Collections: Degas' atelier until 1918; Henry D. Hughes, Philadelphia. *Chester Dale Collection,* 1962. Atelier Stamp: Degas. Painted about 1877. Canvas, 31⅞ x 25⅝" (81.1 x 65.1 cm.).

485

Claude Monet (French, 1840–1926)

735 *Banks of the Seine, Vétheuil.* Signed, and dated 1880. Canvas, 28⅞ x 39⅝" (73.4 x 100.5 cm.). Chester Dale Collection

736 *Vase of Chrysanthemums.* Signed, and dated 1880. Canvas, 39¼ x 28¾" (99.6 x 73 cm.). Chester Dale Collection

737 *The Seine at Giverny.* Signed. c. 1885. Canvas, 32⅛ x 39⅝" (81.6 x 100.3 cm.). Chester Dale Collection

738 *Waterloo Bridge, Gray Day.* Signed, and dated 1903. Canvas, 25⅜ x 39⅜" (65.1 x 100 cm.). Chester Dale Collection

739 *The Houses of Parliament, Sunset.* Signed, and dated 1903. Canvas, 32 x 36⅜" (81.3 x 92.5 cm.). Chester Dale Collection

740 *Woman Seated Under the Willows.* Signed, and dated 1880. Canvas, 31⅞ x 23⅝" (81.1 x 60 cm.). Chester Dale Collection

738

Monet remained true to the Impressionist credo that an artist should transcribe visual sensations as experienced at a specific time and place. This reliance upon sense data as the sole basis of art represents the ultimate extension of nineteenth-century Realism. But there are implicit dangers in this theory: a tendency for scientific observation to replace human emotion, the recording power of the eye to replace the imaginative force of the mind, the analytical theorist to replace the sensuous human being.

740

739

Henri Fantin-Latour

(FRENCH, 1836–1904)

741 STILL LIFE

Many people do not understand why artists take such pleasure in still-life painting. For example, in the picture reproduced here, what was it that really interested Fantin-Latour? Obviously the rendering of actual appearance. But how is that done? The answer lies in the organization of detail, tone, and texture. Detail involves distance and time of vision. Should the artist paint what he would see when closely scrutinizing his subject through a magnifying glass, or when glancing at it quickly from a greater distance with half-closed eyes, or when looking at it repeatedly from a normal distance? The first method leads to those canvases in which a fly invariably crawls across a leaf or petal toward a drop of water, and the second to the broad abstract patterns which Cézanne has handed on to modern painting. Fantin-Latour, however, chooses the third and represents the amount of detail—the petals of the camellias, the skin of the fruit, the wicker of the basket—discernible by normal sight at the distance from which the picture is painted.

The same consistent naturalism appears in the organization of tones. There is a single source of light which defines the local color of each object. As these colors come into shadow each tone is altered consistently, so that the bright and the shadowy pink of the camellias maintains the same proportional relationship as the bright, shadowy green of their leaves, and this tonal accuracy is extended to the areas of light and shadow in the fruit, the basket, the cup, the book, and the table. Much of the reality of the painting depends on these delicate and immensely subtle adjustments.

The third element in conveying actual appearance, variety of texture, is difficult to achieve without destroying the organization of detail and tone. For where the painter wishes to suggest texture he is apt to paint too meticulously, and thus focus undue attention on that area of the picture (see, for example, ter Borch's *The Suitor's Visit*, plate 377). But Fantin-Latour avoids this error and yet manages to suggest the brittle substance of the porcelain cup, the waxy petals of the camellia, and the reticulated skin of the fruit. These three characteristics—consistent selection of detail, consonant organization of tone, and congruous rendering of texture—combine to make this still life one of the supreme expressions of what painters mean by the phrase "art for art's sake."

Collections: Reginald Davis, Paris; A. T. Hollingsworth, London. *Chester Dale Collection*, 1962. Signed, and dated 1866. Canvas, 24⅜ x 29½" (61.9 x 75 cm.).

742

742 **Henri Fantin-Latour** (French, 1836–1904): *Portrait of Sonia*. Signed, and dated 1890. Canvas, 43 x 31⅞″ (109.2 x 81 cm.). Chester Dale Collection

743 **Henri Fantin-Latour**: *Self-Portrait*. Dated 1858. Canvas, 16 x 12⅞″ (40.7 x 32.7 cm.). Chester Dale Collection

744 **Henri Fantin-Latour**: *Mademoiselle de Fitz-James*. Signed, and dated 1867. Canvas, 20⅛ x 16⅞″ (51.1 x 42.8 cm.). Chester Dale Collection

745 **Henri Fantin-Latour**: *Duchesse de Fitz-James*. Signed. 1867. Canvas, 19¾ x 16⅝″ (50.3 x 42.2 cm.). Chester Dale Collection

746 **Paul Cézanne** (French, 1839–1906): *Vase of Flowers*. Signed. c. 1876. Canvas, 28¾ x 23½″ (73 x 59.8 cm.). Chester Dale Collection

743

744

745

Fantin-Latour was popular not only as a still-life painter but also as a portraitist. In his portraits he showed the same skill in observing precisely the amount of detail discernible at the distance from which the picture is painted that one finds in his still lifes. This method often gives his portraits a somewhat photographic look. The vast difference between Fantin-Latour's work and Cézanne's is well illustrated by plate 746. Fantin-Latour painted what he saw on the table in front of him, whereas Cézanne copied a vase of flowers from a magazine illustration and then transformed it into a seedpod which seems to explode with the fertility of nature.

746

Paul Cézanne

(FRENCH, 1839–1906)

747   STILL LIFE

The points made in the discussions on Fantin-Latour will be clearer if one compares the still life reproduced here with his still life in plate 741. In the painting by Fantin-Latour, the texture, tone, and color of the camellias, the fruit, the china, and the blue book are so skillfully organized that merely visual facts take on a quality of poetry. This is Impressionism insofar as the main interest on the part of the artist is in transcribing a visual impression as accurately as possible, using the highest key of color which can be consistently maintained. But it is also more traditional than the work of the Impressionists, closer to eighteenth-century painters like Chardin, who observe their subject with a steady gaze instead of the quick glance used by Impressionist artists (See Manet's advice to Eva Gonzalès, page 454). On the other hand, the still-life painting by Cézanne belongs to a different tradition. It is as far from Impressionism as it is from Chardin. It recalls instead the designs of the great Italian artists, for it has the same gravity and momentum of rhythm we find in the figure paintings of Giotto and Masaccio. The various objects which in Fantin-Latour's still life remain isolated are here united by continuous movement suggested by the pattern in the folds of the cloth and the napkin, a movement controlled and checked by the emphasized rectangular lines in the background. In Cézanne one finds again the permanent equilibrium characteristic of classical design. Cézanne is not dependent on visual memory for his composition as were Impressionists like Degas, for he had instead an extraordinary gift of visual imagination, of that genius for inventing compositions which we find in the major Renaissance artists. Thus the reaction of Cézanne against Impressionism resulted in a new emphasis on form, solidity, and structure—on qualities which were the bone and marrow of Renaissance art.

Collections: Ambroise Vollard, Paris; Maurice Gangnat, Paris; Emil Staub (Staub-Terlinden), Männedorf, Switzerland. *Chester Dale Collection*, 1962. Painted c. 1894. Canvas, 26 x 32¼" (65.5 x 82 cm.).

748

749

750

751

The nineteen canvases by Cézanne in the collection of the National Gallery of Art form one of the most remarkable representations of his work in any museum. Particularly fine are the late paintings (see plates 748, 751, 753, 757, and· 766). These show the deep resonances of color and the strong rhythmic design which Cézanne achieved in the last years of his life.

752

Paul Cézanne (French, 1839–1906)

748 *Still Life with Apples and Peaches.* c. 1905. Canvas, 32 x 39⅝" (81.2 x 100.6 cm.). Gift of Eugene and Agnes Meyer

749 *Man with Pipe.* 1892/96. Canvas, 10¼ x 8" (26.1 x 20.2 cm.). Gift of the W. Averell Harriman Foundation in memory of Marie N. Harriman

750 *At the Water's Edge.* c. 1890. Canvas, 28⅞ x 36½" (73.3 x 92.8 cm.). Gift of the W. Averell Harriman Foundation in memory of Marie N. Harriman

751 *Vase of Flowers.* 1900/1903. Canvas, 39⅞ x 32⅜" (101.2 x 82.2 cm.). Gift of Eugene and Agnes Meyer

752 *The Battle of Love.* c. 1880. Canvas, 14⅞ x 18¼" (37.8 x 46.2 cm.). Gift of the W. Averell Harriman Foundation in memory of Marie N. Harriman

753 *Still Life.* c. 1900. Canvas, 18 x 21⅝" (45.8 x 54.9 cm.). Gift of the W. Averell Harriman Foundation in memory of Marie N. Harriman

753

503

Paul Cézanne

(FRENCH, 1839–1906)

754   THE ARTIST'S FATHER

It is hard to imagine a more ambivalent relationship than that of Paul Cézanne and his father. Emile Zola, Paul's closest friend, describes the elder Cézanne as "mocking, republican, bourgeois, cold, meticulous, stingy. . . . He is, moreover, garrulous and, sustained by his wealth, doesn't care a rap for anyone or anything." This was probably also the younger Cézanne's judgment when in 1866 he was painting the portrait reproduced here; and yet twenty years later, according to friends, he venerated his parent, who had left him what he considered to be a large income.

Louis-Auguste Cézanne started his life as a manufacturer of hats, and by 1848 he had made enough money to buy the local bank, which was in financial difficulties because of the Revolution. He restored its prosperity and hoped his son, too, would become a banker. But when banking made Paul so obviously unhappy, and all he could think of was painting, his father gave him an allowance, small but sufficient to enable him to follow his unprofitable profession. He even agreed to act as a model for his son, whose work he never understood.

With time, relations between father and son, always variable, worsened, and the nadir was reached in 1872 when Paul had a son by Hortense Fiquet. His father was willing to support Paul as a bachelor but unwilling to have a family kept at his expense, especially one his son would not acknowledge. Yet eventually he accepted even this, and in 1886 when Paul at last married Hortense he signed the register. He could scarcely have objected to the long period of illegitimacy of his grandson, since he himself had not married until his own son, Paul, was five years old.

Paul Cézanne painted his father at least three times and drew him often. Of these likenesses the National Gallery portrait is the most overwhelming. The massive body of the sitter, slightly turned in his armchair, suggests such weight and solidity, gives such an effect of three-dimensional existence, that it is difficult to find a comparable portrait by any other artist. These formal qualities are linked to an indefinable tenderness, "as though," to quote John Rewald, "while contemplating him, often without the model's knowledge, the painter had felt the deep-rooted links that nature or fate had established between him and this old man."

Father and son always shared a certain toughness—a revulsion for all sentimentality. When the banker was trying to persuade his son to give up painting, he used to say, "Think of the future; one dies with genius, but one eats with money." After his father's death, Paul, perhaps with subconscious irony, altered this aphorism into his only eulogy for his parent: "My father was a man of genius; he left me an income of twenty-five thousand francs."

Collections: Auguste Pellerin, Paris; Mme René Lecomte, Paris. *Collection of Mr. and Mrs. Paul Mellon*, 1970. Painted 1866. Canvas, 78⅛ x 47" (198.5 x 119.3 cm.).

762

763

510

Paul Cézanne (French, 1839–1906)

762 *Houses in Provence.* c. 1880. Canvas, 25⅝ x 32″ (65 x 81.3 cm.). Collection of Mr. and Mrs. Paul Mellon

763 *Riverbank.* c. 1895. Canvas, 28¾ x 36⅜″ (73 x 92.3 cm.). Ailsa Mellon Bruce Collection

764 *Landscape near Paris.* c. 1876. Canvas, 19¾ x 23⅞″ (50.2 x 60 cm.). Chester Dale Collection

765 *Mont Sainte-Victoire.* c. 1887. Canvas, 26½ x 36″ (67.2 x 91.3 cm.). Gift of the W. Averell Harriman Foundation in memory of Marie N. Harriman

766 *Le Château Noir.* 1900/1904. Canvas, 29 x 38″ (73.7 x 96.6 cm.). Gift of Eugene and Agnes Meyer

Cézanne once wrote, "One can't be too scrupulous, too sincere, or too submissive to nature, but one ought to be nonetheless master of his model and above all of his means of expression. Penetrate to what is before you and express yourself as logically as possible." This might apply to all the landscapes by Cézanne which are reproduced in this volume.

764

765

766

767

768

Camille Pissarro (French, 1830–1903)

767 *Boulevard des Italiens, Morning, Sunlight.* Signed, and dated 1897. Canvas, 28⅞ x 36¼" (73.2 x 92.1 cm.). Chester Dale Collection

768 *Peasant Girl with a Straw Hat.* Signed, and dated 1881. Canvas, 28⅞ x 23½" (73.4 x 59.6 cm.). Ailsa Mellon Bruce Collection

769 *Orchard in Bloom, Louveciennes.* Signed, and dated 1872. Canvas, 17¾ x 21⅝" (45 x 55 cm.). Ailsa Mellon Bruce Collection

770 *Peasant Woman.* Signed, and dated 1880. Canvas, 28¼ x 23⅝" (73.1 x 60 cm.). Chester Dale Collection

771 *The Bather.* Signed, and dated 1895. Canvas, 13⅞ x 10¾" (35.3 x 27.3 cm.). Chester Dale Collection

772 *Hampton Court Green.* Signed, and dated 1891. Canvas, 21⅜ x 28¾" (54.3 x 73 cm.). Ailsa Mellon Bruce Collection

769

Pissarro was much less a "master of his model" than
Cézanne, but he was nonetheless admired and respected
by the significant artists of his generation. Cézanne
wished his landscapes to have the permanence of his
favorite motif, Mont Sainte-Victoire (plate 765),
whereas Pissarro wished his pictures to suggest the
scene exactly as photographed by the retina of the eye.
Sisley shared Pissarro's goal but achieved it less often.
In *Meadow* (plate 776), however, he has created one of
his rare masterpieces.

770

771

772

773

774

775

773 Camille Pissarro (French, 1830–1903): *The Artist's Garden at Eragny.* Signed, and dated 1898. Canvas, 29 x 36⅜" (73.6 x 92.3 cm.). Ailsa Mellon Bruce Collection

774 Camille Pissarro: *Place du Carrousel, Paris.* Signed, and dated 1900. Canvas, 21⅝ x 25¾" (54.9 x 65.4 cm.). Ailsa Mellon Bruce Collection

Alfred Sisley (French, 1839–1899)

775 *Street at Sèvres.* Signed, and dated 1872. Canvas, 15½ x 23½" (39.5 x 59.6 cm.). Ailsa Mellon Bruce Collection

776 *Meadow.* Signed, and dated 1875. Canvas, 21⅝ x 28¼" (54.9 x 73 cm.). Ailsa Mellon Bruce Collection

777 *The Banks of the Oise.* Signed. 1877/78. Canvas, 21⅜ x 25½" (54.3 x 64.7 cm.). Chester Dale Collection

778 *The Road in the Woods.* Signed. 1879. Canvas, 18¼ x 22" (46.3 x 55.8 cm.). Chester Dale Collection

776

778

777

Georges Seurat

(FRENCH, 1859-1891)

779 SEASCAPE AT PORT-EN-BESSIN, NORMANDY

This is one of a group of landscapes, all about the same size, which Seurat painted in 1888. They show various views of Port-en-Bessin and its environs. The two cranes in the upper left-hand corner of the picture control the whole composition. Put your finger over them and you will see that the structure of the landscape has vanished.

Seurat accurately recorded what he was painting, as is proved by photographs taken of the same scene, but he carefully selected the exact location from which to paint. That he was constantly in search of views that would fit into a favorite formula is well illustrated by this seascape, as H. Dorra has pointed out. Here the composition is built around two perpendicular axes, one of which is a golden section, the other a central axis. This compositional device occurs in many of his landscapes.

But photographic veracity does not apply to the subordinate details of the scene. These Seurat arranged arbitrarily. It is improbable, for example, that wind ever blew clouds into those arabesque bands which give such decorative beauty to the sky—a pattern prefiguring Art Nouveau and at the same time echoing the slope of the steep hill.

Seascape may also have been among Seurat's first experiments in painting the border of the canvas to form a frame, for the picture apparently had already been signed before he placed the final touches on its edge, partly obliterating the signature. The problem of the frame preoccupied him. He found that the conventional gold frames falsified the orange tones in his work, whereas the white frames favored by the Impressionists formed too strong a contrast. The solution began to formulate itself with the *Grand Jatte*, when he painted a narrow border of complementary colors to enable the picture to blend with the wall. This idea was more fully developed in his later pictures, which were meant to be self-contained. He wished his variegated dots of complementary colors to create a landscape of carefully controlled space which would not be abruptly cut off at its extremities.

The National Gallery painting was owned originally by Seurat's mother, for whom he felt, judging by his drawings, a deep and tender affection. From Mme Seurat the painting eventually passed to the collection of Félix Fénéon, Seurat's most fervent and articulate admirer.

Collections: Mme Seurat; Léon Appert; Léopold Appert; Félix Fénéon, Paris. *Gift of the W. Averell Harriman Foundation in memory of Marie N. Harriman, 1972. Signed. Painted 1888. Canvas, 25⅝ x 31⅞" (65.1 x 80.9 cm.).*

780

781

782

783

John Rewald has aptly remarked, "Redon lived in a world of beautiful and disquieting dreams that were indistinguishable from reality." But the painter himself wrote, "I have always felt the need to copy nature in small objects, particularly the casual and accidental." The first quotation explains paintings like *Pandora*, *St. Sebastian*, and the puzzling portrait entitled *Evocation of Roussel*; the second explains the three beautiful still lifes of flowers, which delight the eye and present no problem to the brain.

Odilon Redon   (French, 1840–1916)

780   *Pandora.* Signed. 1910/12. Canvas, 56½ x 24¾"
(143.6 x 62.9 cm.). Chester Dale Collection

781   *Saint Sebastian.* Signed. 1910/12. Canvas, 56¾ x
24¾" (144 x 62.8 cm.). Chester Dale Collection

782   *Flowers in a Vase.* Signed. c. 1910. Canvas, 22 x
15½" (55.9 x 39.4 cm.). Ailsa Mellon Bruce Collection

783   *Pansies.* Signed. c. 1905. Pastel, 21½ x 18" (54.6
x 45.7 cm.). Gift of the Adele R. Levy Fund, Inc., as a
tribute to Lessing J. Rosenwald

784   *Evocation of Roussel.* Signed. c. 1912. Canvas,
28⅞ x 21⅜" (73.4 x 54.3 cm.). Chester Dale Collection

785   *Wildflowers.* Signed. c. 1905. Pastel, 24⅜ x 18⅞"
(61.9 x 47.9 cm.). Gift of Loula D. Lasker

786   **Georges Seurat** (French, 1859–1891): *Study for
"La Grande Jatte."* 1884/85. Wood, 6¼ x 9⅞" (15.9 x
25 cm.). Ailsa Mellon Bruce Collection

784

785

786

Vincent van Gogh

(DUTCH, 1853–1890)

787   LA MOUSMÉ

Cézanne was not the only artist to react against Impressionism, against its absorption in the facts of vision. Van Gogh also wished to escape the Impressionist tyranny of the eye, to go beyond the mere transcriptions of appearance. A study of Japanese prints liberated him. From them he learned to paint in masses of flat tone or masses of but slightly broken color, and to treat the picture surface as decoration.

Van Gogh wrote his brother, Theo, "I envy the Japanese the extreme clearness which everything has in their work. It is never tedious, and never seems to be done too hurriedly. Their work is as simple as breathing, and they do a figure in a few sure strokes with the same ease as if it were as simple as buttoning your coat." But van Gogh never attained this facility. He wrote again in July 1888 of *La Mousmé*, "It took me a whole week, I have not been able to do anything else, not having been very well either . . . but I had to reserve my mental energy to do the *mousmé* well. A *mousmé* is a Japanese girl—Provençal in this case—12 to 14 years old." Creation was easier for the Japanese artist. He was a member of a group, where everyone worked in the same tradition, but van Gogh was a lonely individual, never sure of his way, only certain that he must follow his self-destroying search for beauty. It was a quest that cost him first his sanity and then his life, but he knew in the end that he had found the Grail he sought.

Collections: Mme J. van Gogh-Bonger, Amsterdam; Carl Sternheim, La Hulpe, Belgium; Alphonse Kann, St.-Germain-en-Laye, France; J. B. Stang, Oslo. *Chester Dale Collection*, 1962. Painted 1888. Canvas, 28⅞ x 23¾" (73.4 x 60 cm.).

521

Vincent van Gogh

(DUTCH, 1853–1890)

788   GIRL IN WHITE

Every picture by an artist of deep feeling is itself a piece of autobiography. The painting reproduced here was finished less than a month before van Gogh committed suicide. He had been released from the asylum at St-Remy and had placed himself in the care of Dr. Gachet at Auvers-sur-Oise. It was the last stage in a losing battle, the last effort to paint and remain sane.

For a time he seemed better. He liked his new doctor. He painted his portrait. He felt a deep sympathy for a man who also had "the heartbroken expression of our time," as he wrote Gauguin. Although always fearful of another attack, van Gogh seemed happy in his work, hopeful that at last he could resist. Gradually, however, his mind grew clouded again. His letters to Theo became less coherent, tinged with a deepening melancholy. He found that he could paint only "sadness and the extreme of loneliness."

His demon of despair had found him out once more. Perhaps in this picture he decided to paint the portrait of his familiar spirit, to embody all his sorrow in the features of a young peasant girl. It is one of the most beautiful and touching of his pictures. The girl's frail body, her long thin arms with their large, awkward hands, the droop of her shoulders, the huge eyes, vacant and staring, convey an effect of tranquil sadness. All around her is the tender green of early summer. She stands in the midst of nodding heads of wheat like some unhappy spirit of the fields.

In the last few weeks of his life, wheat fields held a deep fascination for van Gogh. He found them hard to paint. As he wrote Gauguin, "It is a question of different greens, of the same value, so as to form a green ensemble which, by its vibration, will make you think of the gentle rustle of ears of wheat swaying in the breeze."

As background in this portrait, they are rendered by the most abstract notation, but with that mystical intensity described by Traherne, "The corn was orient and immortal wheat, which never should be reaped, nor was ever sown." To hold this vision van Gogh worked more feverishly than ever. He knew the danger in this. Shortly before he shot himself he wrote his brother, "Well, my own work, I am risking my life for it and my reason has half foundered in it—that's all right." He was resigned. "Painters have more and more their backs to the wall," he admitted. At last he was ready to accept the terrible truth Emerson has expressed: "The artists must be sacrificed to their art. Like the bees, they must put their lives into the sting they give."

Collections: Mme J. van Gogh-Bonger, Amsterdam; Richard Kisling; Mme H. Glatt-Kisling, Zurich. *Chester Dale Collection*, 1962. Painted 1890. Canvas, 26⅛ x 17⅛" (66.3 x 45.3 cm.).

523

789

789 **Vincent van Gogh** (Dutch, 1853–1890): *Roulin's Baby*. 1888. Canvas, 13¾ x 9⅜" (35 x 23.9 cm.). Chester Dale Collection

790 **Vincent van Gogh**: *The Olive Orchard*. 1889. Canvas, 28¾ x 36¼" (73 x 92 cm.). Chester Dale Collection

791 **Vincent van Gogh**: *Farmhouse in Provence, Arles*. 1888. Canvas, 18⅛ x 24" (46.1 x 60.9 cm.). Ailsa Mellon Bruce Collection

792 **Paul Gauguin** (French, 1848–1903): *Madame Alexandre Kohler*. Signed. 1887/88. Canvas, 18¼ x 15" (46.3 x 38 cm.). Chester Dale Collection

790

791

Van Gogh's "sadness and the extreme of loneliness" are
evident even in paintings where one would normally
expect cheerfulness. *Roulin's Baby* has all the chub-
biness of infancy, but the gaiety one associates, perhaps
wrongly, with roly-poly babies is absent. Instead, those
huge, staring eyes hold a premonition of sorrow to
come. Sad too is the subdued color of *The Olive
Orchard*. The low tonality of this landscape, however,
is explained by the painter in a beautiful analogy, "It is
a canvas worked at from memory because I wanted
something very far away like a vague memory softened
by time."

792

815

Henri Rousseau   (French, 1844–1910)

815   *Rendezvous in the Forest.* Signed. 1889. Canvas, 36¼ x 28¾″ (92 x 73 cm.). Gift of the W. Averell Harriman Foundation in memory of Marie N. Harriman

816   *Boy on the Rocks.* Signed. 1895/97. Canvas, 21¾ x 18″ (55.4 x 45.7 cm.). Chester Dale Collection

Le Douanier Rousseau, as he was called, though technically naive was psychologically sophisticated. His spectral *Boy on the Rocks* and his bizarre *Rendezvous in the Forest* afford glimpses into the nightmare world of the unconscious. One senses that Freud and Jung are in the offing.

816

American School

XIX AND EARLY XX CENTURY

817

818

817 **Unknown Painter** (American, 19th century): *Miss Arnold Holding an Apple.* c. 1830. Wood, 32¼ x 23⅜" (81.7 x 59.5 cm.). Gift of Edgar William and Bernice Chrysler Garbisch

818 **Unknown Painter** (American, 19th century): *Miss Arnold Knitting.* c. 1830. Wood, 35¼ x 22¾" (89.4 x 58 cm.). Gift of Edgar William and Bernice Chrysler Garbisch

819 **Unknown Painter** (American, 19th century): *Portrait of a Man.* Probably 1829. Wood, 19½ x 13½" (49.5 x 33 cm.). Gift of Edgar William and Bernice Chrysler Garbish

820 **Unknown Painter** (American, 19th century): *Blue Eyes.* c. 1840. Wood, oval, 18 x 12¾" (45.8 x 32.5 cm.). Gift of Edgar William and Bernice Chrysler Garbisch

821 **Unknown Painter** (American, 19th century): *The Dog.* Canvas, 35¼ x 41½" (89.4 x 105.3 cm.). Gift of William Edgar and Bernice Chrysler Garbisch

822 **Unknown Painter** (American, 19th century): *The Sargent Family.* 1800. Canvas, 38⅜ x 50⅜" (96.5 x 127.9 cm.). Gift of Edgar William and Bernice Chrysler Garbisch

819

820

The hallucinatory effects that appear in the paintings of
Rousseau (see plates 814–16) are also to be found in the
work of many American anonymous artists. *The Dog*, a
typical American primitive painting, might equally be
ascribed to Rousseau. Occasionally, however, these
native folk painters anticipate European artists of great
sophistication. *Blue Eyes*, for example, is a premature
Modigliani.

821

822

Thomas Eakins continued in his portraits the tradition of the early works of Copley. Probing, analytical, uncompromising, these likenesses are often as detached and unseductive as a psychiatric report. This same passion for visual realism marked American still-life painters, the greatest of whom was William Harnett. As he said, "The whole effect of still-life painting comes from its tone, and the nearer one attains perfection, the more realistic the effect will be." It is because Harnett was able to render this proportional relationship of tones, exactly as they are perceived in nature, that his pictures come so close to ocular truth.

840

839

841

842

843

839 Thomas Eakins (American, 1844–1916): *Monsignor Diomede Falconio.* 1905. Canvas, 72⅛ x 54¼" (183.2 x 138 cm.). Gift of Stephen C. Clark

840 Thomas Eakins: *Louis Husson.* Signed, and dated 1899. Canvas, 24 x 20" (61.3 x 50.6 cm.). Gift of Katharine Husson Horstick

841 Thomas Eakins: *Mrs. Louis Husson.* Signed with initials. c. 1905. Canvas, 24 x 20" (61.3 x 50.6 cm.). Gift of Katharine Husson Horstick

842 Charles Loring Elliott (American, 1812–1868): *William Sidney Mount.* c. 1850. Canvas, 30⅜ x 25" (76.5 x 64 cm.). Andrew W. Mellon Collection

843 William M. Harnett (American, 1848–1892): *My Gems.* Signed, and dated 1888. Wood, 18 x 14" (45.7 x 35.5 cm.). Gift of the Avalon Foundation

844 Frank Duveneck (American, 1848–1919): *William Gedney Bunce.* Probably 1878. Canvas, 30½ x 26" (77.1 x 66 cm.). Andrew W. Mellon Collection

844

Winslow Homer

(AMERICAN, 1836–1910)

845   BREEZING UP

The distinguished achievement of American painting in the second half of the nineteenth century was due in no small part to Winslow Homer, who shares with Thomas Eakins a preeminent position in the tradition of American realism. Homer was trained as an illustrator, and an element of illustration appears in his pictures from beginning to end. His earliest significant work was drawn for *Harper's Weekly* during the Civil War, when he was detailed to the Army of the Potomac as a correspondent. Working for a magazine, he learned to make his illustrations clear and specific. Throughout his life he presented his subjects graphically and made them appear to exist convincingly. Such objective recording has now almost vanished from art; and Homer's pictorial style with its simple, lucid statements has had little if any influence in recent years.

Yet Homer was able to suggest mood, feeling, atmosphere, as vividly as any Abstract Expressionist. Three small boys and a fisherman in a sailboat evoke the pleasure of sailing before a fair breeze; a dory with men peering over the side into a foggy sky conveys the loneliness and vastness of the sea; a huntsman with his dog silhouetted against the mountain suggests the exhilaration of sport. One could elaborate endlessly.

But the important point is that a certain mood is induced in the spectator's mind by recognizable images. Representation in the visual arts is, of course, traditional. The basic language of painting with rare exceptions has always been representational, an imagery of identifiable objects. At times, however, painting has tried to usurp the function of other arts: poetry, for example, with the Pre-Raphaelites, and music with the Abstract Expressionists. With Winslow Homer, there is no confusion of the arts. He simply represents actual scenes with such vividness, with such grasp of significance, that their pervading mood is inescapable.

Collections: Charles Stewart Smith, New York; Howard Caswell Smith, Oyster Bay, New York. *Gift of the W. L. and May T. Mellon Foundation*, 1943. Signed, and dated 1876. Canvas, 24⅛ x 38⅛" (61.5 x 97 cm.).

557

846

Two streams of American painting, the romantic and the realistic, are illustrated by these reproductions. Blakelock is a romantic. In the gathering dusk his garden glows with a murky light. A commonplace scene is imbued with a mystery and melancholy foreshadowing the artist's madness and suicide. Kensett and Moran, who belong to the opposite tradition, see nature with the sharp focus of a laser beam. Newport, Lake George, and a turbulent sea are represented objectively and without emotional overtones. Martin Johnson Heade, like Church (see plate 831), had traveled in South America, and in plate 851 he captures the effect of light and shadow on one of the world's most beautiful bays.

847

848

846 **Winslow Homer** (American, 1836–1910): *Hound and Hunter.* Signed, and dated 1892. Canvas, 28¼ x 48⅛" (71.8 x 122.2 cm.). Gift of Stephen C. Clark

847 **Winslow Homer**: *Right and Left.* Signed, and dated 1909. Canvas, 28¼ x 48⅜" (71.8 x 123 cm.). Gift of the Avalon Foundation

848 **Thomas Moran** (American, 1837–1926): *The Much Resounding Sea.* Signed, and dated 1884. Canvas, 25 x 62" (64 x 148.8 cm.). Gift of the Avalon Foundation

849 **Ralph Albert Blakelock** (American, 1847–1919): *The Artist's Garden.* Signed. c. 1880. Canvas, 16 x 24" (40.5 x 61.3 cm.). Gift of Chester Dale

850 **John Frederick Kensett** (American, 1816–1872): *Beacon Rock, Newport Harbor.* Signed with initials, and dated 1857. Canvas, 22½ x 36" (57.1 x 91.5 cm.). Gift of Frederick Sturges, Jr.

851 **Martin Johnson Heade** (American, 1819–1904): *Rio de Janeiro Bay.* Signed, and dated 1864. Canvas, 17⅞ x 35⅞" (45.1 x 91 cm.). Gift of the Avalon Foundation

849

850

851

James McNeill Whistler

(AMERICAN, 1834-1903)

852   THE WHITE GIRL (SYMPHONY IN WHITE, NO. 1)

There have always been two opposed traditions in American painting. Eakins and Homer represent one: a rugged, native vitality; Whistler and Mary Cassatt illustrate the second: a genteel, Europeanized urbanity. Although Whistler's fame is brighter in Europe than in America, his sophisticated selection of what seems best, wherever found, is of exceptional significance to this country, for it marks the coming of age of American painting.

Whistler would never have understood or approved of Homer's or Eakins' works. He tried to avoid what they sought, qualities he described as "damned realism, and beautiful nature and the whole mess." He preached a return to "that wondrous thing called the masterpiece, which surpasses in perfection all that they [the gods] have contrived in what is called Nature." In other words, Whistler wished to demonstrate that the inventive force of the artist is more important than the recording power of his eye. To do this he combined the patterns of Japanese prints with that mastery of value relations which distinguishes the painting of Velázquez. This eclecticism is predictable from even so early a work as *The White Girl*, a portrait of his mistress Joanna Heffernan. It was shown in 1863 at the Salon des Refusés with what we now consider to be many of the finest French paintings of the second half of the nineteenth century. It proved to be the sensation of that exhibition, the most revolutionary held in France in a hundred years.

True, the public was hostile, and Zola has reported how people nudged one another and became almost hysterical with laughter in front of the painting. But the wisest connoisseurs and critics were enthusiastic, and with *The White Girl* Whistler became the first American painter since the eighteenth century to attain renown and leadership among European artists.

Collection: Thomas Whistler, Baltimore. *Harris Whittemore Collection*, 1943. Signed, and dated 1862. Canvas, 84½ x 42½" (214.7 x 108 cm.).

863

864

865

Mary Cassatt, like her friend Degas, studied the old masters assiduously. This is evident in *Girl Arranging Her Hair*, which was shown in 1886 in the last Impressionist exhibition. Miss Cassatt has taken an awkward adolescent and placed her in the pose of Michelangelo's *Bound Slave*, a statue she had often seen in the Louvre. Degas, entranced with her blending of the contemporary and the classical, bought the painting and kept it until he died. But the picture is not characteristic of Miss Cassatt's work. More in her usual style is *The Loge*. It shows her particular qualities: an elaborate and fragile refinement, a mood of social fastidiousness, which suggests the novels of her fellow expatriates Henry James and Edith Wharton.

John Singer Sargent

(AMERICAN, 1856–1925)

866   MRS. ADRIAN ISELIN

Sargent's painting of Mrs. Iselin epitomizes the American mothers described in the novels of Henry James: ruthless guardians of their young, determined managers of financial and social advancement. Thirty years after Sargent had painted this portrait he was asked if he remembered it. He thought for a moment before he replied, "Of course! I cannot forget that dominating little finger." And with what skill he has shown it tapping the edge of the table!

Mrs. Iselin's grandson has recounted how reluctant she was to have her portrait painted. When Sargent came for the first sitting, she entered the room in an extremely irritated manner, followed by her maid carrying her best French frocks, and haughtily told the artist to choose a dress. Sargent replied that he wanted to paint her just as she was. He did not mention that he intended to portray her resentful expression at having to pose, her air of contempt for the painter, and her large and ugly ear.

In those early days the young portraitist was more courageous and less bored than he would become in later years. He painted his sitters as he saw them, disregarding their feelings and their wishes. He was at his best when the character and the mood he wanted to portray were obvious. Mrs. Iselin was a perfect model. She was firm, self-confident, perhaps a little aggressive. One admires her without feeling the least sympathy for her forceful personality, which Sargent has caught unforgettably.

Technically the painting is brilliant, but it reveals the flaw which Henry James astutely perceived and described in an essay published the year before the portrait was painted. After praising Sargent's astounding dexterity, the novelist asked, "Yes, but what is left?" He observed that "it may be better for an artist to have a certain part of his property invested in unsolved difficulties." And he concluded his essay saying, "The highest result [in portraiture] is achieved when to this element of quick perception a certain faculty of brooding reflection is added." This "faculty of brooding reflection" was exactly what Sargent lacked, and as a consequence his work for all its brio remains superficial.

Collections: Family of the sitter, New York City and New Rochelle. *Gift of Ernest Iselin*, 1964. Signed, and dated 1888. Canvas, 60½ x 36⅝" (153.7 x 93 cm.).

867

868

869

867 John Singer Sargent (American, 1856–1925): *Mrs. Joseph Chamberlain*. Signed, and dated 1902. Canvas, 59¼ x 33″ (150.6 x 83.9 cm.). Gift of the sitter, Mary Endicott Chamberlain Carnegie

868 John Singer Sargent: *Street in Venice*. Signed. 1882. Wood, 17¾ x 21¼″ (45.1 x 53.9 cm.). Gift of the Avalon Foundation

869 John Singer Sargent: *Mrs. William Crown-inshield Endicott*. Signed, and dated 1901. Canvas, 64¼ x 45⅛″ (163.6 x 114.3 cm.). Gift of Louise Thoron Endicott in memory of Mr. and Mrs. William Crown-inshield Endicott

870 Childe Hassam (American, 1859–1935): *Allies Day, May 1917*. Signed, and dated May 17, 1917. Canvas, 36¾ x 30¼″ (93.2 x 77.3 cm.). Gift of Ethelyn McKinney in memory of her brother, Glenn Ford McKinney

871 John Singer Sargent: *Repose*. Signed, and dated 1911. Canvas, 25⅛ x 30″ (63.8 x 76.2 cm.). Gift of Curt H. Reisinger

870

871

John Singer Sargent was at his best in sketches like *Repose* and *Street in Venice*, painted for his own pleasure. He enjoyed displaying his virtuousity of brushwork, especially when he felt no responsibility for a portrait. Compromising more and more in his portraits of the rich and famous, he painted not what he saw in front of him, but what his sitter thought his or her appearance to be. Artists in the past have done this, but they did not have Sargent's wish to match what he observed of variations of shadow, and alterations of color. The task of copying appearance yet trying to flatter the sitter became too tedious, and Sargent at the end of his life abandoned portraiture and took up architectural decoration, for which he had no talent whatever.

George Bellows

(AMERICAN, 1882–1925)

872   BOTH MEMBERS OF THIS CLUB

Few artists have been proficient athletes, but George Bellows was an exception. He starred at school and college in basketball and baseball, and in the opinion of friends might have gone on to play in the major leagues. From an early age, however, he was determined to be a painter. He enrolled in the New York School of Art and studied under Robert Henri, who taught him that "anything . . . which has the power to hold or receive human attention may be the subject of a work of art." He enjoyed painting prizefights, depicting, as he said, "two men trying to kill each other"; and in this painting of a fight at Tom Sharkey's Athletic Club, near the artist's studio in New York City, he has shown not only a vicious combat but also the frenzied delight of the spectators. These half-demented faces are brilliantly executed, with Hogarth's sense of exaggeration and the slashing brushwork of Goya's nightmare scenes.

The original title, *A Nigger and a White Man*, was later changed to *Both Members of This Club*. Bellows undoubtedly intended an ironic commentary on integration in 1909, when the picture was painted, as well as on a device to circumvent a New York State law which made public boxing illegal from 1900 to 1910. Fights were therefore staged at "private" clubs, such as Sharkey's, where both spectators and boxers were members, the latter usually only for the night of the fight. In this picture it has been impossible to identify the two boxers.

George Bellows painted six boxing pictures and made sixteen lithographs and innumerable drawings of prizefights. In his book *George Bellows and the Ashcan School of Painting*, Donald Braider noted that many authorities consider *Both Members of This Club* "his best in this genre." It is certainly much better than his later efforts, when all the vigor of his early style had been devitalized by the anemic theories of Dynamic Symmetry and the cerebral color harmonies of the Tone Solid, put forward by Professors Jay Hambidge and Denman Ross, respectively. Bellows died at forty-two, but his demise as an artist took place much earlier.

Collection: Mrs. George Bellows, New York. *Gift of Chester Dale*, 1944. Signed. Painted 1909. Canvas, 45¼ x 63⅛" (115 x 160.5 cm.).

573

873 George Bellows (American, 1882–1925): *The Lone Tenement.* Signed. 1909. Canvas, 36⅛ x 48⅛" (91.8 x 122.3 cm.). Gift of Chester Dale

874 William Glackens (American, 1870–1938): *Family Group.* 1910–11. Canvas, 72 x 84" (182.8 x 213.3 cm.). Gift of Mr. and Mrs. Ira Glackens

875 George Luks (American, 1866–1933): *The Miner.* Signed. 1925. Canvas, 60¼ x 50⅜" (153.1 x 128 cm.). Gift of Chester Dale

876 Robert Henri (American, 1865–1929): *Snow in New York.* Signed, and dated Mar 5 1902. Canvas, 32 x 25¾" (81.2 x 65.3 cm.). Gift of Chester Dale

877 John Sloan (American, 1871–1951): *The City from Greenwich Village.* 1922. Canvas, 26 x 33¾" (66 x 85.7 cm.). Gift of Helen Farr Sloan

873

874

875

876

George Bellows, although not one of the original members, later became closely associated with a group known as The Eight, which included the best American painters working just before and after World War I. Robert Henri was their teacher and spokesman, and the most gifted members were William Glackens, George Luks, and John Sloan. All at one time or another held jobs as cartoonists or magazine illustrators, and the atmosphere of the "city desk" colors their interpretation of the American scene. Their brushwork is vehement and their point of view often tough, with something of the truculence of the newspaper reporter. They were dubbed with considerable aptness, "The Ashcan School."

The Eight were instrumental in bringing together in New York an exhibition of contemporary American painting (including Glackens's *Family Group*) and Post-Impressionist, Fauve, and Cubist works from Europe. The show opened at the Armory in February 1913, and it had a tremendous impact on artists and public alike. Walt Kuhn, Marsden Hartley, and Max Weber were among those who felt the influence of the Armory Show, and they represent the new trend toward Modernism in American painting.

877

878

879

878 Walt Kuhn (American, 1877–1949): *The White Clown.* 1929. Canvas, 40¼ x 30¼" (102.3 x 76.9 cm.). Gift of the W. Averell Harriman Foundation in memory of Marie N. Harriman

879 Max Weber (American, 1880–1961): *Rush Hour, New York.* 1915. Canvas, 36¼ x 30¼" (92 x 76.9 cm.). Gift of the Avalon Foundation

880 Marsden Hartley (American, 1877–1943): *The Aero.* c. 1914. Canvas, 39½ x 32" (100.3 x 81.2 cm.). Andrew W. Mellon Fund

881 Marsden Hartley: *Mount Kitadhin.* 1942. Oil on Masonite, 30 x 40⅛" (76 x 101.9 cm.). Gift of Mrs. Mellon Byers

880

881

XX Century

Pierre Bonnard

(FRENCH, 1867-1947)

882   THE LETTER

The styles of Bellows and Bonnard provide a study in contrasts. Bellows was sometimes too brutal, Bonnard occasionally too bland. *Both Members of This Club*, (plate 872) is strident, virile, explicit; *The Letter* is subtle, feminine, intimate.

Intimacy in art is a quality difficult to convey. The subject matter of the intimate picture is, of necessity, slight, made up of recurring incidents in everyday life, scenes so fleeting that they pass almost without notice. But these must be seen with tenderness and sympathy. They must stimulate us to enter imaginatively the small, serene world in which they take place. Only a painter like Bonnard, gifted with exceptional sensitivity, can catch in his memory the instantaneous gesture, the unconscious pose, the singularity of appearance essential to such subjects.

In the picture reproduced here, Bonnard was fascinated by the appearance of a girl sitting at her desk. She seems absorbed and puzzled. One senses she is not writing a love letter. Perhaps it is only a thank-you note. Her shadow of a smile suggests that she wants it to be a little unconventional, a little whimsical but there is a momentary hesitation, her thought remains elusive. Her mood is conveyed by the hovering pen, the slight smile, the way the eyes seem to reread what has been written.

Bonnard never painted from a model. For this reason he was constantly making quick notations of things seen, notes in pen, pencil, and ink of each salient feature of the motif. These sketches, often indecipherable to anyone but himself, would fix in his mind the significant image caught by his alert vision. From these he would construct a formal harmony of line and color. His problem, however, was to preserve the spontaneity of his first inspiration, to hold, in spite of careful calculations, his gay, almost impish reaction to his subject.

This may explain his unconventional way of painting, as though the very informality of his methods would assist him in retaining the freshness of his original conceptions. He almost never worked at an easel. He tacked his canvases on the wall, indifferent to even the brightest wallpapers. At times he worked in his dining room, at times in a hotel bedroom, but hardly ever in a studio. He would often paint several pictures on one canvas and then cut them apart. Cursory as these methods may seem, Bonnard was at the same time exacting in self-criticism. He would, for example, go to a museum where his pictures were hanging and, while a friend distracted the guard, repaint certain passages which displeased him!

Collection: Alexandre Natanson, Paris. *Chester Dale Collection*, 1962. Signed. Painted about 1906. Canvas, 21⅝ x 18¾" (55 x 47.5 cm.).

883

884

Bonnard, particularly in his early work, wanted to catch the character of the scenes he painted, and to express their inner meaning even if this entailed a certain awkwardness in the composition. But he was basically a decorator. As Albert Aurier astutely observed, Bonnard is "a delightful ornamentalist, as skillful and resourceful as a Japanese and capable of embellishing all the ugly things of our life with the ingenuous and iridescent flowerings of his imagination."

Pierre Bonnard (French, 1867--1947)

883 *Bouquet of Flowers.* Signed. c. 1926. Canvas, 27⅝ x 18⅝" (70.3 x 47.4 cm.). Ailsa Mellon Bruce Collection

884 *The Artist's Sister and Her Children.* Signed, and dated 1898. Cardboard on wood, 12 x 10" (30.5 x 25.4 cm.). Ailsa Mellon Bruce Collection

885 *The Cab Horse.* Signed. c. 1895. Wood, 11¾ x 15¾" (29.7 x 40 cm.). Ailsa Mellon Bruce Collection

886 *Two Dogs in a Deserted Street.* Signed. c. 1894. Wood, 13⅞ x 10⅝" (35.1 x 27 cm.). Ailsa Mellon Bruce Collection

887 *Stairs in the Artist's Garden.* 1942/44. Canvas, 24⅞ x 28¾" (63.3 x 73.1 cm.). Ailsa Mellon Bruce Collection

888 *Children Leaving School.* Signed. c. 1895. Cardboard on wood, 11⅜ x 17⅜" (28.9 x 44 cm.). Ailsa Mellon Bruce Collection

889 *A Spring Landscape.* c. 1935. Canvas, 26⅝ x 40½" (67.6 x 103 cm.). Ailsa Mellon Bruce Collection

885

886

887

888

889

Edouard Vuillard

(FRENCH, 1868–1940)

890   THÉODORE DURET

Bonnard we associate with youth, with pictures like *The Letter*; but Vuillard, his close friend, was at his best when he was exploring the increasing frailty and infirmity of age. He seems to have felt a tender sympathy for those who were on the downward slope of life, and repeatedly painted them as they hastened onward at an ineluctably faster speed. He observed his mother in scores of paintings, noting her face with its ever deepening lines; her back bending more and more, from rheumatism; the gradual graying of her hair; and her growing resemblance to his grandmother, whom he drew when he was a young man.

Old men equally fascinated him. His likeness of Théodore Duret, the art critic and champion of the Impressionists, is among the most sensitive representations of age since the late portraits of Rembrandt. Duret sits in his study, surrounded by his works of art. Directly behind him are three paintings, the smaller ones unidentified, the larger one, *Telemachus and Mentor* by Tiepolo, now belonging to the Rijksmuseum, Amsterdam. Reflected in the mirror is Duret's portrait by Whistler, later acquired by the Metropolitan Museum, New York. In Whistler's painting, Duret is shown carrying over his arm a pink cloak, which is the key to Vuillard's own color scheme, and in his hand an opera hat. He looks a typical boulevardier. Thirty years pass, and Duret has totally changed. He appears meager; his hands seem to tremble; his eyes are red rimmed. His weightless, insubstantial body is rendered no more definitely than his surroundings. Thus this apparition of old age dissolves into its chromatic constituents, takes on the protective coloration characteristic of Vuillard's figures, and becomes one substance with all the other details of the scene. There is an effect of imprecision, enhanced by the use of cardboard as a ground. Because of its absorbency, outlines are blurred, and the result is a uniformity of texture, which Vuillard loved.

That nothing is precisely seen does not affect the precision of the design. The carefully constructed composition defines the mood of the portrait. Vuillard wished to indicate the claustral life of a scholar. Consequently Duret is shown as tightly constricted by the angles of the desk piled high with books, papers, reviews, the paraphernalia of his trade. The two wings of the writing table are like the blades of a scissors, seemingly ready to sheer the sitter in two, to destroy him. His favorite cat, Lulu, sits on his knee, an intimation of his solitude, his loneliness. It is a masterpiece of psychological portraiture; as Claude Roger-Marx has said, it "is worthy of inclusion with the great portraits of writers at work—with the Zola of Manet, the Duranty of Degas, and the Gustave Geffroy of Cézanne."

Collection: Théodore Duret, Paris. *Chester Dale Collection*, 1962. Signed, and dated 1912. Cardboard mounted on wood, 37½ x 29½" (95.2 x 74.8 cm.).

583

906

907

908

591

909

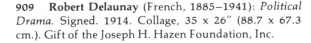

910

Although Paris in the last three hundred and fifty years has produced no Rubens, Rembrandt, or Velázquez, it has been, all in all, the most creative city for painting over the longest period in history. These reproductions show the work of a few of the artists who, in this century, formed the School of Paris. With Modigliani, Matisse, Braque, and Picasso, they provided for many years the dominant movements in the art of our time, whether Expressionism, Cubism, abstraction, or the more conventional vision of Utrillo and Derain. Until World War II, when New York became a new center of creativity, these painters, Parisian by birth or adoption, dominated the world of art.

909   Robert Delaunay (French, 1885–1941): *Political Drama.* Signed. 1914. Collage, 35 x 26" (88.7 x 67.3 cm.). Gift of the Joseph H. Hazen Foundation, Inc.

910   André Derain (French, 1880–1954): *Flowers in a Vase.* Signed. 1932. Canvas, 29½ x 37" (75 x 94 cm.). Chester Dale Collection

911   André Derain: *The Old Bridge.* Signed. 1910. Canvas, 31⅞ x 39½" (81 x 100.3 cm.). Chester Dale Collection

912   Chaim Soutine (Russian, 1893–1943): *Portrait of a Boy.* Signed. 1928. Canvas, 36¼ x 25⅝" (92.1 x 65.1 cm.). Chester Dale Collection

913   Maurice Utrillo (French, 1883–1955): *Marizy-Sainte-Geneviève.* Signed. c. 1910. Canvas, 23½ x 31⅞" (59.7 x 81 cm.). Chester Dale Collection

914   Maurice Utrillo: *Street at Corte, Corsica.* Signed. 1913. Canvas, 24 x 31¾" (60.8 x 80.7 cm.). Ailsa Mellon Bruce Collection

915   Raoul Dufy (French, 1877–1953): *Regatta at Cowes.* Signed, and dated 1934. Canvas, 32⅛ x 39½" (81.6 x 100.3 cm.). Ailsa Mellon Bruce Collection

911

912

913

914

915

Henri Matisse

(FRENCH, 1869-1954)

916   BEASTS OF THE SEA

More than seventy years ago Henri Matisse, king of the Fauves or "Wild Beasts," as he and his friends were called, challenged the doctrine generally accepted since the Renaissance that the suggestion of a third dimension through modeling is basic in painting. He pointed out that shading and perspective, at least as taught in art schools, tend to weaken the effect of line, color, and pattern. Instead he wished "to study each element of construction separately: drawing, color, values, composition; to explore how these elements could be combined into a synthesis without diminishing the eloquence of any one of them by the presence of the others."

Matisse's mastery of two-dimensional representation led logically to his exploration of the possibilities of collage. His first use of scissors and paper was in 1931, but only as a means to an end. He wanted to work out the placement of the figures in his decorations for the Barnes Gallery in Merion, Pennsylvania. Toward the end of his life, however, in ill health and unable to work at his easel, he turned to collage as an art in itself. He found, as he explained, that by using colored paper and scissors, "instead of establishing a contour, and then filling it with color . . . I draw directly in the color."

In 1950, when he was over eighty, he cut out one of his most beautiful collages, which he called *les bêtes de la mer*. It is a memory of the South Seas, which he had visited twenty years earlier. There are symbols of the aquatic life at the bottom of the ocean, of the surface of the water, of the island itself (perhaps Tahiti) and of the sky above. Matisse has described looking into a lagoon. He recounts how the water was "greyish jade-green, colored by the bottom, which lies very close, the branched coral and their variety of soft pastel tints, around which pass shoals of small fish, blue, yellow, and striped with brown, looking as though they were enamelled. And dotted about everywhere the dark brown of the sea-cucumbers, torpid and almost inert . . ." In the artist's description note that the colors of nature are muted, like the pastel tints he mentions, but in the collage colors blaze forth vividly. The artist observing his visual data, in Matisse's words, "must render the emotion they awaken . . . the emotion of the ensemble, the specific character of every object—modified by its relation to the others—all interlaced like a cord or a serpent." In other words the artist's transcription from nature must never be literal.

In *Beasts of the Sea* Matisse combines the most dissonant colors. Playing them against each other, he attains tonal resonances unique in art. Such chromatic harmonies in pigment and collage are Matisse's great contribution to painting; and they explain why he, of all contemporary artists, had the greatest influence on the color painters of the nineteen-sixties.

Collection: Family of the artist. *Ailsa Mellon Bruce Fund*, 1973. Constructed 1950. Paper on canvas (collage)   116⅜ x 60⅝" (295.5 x 154 cm.).

917

918

920

919

Henri Matisse (French, 1869–1954)

917 *Pot of Geraniums.* Signed. 1912. Canvas, 16¼ x 13⅛" (41.3 x 33.3 cm.). Chester Dale Collection

918 *Still Life with Pineapple.* Signed. 1924. Canvas, 19⅞ x 24¼" (50.5 x 61.5 cm.). Gift of the W. Averell Harriman Foundation in memory of Marie N. Harriman

919 *Woman with Amphora and Pomegranates.* 1952. Paper on canvas (collage), 96 x 37⅞" (243.6 x 96.3 cm.). Ailsa Mellon Bruce Fund

920 *Les Gorges du Loup.* Signed. 1920/25. Canvas, 19¾ x 24" (50.2 x 60.9 cm.). Chester Dale Collection

921 *La Coiffure.* Signed. 1901. Canvas, 37½ x 31½" (95.2 x 80.1 cm.). Chester Dale Collection

922 *Odalisque with Raised Arms.* Signed. 1923. Canvas, 25⅝ x 19¾" (65.1 x 50.2 cm.). Chester Dale Collection

923 *Venus.* Signed with initials. 1952. Paper on canvas (collage), 39⅞ x 30⅛" (101.2 x 76.5 cm.). Ailsa Mellon Bruce Fund

924 *Still Life: Apples on Pink Tablecloth.* Signed. c. 1922. Canvas, 23¾ x 28¾" (60.4 x 73 cm.). Chester Dale Collection

921

922

Matisse's painting bears a superficial and deceptive resemblance to the work of a child. But the revolution he introduced into art is rooted in studies which began when he was a copyist in the Louvre, and which he continued to do through his last years, when he executed his greatest designs—for a Dominican chapel at Vence, in southern France. Like Michelangelo, however, Matisse was always at pains to hide the effort that had gone into his work. He wished his paintings "to have the lightness and joyousness of springtime, which never lets anyone suspect the labor it has cost." In this statement he described his greatest gift: almost alone among twentieth-century artists he was able to convey his own delight in a person, or a place, or a flower, to communicate a joyousness of vision which eighty-five years and two wars did not diminish.

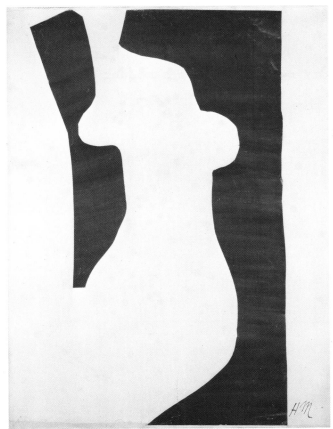

923

924

Georges Braque

(FRENCH, 1882–1963)

925   NUDE WOMAN WITH BASKET OF FRUIT

Braque's father and grandfather were housepainters, and he learned from them the meaning of craftsmanship. They gave him his command of texture, and above all they taught him patience and perseverance. He was always slow but determined. He used to box with Derain, and he would wear him down with a ponderous and impenetrable defense until his more powerful but wilder opponent could be felled with a single well-aimed blow. This tenacious slowness was characteristic of Braque's approach to painting. As he said, "Progress in art consists not in extending one's limits, but in knowing them better."

His fortieth birthday occurred in 1922, when the Salon d'Automne held a special exhibition in recognition of his achievement. The same year, at the height of his powers, he began his series of Canephori (Ceremonial Basket Bearers). Sensuality as we find it in the Old Masters, the late works of Titian and Rubens, for example, is difficult, though not impossible, to combine with the increasing abstraction characteristic of contemporary painting. And yet Braque's monumental, partially draped figures, abstract as they are, have a compelling eroticism that is impossible to forget. The giantess reproduced here might well represent "wide-bosomed Earth, the everlasting foundation of us all," as John Russell has pointed out, or conjure up "member-loving Aphrodite." In either role she suggests some modern symbol of fertility.

But the remarkable fact is the way these two-dimensional goddesses with their deliquescent outlines seem to have a visionary existence. Although nothing is modeled and there is no deviation from the flatness of the *espace pictural*, yet skillfully selected color patches and brilliantly related contours suggest volume, so that one can easily imagine the figures translated into sculpture, statues such as one sees in the gardens of Versailles. Apollinaire once said, "No one is less concerned than he [Braque] with psychology, and I fancy a stone moves him as much as a face does." Such indifference to personality led him to create universal types of femininity.

The series of the Canephori ended around 1927. According to Jean Leymarie, "Among many variants of unequal value, some less firmly designed than others, though all are imbued with a decorative stateliness, the finest is the Canephorus of 1926 in the Chester Dale Collection in Washington, outstanding for its power and robust vigour." And also, I might add, for its amplitude and fluidity of form.

Collection: Paul Rosenberg, Paris. *Chester Dale Collection*, 1962. Signed, and dated 1926. Canvas, 63¾ x 29¼" (162 x 74.3 cm.).

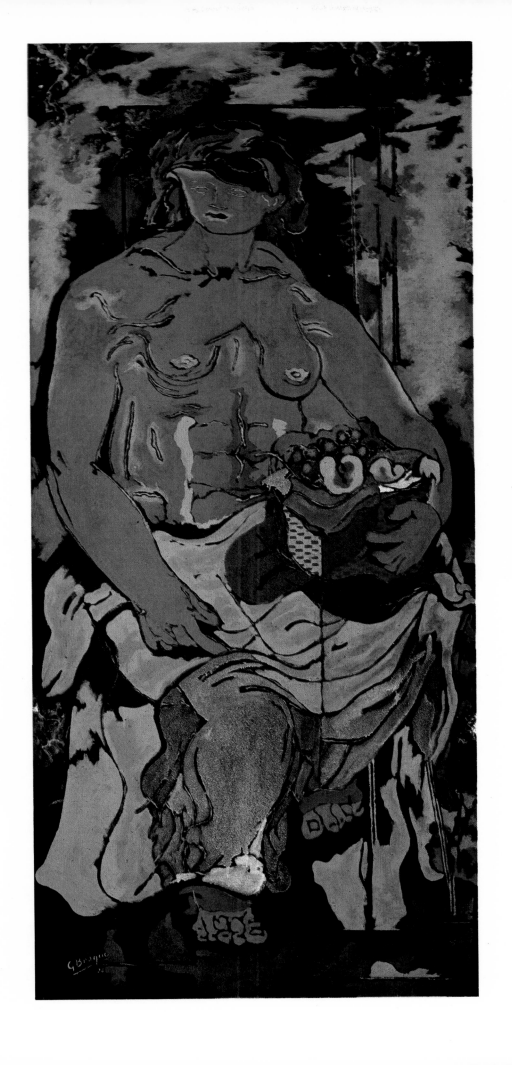

599

926

927

Braque was a master of powerful, chromatic tonalities, subdued in intensity, yet so strong in effect that one has difficulty in hanging his paintings beside those of other artists. Just as he used to knock out Derain when they were sparring, so his pictures knock out Derain's when their work is juxtaposed. But Derain had a facility denied to Braque. His still life shows how cleverly he manages to combine Cubism with representation.

928

929

930

Georges Braque (French, 1882–1963)

926 *Nude Woman with Fruit.* Signed, and dated 1925. Canvas, 39½ x 32″ (100.3 x 81.3 cm.). Chester Dale Collection

927 *Peonies.* Signed, and dated 1926. Wood, 22⅛ x 27¼″ (56.2 x 69.3 cm.). Chester Dale Collection

928 *Still Life: The Table.* Signed, and dated 1928. Canvas, 32 x 51½″ (81.3 x 130.8 cm.). Chester Dale Collection

929 *Still Life: Le Jour.* Signed, and dated 1929. Canvas, 45¼ x 57¾″ (115 x 146.7 cm.). Chester Dale Collection

930 **André Derain** (French, 1880–1954): *Harlequin.* Signed. 1919. Canvas, 29⅛ x 24″ (74 x 61 cm.). Chester Dale Collection

931 **André Derain**: *Still Life.* Signed. 1913. Canvas, 28⅞ x 36⅜″ (73.4 x 92.4 cm.). Chester Dale Collection

931

Lyonel Feininger

(AMERICAN, 1871–1956)

932   ZIRCHOW VII

Feininger was born in New York, and at twelve he became a concert violinist. When he was sixteen he went to Germany to study music but soon abandoned this career to become a painter, studying first in Hamburg and then in Berlin. He taught for a time at the Weimar Bauhaus and founded the group "The Blue Four" with Klee, Kandinsky, and Jawlensky. His life until 1936 was spent almost entirely in Germany, but in 1937 he returned permanently to the United States.

His son Lux has written the following letter to Ralph Colin, the family lawyer, in answer to my request for information about *Zirchow VII.*

"The date of the painting, 1918, marks a period in Lyonel Feininger's life almost completely overshadowed by his horror of the world war. He had arrived at the conviction that, apart from right and wrong, war itself was totally bad and was a sign of the badness of society. His painting, as many letters particularly from this period testify, was his sole refuge from his spiritual affliction. 'Expression of the deepest kind of inner longing' is a term recurring in letters to the poet Knoblauch, to the painter Alfred Kubin, and many others. What this longing was, one must constantly guess, for it is never stated otherwise than as existing. In this particular painting, a depth of structural unity, of interpenetration of light and substance, presented in deeply glowing color, is achieved which is indeed outstanding in even this, one of my father's very strongest, periods. He therefore rightly considered this to be one of his very major works. It was painted in Zehlendorf, that small suburb of Berlin, in those years an almost rural village, in which he was, as an 'enemy alien,' severely restricted in his movements and, nominally, under daily police sur-veillance . . . . Travel was forbidden. Hunger was severely felt by everyone at this stage, mostly so in the large urban areas, where the strictest rationing of all foods and unavailability of many essential dietary items caused considerable suffering. The vision of unity and reconciliation which is in this and other paintings of L. F. is to be seen against this background, like the rainbow against the thunder cloud. The theme, the church of Zirchow, a Thuringian village, was sketched by my father in the happy times he had spent in Weimar in the years 1905, 1913, and 1914. In the act of evocation which, in my father's painting, is a synonym for 'composition,' the sketches made so many years earlier played an essential part. It is essential for the understanding of Feininger's art to realize that the underlying thought of it is religious in the deepest and truest sense of the word, and that this has nothing whatever to do with membership in church or synagogue, both of which my father repudiated as almost blasphemously contradicting the spirit of the bible. For the period of world war I one may say that his outlook was Tolstoyian."

Collection: Mrs. Julia Feininger, New York. *Gift of Julia Feininger,* 1966. Painted 1918. Canvas, 31¾ x 39⅝" (80.7 x 100.6 cm.).

Piet Mondrian

(DUTCH, 1872–1944)

933   LOZENGE IN RED, YELLOW, AND BLUE

It is noteworthy that the roots of modern Expressionism can be traced to a Dutch artist, Vincent van Gogh, and that the opposite stylistic trend, coldly intellectual and purely optical, can be traced to another Dutchman, Piet Mondrian.

The painting reproduced here, dated about 1925, is one of about twenty paintings by Mondrian that are square and stand on one corner. The first was done in 1918, but most were painted in 1925 and 1926. He returned to this compositional pattern at the end of his life with *Victory Boogie-Woogie* (Collection of Mr. and Mrs. Burton G. Tremaine), which he was working on when he died.

Mondrian's abstractions are exercises in optical balance. Around an imaginary center the primary colors, blue, red, and yellow, to which he limited his palette, are carefully equalized in their placing, value, intensity, and amount. Thus the eye is drawn equally over the whole of the picture's surface. This gives the effect of dynamic movement held in tension.

Such paintings represent the complete dehumanization of art. Mondrian "systematically eliminated the world of nature and man." As he said once, "Yes, all in all, Nature is a damned wretched affair. I can hardly stand it."

Mondrian's ideas parallel those of Spinoza. It is interesting that the philosopher and the painter, separated by 250 years, should have arrived at much the same conclusion, to quote from Spinoza's *Ethics* "that the mind can create of its own force, sensations of ideas which do not belong to anything." Here one finds the philosophical basis of Mondrian's work.

The psychological background, however, is more interesting and perhaps more significant. Mondrian grew up in the shadow of a domineering father who was a gifted draftsman and academic realist. Much of the son's progress toward complete abstraction may well have been a rebellion against paternal and family influences. It is interesting to note that he kept his diploma from the State Academy of Fine Arts in Amsterdam until his death—proof to himself that he was as competent an academic painter as either his father or his uncle, who had been his teachers. Nevertheless, he had to express his own personality, to destroy the academic tradition which had been thrust upon him. Many artists of Mondrian's generation were engaged, figuratively speaking, in blowing up the academies, but pictures like the one reproduced sparked the most effective explosions.

Collections: Bienert, Dresden; Jon Nicholas Streep, New York; John L. Senior, Jr., New York. *Gift of Herbert and Nannette Rothschild*, 1971. Painted about 1925. Canvas on fiberboard, 56¼ x 56″ (142.8 x 142.3 cm.).

605

Pablo Picasso

(SPANISH, 1881–1973)

934 FAMILY OF SALTIMBANQUES

In 1905 Picasso intended to paint two large pictures but completed only one, the *Family of Saltimbanques*. Roughly seven feet square, it is the most impressive achievement of his early period. His many studies of the friends he had made at the Cirque Medrano—clowns, jugglers, and strolling players—are here gathered together in an empty, treeless landscape under a blue sky from which a fog seems to be clearing. On one side is a group comprising Harlequin holding the hand of a little girl, next to him the director of the troupe with a heavy paunch, dressed in red tights and wearing the mock crown of the bronze jester sculptured at about the same time, and at his side two adolescent acrobats. The composition is balanced precariously by a solitary girl (inspired perhaps by a Tanagra statuette), who is seated further in the foreground. These detached figures are unified by their mood of contemplation and by their inner loneliness.

Harlequin has the profile of Picasso himself. Jung has pointed out that the artist's desire to paint himself repeatedly in this disguise reveals a subconscious wish to play the role of Harlequin, "to juggle with everything," as Roland Penrose has perceptively said, "while remaining aloof and irresponsible."

The enigma of these circus people standing together as though awaiting some command or some mysterious event fascinated the German poet Rainer Maria Rilke. In 1918 he asked a friend who owned the painting whether he might live in the same room with it. Later he told her that the *Saltimbanques*, "the loveliest Picasso in which there is so much Paris that for moments I forget," had inspired him to write the fifth of his *Duino Elegies*, which begins:

> But tell me, who *are* they, these acrobats, even a little
> more fleeting than we ourselves—so urgently, ever since childhood,
> wrung by an (oh, for the sake of whom?)
> never-contented will? That keeps on wringing them,
> bending them, slinging them, swinging them,
> throwing them and catching them back; as though from an oily
> smoother air, they come down on the threadbare
> carpet, thinned by their everlasting
> upspringing, this carpet forlornly
> lost in the cosmos.

Collections: André Level, Paris; "Peau de l'Ours," Paris; Hertha von Koenig, Munich. *Chester Dale Collection*, 1962. Signed. Painted 1905. Canvas, 83¾ x 90⅜" (212.8 x 229.6 cm.).

607

Sculpture

The National Gallery of Art possesses a broad array of masterworks representing all sculptural media from the fourteenth century to the twentieth. The earliest of the works illustrated in this section are capital examples of northern and southern Italian relief-carvings of the Trecento, while international developments in late medieval sculpture are represented by two exceptional stone groups—the *Trinity* and *St. George*, both made to Spanish commissions. (The *St. George* is the largest free-standing Nottingham alabaster at present known.) The Gallery's greatest concentration of sculptural masterpieces represents the cultural flowering of Renaissance Italy. The stars in this constellation are a possible early work by Jacopo della Quercia; the finest example of a widespread type of half-length Madonna composition; the famous Martelli *David* and a fine group of relief plaquettes associated with Donatello; in addition to works by Desiderio, Antonio Rossellino, Verrocchio, Francesco di Giorgio (including a group of bronzes incorporating perhaps his finest relief), Riccio, and Mino (represented by four wonderful marbles culminating in one of the earliest dated busts of the Florentine Renaissance, his *Astorgio Manfredi* of 1455).

This singular density of first-rate Quattrocento

947 **Attributed to Adriaen de Vries** (Dutch-Florentine, c. 1560–1627): *Mercury*. c. 1603/13. Bronze, without base, 69⅝ x 19 x 37¼" (177 x 48.5 x 94.9 cm.). Andrew W. Mellon Collection

figural sculpture provides a splendid foil to a composite collection of Renaissance small bronzes, medals, and especially plaquettes, in which the Gallery's holdings are unmatched in breadth and quality. With almost 1,500 of these rare treasures of miniature sculpture, among them such unique specimens as Costanzo's medal of Mohammed II, and with the superlative portrait of Leon Battista Alberti taking pride of place in a group of reliefs and plaquettes acknowledged to be the finest such series in existence, the National Gallery's collection puts Washington on a rank with Florence, Vienna, and London as an internationally important center for the enjoyment and study of Renaissance bronzes. bronzes.

The sixteenth century is more selectively but still impressively represented, by fine works associated with the Venetian period of Jacopo Sansovino, by the noble terra-cotta *Knight* of his contemporary Vittoria, by masterpieces from Florence, such as Danti's *Descent from the Cross*, and by beautiful works from central and northern Europe such as Riemenschneider's *St. Burchard*, Vischer's *Orpheus* relief, and the magnificent *Mercury* made after Giambologna's model, perhaps for the Emperor Rudolf II in Prague.

Adriaen de Vries, the possible author of the Mellon *Mercury*, inaugurates a series of rare seventeenth-century masterworks with his signed and dated *Virtue and Vice* of 1610, a sequence continued with a celebrated youthful bust by Bernini, with the graceful fountains designed by Le Brun for the Théâtre de l'Eau at Versailles, and with Foggini's elaborate marble portraits of the Florentine Grand Ducal rulers. Much of the Gallery's recent activity has been focussed on expanding these areas of High Renaissance and Baroque sculpture, so that we have now added to our holdings such treasures as Antonio Lombardo's important *Allegory* of 1512 and an early terra-cotta bust of St. Matthias by Algardi.

Eighteenth- and nineteenth-century sculpture is another area of long-standing strength for the Gallery. In addition to splendid Italian productions such as the Berninesque *Thetis*, it houses masterpieces by many preeminent French artists, including cabinet and garden figures, Academy reception-pieces such as Robert Le Lorrain's *Galatea*, and portraits of royal figures as well as of other individuals representing many levels of eighteenth-century society. The Gallery's collection of original maquettes and early marbles and bronzes by Rodin is outstanding, and fine works by Carpeaux, Gauguin, and Saint-Gaudens provide a wider chronological and geographic frame of reference for the later nineteenth century.

From more recent times, the Gallery's collection includes an entirely autograph late masterpiece by Lehmbruck; an early and magnificent marble *Bird*—together with a large portrait—by Brancusi; an important Surrealist sculpture which Giacometti executed at the turning point of his career; and a strikingly beautiful *Cubi* by David Smith. These later works dramatically extend the significance of the sculpture holdings at the National Gallery of Art. Already the repository of one of the greatest Renaissance collections, its interest and appeal is thus carried forward, at the same astonishing level of quality, to the threshold of our own day.

Douglas Lewis
Curator of Sculpture

948

948 Giovanni di Balduccio (Pisan, active 1317–1349): *Charity*. 1328–34. Marble relief, 17¾ × 13⅞″ (45.1 × 35.3 cm.). Samuel H. Kress Collection

949 English School (last quarter XIV century): *St. George and the Dragon*. Alabaster, painted and gilded, 32 × 23¾ × 8⅛″ (81.5 × 60.5 × 20.5 cm.). Samuel H. Kress Collection

949

950

951

952

950 Spanish School (early XIV century): *The Holy Trinity*. c. 1300. Alabaster, 33½ x 14 x 11½" (85.3 x 35.7 x 29.2 cm.). Samuel H. Kress Collection

951 Tino di Camaino (Tuscan, c. 1285–1337): *Madonna and Child with Queen Sancia, Saints and Angels*. c. 1335–45. Alabaster relief, 20¼ x 14⅞" (51.4 x 37.8 cm.). Samuel H. Kress Collection

952 Jacopo della Quercia (Sienese, 1367?–1438): *Madonna of Humility*. Early XV century. Marble, 22⅞ x 19¼ x 11⅛" (58.4 x 48.8 x 28.3 cm.). Samuel H. Kress Collection

953 **Florentine School** (XV century): *Madonna and Child*. 1425. Wood, carved, painted, and gilded, 40⅜ x 24½″ (125 x 62.3 cm.). Samuel H. Kress Collection

954 **Leon Battista Alberti** (Florentine, 1404–1472): *Self-Portrait*. c. 1435. Bronze plaque with black patina, 7⅞ x 5⅜ ″ (20.1 x 13.6 cm.). Samuel H. Kress Collection

955 **Florentine School** (XV century):*Madonna and Child*. c. 1425. Terra cotta, painted and gilded, 47½ x 18½ x 13⅛″ (120.8 x 47.2 x 33.5 cm.). Andrew W. Mellon Collection

956 **Mino da Fiesole** (Florentine, 1429–1484): *Charity*. c. 1465–70. Marble relief, 49¾ x 17" (126 x 43 cm.). Andrew W. Mellon Collection

957 **Mino da Fiesole**: *Faith*. c. 1465–70. Marble relief, 49¾ x 17" (126 x 43 cm.). Andrew W. Mellon Collection

958

960

959

958 **Mino da Fiesole**: *Astorgio Manfredi*. Dated 1455. Marble, 20¼ x 21¼ x 10⅞″ (51.5 x 54.2 x 27.7 cm.). Widener Collection

959 **Upper Rhenish School**: *The Dead Christ Supported by an Angel (The Trinity)*. c. 1440. Alabaster relief, painted and gilded, 12¼ x 8⅞ x 3⅞″ (31.1 x 22.6 x 9.8 cm.). Gift of Mrs. Ralph Harman Booth

960 **Mino da Fiesole**: *The Virgin Annunciate*. c. 1458. Marble, 20 x 14½ x 5⅜″ (51 x 37 x 13.6 cm.). Samuel H. Kress Collection

961   Antonio Rossellino (Florentine, 1427–1478/79): *The Young St. John the Baptist.* c. 1470. Marble, 13⅝ x 11¾ x 6¼" (34.7 x 29.8 x 16.1 cm.). Samuel H. Kress Collection

962   Antonio Rossellino: *Madonna and Child.* c. 1477–81. Marble relief, 33 x 22" (84 x 56 cm.). Samuel H. Kress Collection

963   Desiderio da Settignano (Florentine, 1428–1464): *St. Jerome in the Desert.* c. 1461. Marble relief, 16¾ x 21½ (42.7 x 54.8 cm.). Widener Collection

964   Desiderio da Settignano: *Bust of a Little Boy.* c. 1455–60. Marble, 10⅜ x 9¾ x 5⅞" (26.3 x 24.7 x 15 cm.). Andrew W. Mellon Collection

965   Desiderio da Settignano: *The Christ Child.* c. 1460–64. Marble, 12 x 10⅜ x 6⅜" (30.5 x 26.5 x 16.3 cm.). Samuel H. Kress Collection

962

961

963

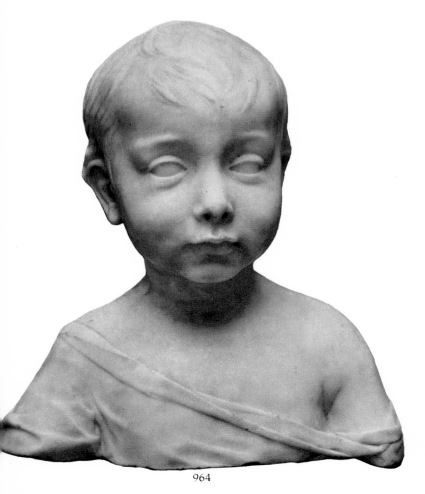

964

965

966

967

968

628

969

970

966   **Donatello** (Florentine, c. 1386–1466): *The David of the Casa Martelli*. Third quarter XV century. Marble, 64 x 19¾ x 16⅝″ (162.8 x 50.4 x 42.4 cm.). Widener Collection

967   **Francesco di Giorgio** (Sienese, 1439–1501/02): *St. Jerome*. c. 1477–85. Bronze relief, 21⅝ x 14¾″ (55 x 37.3 cm.). Samuel H. Kress Collection

968   **Costanzo da Ferrara** (worked chiefly in Naples, XV century): *Mohammad II, Sultan of the Turks*. c. 1480. Bronze medal, obverse, diam. 4⅞″ (12.3 cm.). Samuel H. Kress Collection

969   **Francesco di Giorgio**: *St. John the Baptist*. Last quarter XV century. Bronze plaquette with black patina, diam. 8″ (20.3 cm.). Samuel H. Kress Collection

970   **Francesco di Giorgio**: *Sebastian*. Last quarter XV century. Bronze plaquette with black patina, diam. 8″ (20.3 cm.). Samuel H. Kress Collection

971   **Lorenzo di Pietro, called Vecchietta** (Sienese, c. 1412–1480): *Winged Figure Holding a Torch*. c. 1470. Bronze, without base, 17⅞ x 6⅞ x 8¼″ (45.6 x 17.7 x 21 cm.). Samuel H. Kress Collection

971

972 Andrea della Robbia (Florentine, 1435–1525):
The Adoration of the Child. c. 1480. Glazed terra-cotta
relief, including base, 50⅜ x 30½" (127.8 x 77.4 cm.).
Samuel H. Kress Collection

973 After Andrea del Verrocchio: *Alexander the
Great.* XVI century. Marble relief, 21 x 14½" (55.9 x
36.7 cm.). Gift of Therese K. Straus

975

976

977

974 Studio of Benedetto da Maiano: *St. John the Baptist*. c. 1480. Terra cotta, painted, 19¼ x 20½ x 10¼″ (48.9 x 52 x 26 cm.). Andrew W. Mellon Collection

975 Domenico Gagini (Lombard, mentioned 1448–1492): *The Nativity*. c. 1458. Marble relief, 35½ x 20½″ (90 x 52 cm.). Samuel H. Kress Collection

976 Andrea del Verrocchio (Florentine, c. 1435–1488): *Giuliano de' Medici*. c. 1475. Terra cotta, 24 x 26 x 11⅛″ (61 x 66 x 28.3 cm.). Andrew W. Mellon Collection

977 Andrea del Verrocchio: *Lorenzo de' Medici*. c. 1480. Terra cotta, painted, 25⅞ x 23¼ x 12⅞″ (65.8 x 59.1 x 32.7 cm.). Samuel H. Kress Collection

978

978   Il Riccio (Andrea Briosco) (Paduan, 1470–1532): *The Entombment*. c. 1506–16. Bronze relief, 19⅞ x 29¾" (50.4 x 75.5 cm.). Samuel H. Kress Collection

979   Francesco da Sant'Agata (Paduan, active c. 1520): *Hercules and Antaeus*. Bronze, 15 x 4¾ x 10½" (38 x 12 x 26.5 cm.). Widener Collection

980   Francesco da Laurana (Venetian, c. 1425–1502): *A Princess of the House of Aragon*. 1472–75. Marble, 17½ x 17¾ x 8⅝" (44.4 x 45.2 x 22.1 cm.). Andrew W. Mellon Collection

981   Giovanni Antonio Amadeo (Lombard, 1447–1522): *Lodovico Sforza, Called Il Moro*. 1491–94. Marble relief, diam. 24" (61 cm.). Andrew W. Mellon Collection

982   Pietro Lombardo (Lombard-Venetian, c. 1435–1515): *A Singing Angel*. c. 1490. Marble, 33⅞ x 11 x 11¾" (86 x 28 x 30 cm.). Samuel H. Kress Collection

979

980

981

982

983

983 **Antonio Lombardo** (Venetian, c. 1458–1516): *Peace Establishing Her Reign: Allegory of the Victory of Ravenna.* 1512. Bronze, 15⅞ x 13¼ x 30″ (40.6 x 33.9 x 76 cm.). Ailsa Mellon Bruce Fund

984 **Jacopo Sansovino** (Florentine-Venetian, 1486–1570): *Venus Anadyomene.* c. 1527. Bronze, 65½ x 17¼ x 13¼″ (166 x 44 x 33.7 cm.). Andrew W. Mellon Collection

985 **Peter Vischer the Younger** (German, 1487–1528): *Orpheus and Eurydice.* c. 1515. Bronze, 7¾ x 5¾″ (19.5 x 15 cm.). Samuel H. Kress Collection

986 **Tilman Riemenschneider** (German, c. 1460–1531): *St. Burchard of Würzburg.* c. 1510. Wood, 32⅜ x 18½ x 11⅞″ (82.3 x 47.2 x 30.2 cm.). Samuel H. Kress Collection

987 **Benedetto da Rovezzano** (Florentine, 1474–c. 1554): *Relief from an Altar or Tabernacle.* c. 1505–13. Marble, 22 x 51″ (56 x 129.5 cm.). Widener Collection

984

1008 Jean-Antoine Houdon (French, 1741–1828): *Giuseppe Balsamo, Conte di Cagliostro.* Signed, and dated 1786. Marble, 24¾ x 23 x 13½" (62.9 x 58.9 x 34.3 cm.). Samuel H. Kress Collection

1009 Jean-Antoine Houdon: *Diana.* Signed, and dated 1778. Marble, with base 32⅛ x 17¾ x 12⅝" (81.6 x 45.1 x 32.2 cm.). Gift of Syma Busiel

1010 Clodion (French, 1738–1814): *A Vestal.* Signed, and dated 1770. Marble, 37½ x 16½ x 13¾" (95.5 x 42.1 x 35 cm.). Samuel H. Kress Collection

1011 Clodion: *La Surprise.* Signed, and dated 1799. Terra cotta, including base, 14½ x 10⅛ x 8" (37 x 25.9 x 20.3 cm.). Gift of Mrs. Jesse Isidor Straus

1012 Jean-Antoine Houdon: *Alexandre Brongniard.* Signed, and dated 1777. Marble, 15⅜ x 11¼ x 7⅜" (39.2 x 28.7 x 19 cm.). Widener Collection

1013 Jean-Antoine Houdon: *Louise Brongniard.* 1777. Marble, 14⅛ x 9⅞ x 7⅝" (37.7 x 25.3 x 19.5 cm.). Widener Collection

1011

1012

1013

1014 **Jean-Baptiste Carpeaux** (French, 1827–1875): *Neapolitan Fisherboy.* Signed, and dated 1861. Marble, 36¼ x 16½ x 18⅜″ (92 x 42 x 47 cm.). Samuel H. Kress Collection

1015 **Jean-Baptiste Carpeaux**: *Girl with a Shell.* Signed, and dated 1867. Marble, 40¾ x 16⅞ x 20¼″ (103.5 x 43 x 51.5 cm.). Samuel H. Kress Collection

1015

1016 **Paul Gauguin** (French, 1848–1903): *Eve.* 1890. Ceramic, painted, 23⅞ x 11 x 10¾″ (60.6 x 27.9 x 27.3 cm.). Ailsa Mellon Bruce Fund

1017 **Auguste Rodin** (French, 1840–1917): *The Evil Spirits.* Signed. 1899. Marble, 28 x 29¾ x 23¼″ (71.2 x 75.7 x 59 cm.). Gift of Mrs. John W. Simpson

1018 **Auguste Rodin**: *Bust of a Woman.* Signed, and dated 1875. Terra cotta, 19¼ x 14⅛ x 10⅝″ (48.9 x 35.6 x 33.6 cm.). Gift of Mrs. John W. Simpson

1014

1016

1017

1018

647

1019

1020

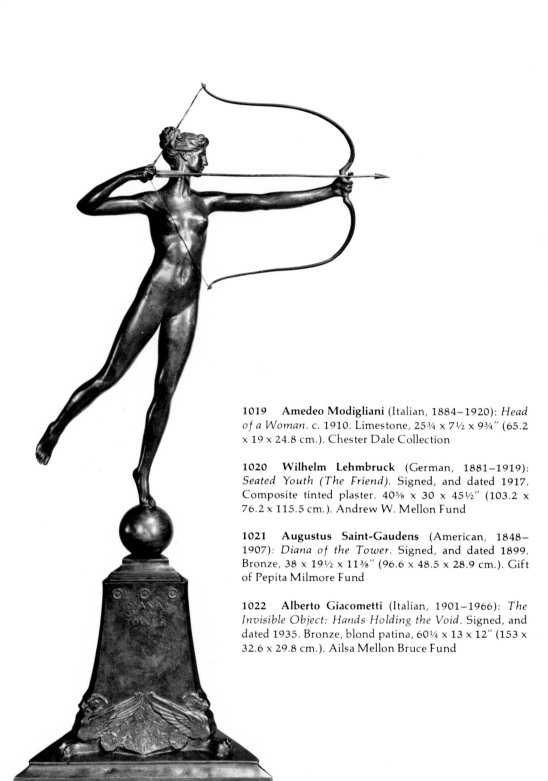

1021

1019 **Amedeo Modigliani** (Italian, 1884–1920): *Head of a Woman*. c. 1910. Limestone, 25¾ x 7½ x 9¾″ (65.2 x 19 x 24.8 cm.). Chester Dale Collection

1020 **Wilhelm Lehmbruck** (German, 1881–1919): *Seated Youth (The Friend)*. Signed, and dated 1917. Composite tinted plaster. 40⅝ x 30 x 45½″ (103.2 x 76.2 x 115.5 cm.). Andrew W. Mellon Fund

1021 **Augustus Saint-Gaudens** (American, 1848–1907): *Diana of the Tower*. Signed, and dated 1899. Bronze, 38 x 19½ x 11⅜″ (96.6 x 48.5 x 28.9 cm.). Gift of Pepita Milmore Fund

1022 **Alberto Giacometti** (Italian, 1901–1966): *The Invisible Object: Hands Holding the Void*. Signed, and dated 1935. Bronze, blond patina, 60¼ x 13 x 12″ (153 x 32.6 x 29.8 cm.). Ailsa Mellon Bruce Fund

1022

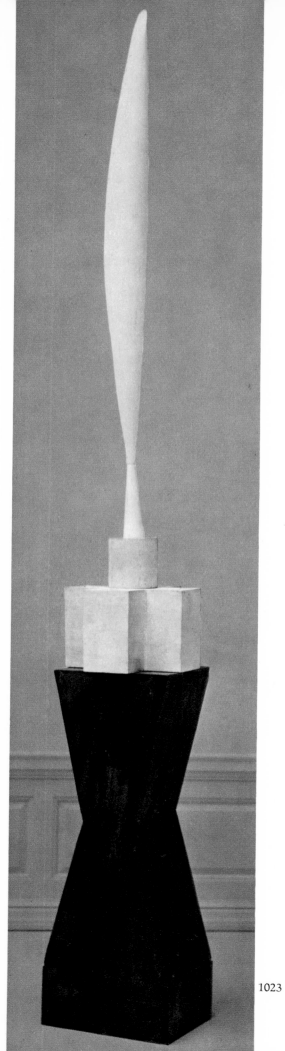

1023

1024

650

1025

1023 **Constantin Brancusi** (Rumanian, 1876–1957):
Agnes E. Meyer. 1929. Black marble, height 90⅝″
(230.1 cm.). Gift of Eugene and Agnes Meyer

1024 **Constantin Brancusi**: *Bird in Space.* 1925. Marble, stone and wood, height 136½″ (344.6 cm.). Gift of
Eugene and Agnes Meyer

1025 **David Smith** (American, 1906–1965): *Cubi
XXVI.* 1965. 9′ 11⅜″ x 12′ 7¼″ (303.2 x 384.2 cm.).
Promised Gift of Helen B. Stern

Drawings

XIII TO XX CENTURY

Drawings

A major collection of graphic arts, in contrast with paintings and sculpture, necessarily includes many more individual works, and usually depends upon the generosity of many more individual donors. In this introduction, it may be most useful to give a summary account of the coming to the National Gallery of the many thousands of works of graphic art that constitute its collection. With the generous support of numerous friends, the Gallery's holdings have grown with striking rapidity.

At the time of this interim report on our progress, the collections of the Department of Graphic Arts comprise prints, drawings, illustrated books, and photographs. Since this section can reproduce only a small selection, the choice has been restricted to drawings, even excluding many types of works that are normally grouped under this heading. A number of our later pastels, gouaches, and collages appear above in the paintings section, for example, the fine works by La Tour, Degas, Renoir, Toulouse-Lautrec, Vuillard, and Matisse. We have not included our monotypes, nor impressions of prints with drawings over them. From the fine group of medieval and Renaissance miniatures and drawings for illumination in the Rosenwald Collection, we have included only a token, the magnificent thirteenth-century leaf from the Arenberg Psalter.

The first gifts of graphic art to the new National Gallery of Art, in 1941, consisted mainly of old master prints, donated by Ellen Bullard, Philip Hofer, Paul Sachs, and especially W. G. Russell Allen, whose contribution provided a large and excellent survey. Our first important gift of drawings came in 1942, from Mrs. John W. Simpson: eight fine Rodins which exemplify his marvelous economy of line, a touchstone for authentic Rodins in that most of them had been given directly to the Simpsons by the artist. The first truly major gift, Joseph E. Widener's superbly select collection of graphic art, followed in the fall of the same year. With the exception of a few early works, the beautiful Dürer *Young Woman in Netherlandish Dress* and eight fine Rembrandts, the main strength of the Widener collection is in the eighteenth century. An extraordinary group of eighteenth-century French illustrated books—with so many special copies, early proofs, and luxurious bindings typical of the period—is complemented by an equally fine collection of French prints and spiced with large groups of drawings for the book illustrations, including designs by Boucher, Gravelot, Eisen, and Moreau le Jeune.

Within a year of the Widener donation came the first of the most important series of gifts the department has received to date, the extraordinary collection of Lessing J. Rosenwald. For the next three

1044

1045

1046

665

1048

1047

1049

1047 Luca Cambiaso (Genoese, 1527–1585). *The Martyrdom of St. Lawrence*. Before 1581. Pen and brown ink and wash, 15¼ x 9⅝″ (38.8 x 24.4 cm.). Ailsa Mellon Bruce Fund

1048 Agostino Carracci (Bolognese, 1557–1602): *Wooden Landscape with a Boat*. c. 1585–90. Pen and brown ink, 8½ x 12⅞″ (21.6 x 32.7 cm.). Anonymous Promised Gift

1049 Jacopo Tintoretto (Venetian, 1518–1594): *Standing Youth with His Arm Raised, Seen from Behind*. Black chalk on buff paper, 14¼ x 8⅝″ (36.3 x 21.9 cm.). Ailsa Mellon Bruce Fund

1050

1051

1050 Bartholomeus Breenbergh (Dutch, 1599–1658/9): *Landscape with Large Rock*. 1619–c. 1629. Pen and brown ink and wash, some black chalk, 9¾ x 10⅝″ (24.9 x 27 cm.). Ailsa Mellon Bruce Fund

1051 Rembrandt van Ryn (Dutch, 1606–1669): *Self-Portrait*. c. 1637. Red chalk, 5⅛ x 4¾″ (12.9 x 11.9 cm.). Rosenwald Collection

1052 Jacques de Gheyn II (Flemish, 1565–1629): *Landscape with Sleeping Peasants*. c. 1603. Pen and brown ink on buff paper, 10⅛ x 15¼″ (25.7 x 38.7 cm.). Anonymous Promised Gift

1052

1053

1054

Rembrandt van Ryn (Dutch, 1606–1669)

1053 *Saskia Lying in Bed.* c. 1638. Pen and brush in bistre, wash, 4⅞ x 7⅛" (12.5 x 18 cm.). Ailsa Mellon Bruce Fund

1054 *The Preacher Jan Cornelius Sylvius.* c. 1644/45. Pen and bistre drawing, 5¼ x 4⅞" (13.4 x 12.2 cm.). Rosenwald Collection

1055 *View over the Amstel from the Rampart.* c. 1646. Pen and wash of brown india ink, 3½ x 7¼" (8.9 x 18.5 cm.). Rosenwald Collection

1056 *Landscape with Cottage and Hay Barn.* c. 1650. Pen and gray-brown bistre, wash, 4⅛ x 7" (10.5 x 17.9 cm.). Rosenwald Collection

1057 *Eliezer and Rebecca at the Well.* c. 1640–50. Pen and brown ink and brown wash with white body color, 8 x 12⅞" (20.4 x 32.6 cm.). Widener Collection

1058 *Lot and His Family Leaving Sodom.* c. 1655. Pen and bistre, 7¼ x 11" (19.7 x 27.9 cm.). Widener Collection

1055

1056

1057

1058

1082

1083

1084

1085

1085 **Honoré Daumier** (French, 1808–1879): *Two Lawyers*. Crayon and gray and brown and pink washes, 10½ x 9¼" (26.5 x 23.5 cm.). Gift of Myron A. Hofer in memory of his mother, Mrs. Charles Hofer

1086 **Edouard Manet** (French, 1832–1883): *The Man in the Tall Hat*. Watercolor, 14⅛ x 10⅛" (35.7 x 25.7 cm.). Rosenwald Collection

1087 **Edgar Degas** (French, 1834–1917): *The Artist's Brother, René*. 1855. Pencil, 11½ x 9" (29.3 x 23 cm.). Promised Gift of Mr. and Mrs. Paul Mellon

1088 **Edgar Degas**: *Jockey*. c. 1898. Washed pastel and brown wash, 11 x 7⅞" (28 x 20.1 cm.). Gift of Mrs. Jane C. Carey for the Addie Burr Clark Memorial Collection

1089 **Mary Cassatt** (American, 1844–1926): *Tramway*. c. 1891. Black crayon, 14⅜ x 10⅝" (36.5 x 27 cm.). Rosenwald Collection

1086

1088

1087

1089

1090

1092

1091

1093

1090 **Vincent van Gogh** (Dutch, 1853–1890): *Harvest–The Plain of La Crau.* c. 1888. Reed pen, 9⅝ x 12½″ (24.3 x 31.6 cm.). Promised Gift of Mr. and Mrs. Paul Mellon

1091 **Paul Gauguin** (French, 1848–1903): *Nave Nave Fenua.* c. 1894–1900. Ink drawing with watercolor, 16½ x 10¼″ (41.9 x 26 cm.). Rosenwald Collection

1092 **Winslow Homer** (American, 1836–1910): *Incoming Tide: Scarboro, Maine.* 1883. Watercolor, 15 x 21½″ (38.1 x 54.8 cm.). Gift of Mrs. Charles R. Henschel in memory of her husband

1093 **Winslow Homer**: *Sketch for Hound and Hunter.* 1892. Watercolor, 13⅞ x 20″ (35.4 x 50.8 cm.). Gift of Mrs. Charles R. Henschel in memory of her husband

1094 **Odilon Redon** (French, 1840–1916): *Head of a Veiled Woman.* Charcoal on tan paper, 20½ x 14¾″ (52.2 x 37.5 cm.). Rosenwald Collection

1094

1095

1096

1097

1098

1095 **Edvard Munch** (Norwegian, 1863–1944): *Two Women's Heads.* Colored crayon, 11¼ x 14⅞" (28.3 x 37.4 cm.). Anonymous Promised Gift

1096 **Pablo Picasso** (Spanish, 1881–1973): *Self-Portrait.* c. 1902. Crayon and watercolor, 12 x 9⅜" (30.4 x 23.8 cm.). Ailsa Mellon Bruce Collection

1097 **Auguste Rodin** (French, 1840–1917): *Dancing Figure.* 1905. Pencil with brown wash, 12¾ x 9⅞" (32.5 x 25 cm.). Gift of Mrs. John W. Simpson

1098 **Henri Matisse** (French, 1869–1954): *Young Girl with Long Hair.* 1926. Pencil, 21¼ x 14½" (54 x 37 cm.). Rosenwald Collection

1099 **Egon Schiele** (Austrian, 1890–1918): *Seated Nude.* 1918. Black crayon, 17 x 11" (43 x 27.5 cm.). Anonymous Promised Gift

1099

1100

1100 **Ernst Ludwig Kirchner** (German, 1880–1938): *Nude Woman in Tub.* c. 1923. Pen, wash, colored crayon, 21½ x 14⅛" (52 x 36 cm.). Anonymous Promised Gift

1101 **Joan Miró** (Spanish, born 1893): *Three Women.* 1934. Ink and pastel, 24½ x 18" (62.2 x 45.7 cm.). Gift of Frank and Jeannette Eyerly

1102 **Arshile Gorky** (American, 1904–1948): *The Plow and the Song.* 1947. Pencil, charcoal, pastel, and oil on paper, approximately 48 x 59" (121.9 x 142.2 cm.). Gift of the Avalon Foundation

1103 **John Marin** (American, 1870–1953): *Woolworth Building No. 29.* Watercolor, 18¾ x 15⅝" (47.6 x 39.8 cm.). Gift of Eugene and Agnes Meyer

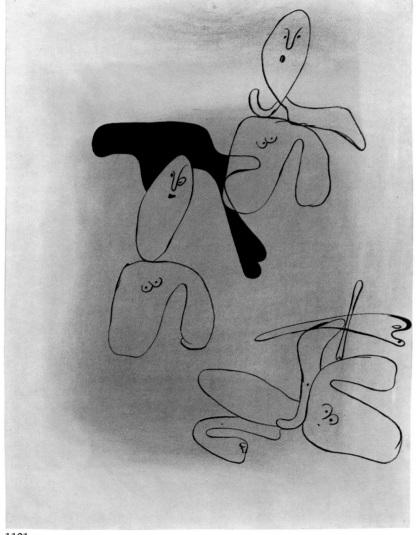

1101

1102

1103

Index to the Text

All numbers in this Index refer to *pages*.